TENNYSON'S GIFT

It is July 1864 and the Isle of Wight is buzzing with eccentric creative types. Tennyson recites poetry to furniture while his invalid wife hides bad reviews in teapots and buries them in the garden with a teaspoon.

Also at Freshwater Bay are the creepy Charles Dodgson (aka Lewis Carroll) and Julia Margaret Cameron, a photographer determined to capture an image of the bard in a suitably heroic pose.

Into this cauldron of unrequited love and egotism step the acclaimed painter G. F. Watts and his unlikely sixteen-year-old actress wife Ellen Terry; also the American father-and-daughter team of phrenologists, Lorenzo and Jessie Fowler.

TENNYSON'S GIFT

Lynne Truss

WINDSOR
PARAGON

First published 1996
by
Penguin Books
This Large Print edition published 2005
by
BBC Audiobooks Ltd by arrangement with
Profile Books Ltd

ISBN 1 4056 1054 9 (Windsor Hardcover)
ISBN 1 4056 2043 9 (Paragon Softcover)

British Library Cataloguing in Publication Data available

Printed and bound in Great Britain by
Antony Rowe Ltd., Chippenham, Wiltshire

Celebrities seem to come like misfortunes—
it never rains but it pours.
LEWIS CARROLL, *Diaries*, October 1863

There is a terrible truthfulness about
photography that sometimes
makes a thing ridiculous.
GEORGE BERNARD SHAW

The action takes place at Freshwater Bay, Isle of Wight, in the last week of July 1864

Part One

HATS ON

One

A blazing dusty July afternoon at Freshwater Bay; and up at Dimbola Lodge, with a glorious loud to-do, the household of Mrs Julia Margaret Cameron is mostly out of doors, applying paint to the roses. They run around the garden in the sunshine, holding up skirts and aprons, and jostle on the paths. For reasons they dare not inquire, the red roses must be painted white. If anyone asked them to guess, they would probably say, 'Because it's Wednesday?'

'You're splashing me!'

'Look out!'

'We'll never get it done in time!'

'What if she comes and we're not finished?'

'It will be off with our heads!'

The smell of paint could probably stop an engine on the Great Western; so it is no surprise that it stops the inquisitive Reverend Dodgson, who happens to be sidling by the house at this moment, on his way up the lane from the sparkling afternoon sea. In fact the smell wafts so strongly through the tall briar hedge that it almost knocks his hat off. He pauses, tilts his head, and listens to the commotion with a faraway, satisfied smile. If you knew him better, you would recognize this unattractive expression. It is the smirk of a clever dysfunctional thirty-two-year-old, middle-aged before his time, whose own singular insights and private jokes are his constant reliable source of intellectual delight.

'O-O—Off with our heads?' he muses, and opens a small notebook produced with a parlour magician's flourish from an inside pocket.

'Off with our h—heads?' He makes a neat note with a tiny pencil.

'H-H-H—Extraordinary.'

It is a very warm day, but Dodgson's only thoughtful concession to holiday garb is a pale boater added to his clerical black. Perspiration gathers at his collar and in his arm-pits, but since this is just the sort of discomfort a real mid—Victorian gentleman is obliged to put up with, he refuses to take notice. Dodgson is a sober dresser always, and today he is on a mission of importance. The only thing that worries him is the straw hat—a larky addition which seemed a good idea at the time. He takes off the hat and studies it. He doesn't know what to do.

The trouble with the Poet Laureate—on whom Dodgson plans shortly to call—is judging the etiquette. Will the fashionable summer hat be a help or hindrance? Tennyson is well known for his testiness; he is a great sore-headed bear of a man who expects his full due as Top Poet. Yet at the same time he has extreme short sight and filthy clothes covered in dog hair and smelling of stale pipe tobacco. Does it matter, therefore, what a supplicant wears? Dodgson tucks the hat carefully under his arm, touches his neat hair with one hand, and then the other, and replaces the hat. A small curl on his large temple lies exactly as it should. There never was such a fastidious fellow as Dodgson when it comes to attire. It has often been remarked. When he touches his hair like that, he does it with such concentration that he seems to be checking he still has his head fixed on.

'The Poet Laureate? Oh, very good, Dodo. Why not drop in on Her Majesty, too?' his Christ Church colleagues sniggered supportively, before he left Oxford for the Isle of Wight. Was this sarcasm? Did they think, perhaps, that he was making it up?

But yes, he is proud of it. The object of this smooth-faced stammering non-entity is indeed Alfred Tennyson, the greatest wordsmith in the land, the man who claims—with justice—to know the rhythmic value of every word in English except 'scissors'. The man who had the extraordinary literary luck to write *In Memoriam* before Queen Victoria got bereaved and needed it. And if Dodgson is vain of the acquaintance (and inflates it), it is understandable. He forged this relation single-handed, Tennyson offering him no encouragement of any kind. A lesser man would have given up long since, and pushed off back to his Euclid.

But when Dodgson sets his heart on befriending a fellow of celebrity or talent, he forgives all bad-tempered rebuffs, however pointed those rebuffs might be.

'Be off with you! What are you doing in my drawing room?' Christina Rossetti once demanded in Chelsea. (He soon overlooked this outburst of hot-blooded Latin temperament.)

'What was your name again?' asked John Ruskin at Coniston, a clever remark worthy of the foremost critic of the age, at which Dodgson smiled indulgently.

'I'll set the dog on you,' quipped Elizabeth

Barrett Browning.

Yes, between unequals in the social arena, the proverbial 'nothing ventured' is quite correct, and Dodgson proves it tirelessly. 'Nothing will come of nothing, speak again,' Dodgson is pleased to repeat to himself sometimes. It shows he knows Shakespeare as well as maths.

And now, this undaunted fellow carries under his arm a manuscript of a new book for children, about a girl called Alice. And he is bearing it like a great magical gift up the lane to Farringford, Tennyson's house, two hundred yards further from the sea. He feels like a knight returning with the Holy Grail; positive that his king will be terrifically impressed.

'You're not going to show Tennyson your *silly book*?' they said, those Oxford know-nothings. (Dodgson just can't stop remembering their jibes somehow.)

'N—Not exactly,' he replied.

No, the idea was to reacquaint himself breezily with Tennyson ('Dodgson? Is it you? Well met, my dear young fellow!'). And then, after some pleasant bread and butter on the lawn, a chat about the latest American poetry, and a kind offer of dinner and bed from Tennyson's saintly wife Emily, Dodgson would humbly ask permission (*ahem*) to dedicate his little book of nonsense to the laureate's sons. 'To my very dear and very close friends Hallam and Lionel T,' was the modest idea, although of course every reader would guess at once the full name of these famous children, and be tremendously envious of the author's sky-high literary connections.

'It's not much to ask,' Dodgson told his amazed

collegiate cronies.

'Want to bet?'

'It's no more than asking a person to p—pose for a ph—ph'

'Photograph?'

'Yes.'

'You mean it doesn't cost them anything, yet it profits *you*?'

'W-W—Well, I w—wouldn't—.'

'Best of luck,' they had laughed, interrupting.

'I'll have you know, I am a gr—great friend of L—Lionel T-T—,' he began. But nobody was listening. They all knew Dodgson's Lionel Tennyson story, and thought it a lot less flattering than Dodgson did. Evidently the poet's glamorous ten-year-old younger son once agreed to correspond with Dodgson, but imposed an interesting condition: that he could first strike Dodgson's head with a croquet mallet.

'More paint here!'

'Slap it on, jump to it!'

Back in Freshwater, outside Mrs Cameron's house, Dodgson wonders what on earth is going on. After weeks of drought, the hedgerow is singed brown; it crackles as he presses his body close to hear. Perhaps Mrs Cameron has ordered her grass to be painted green, so that it will look fresh and emerald from an upstairs window. Knowing of his fellow photographer's boundless and misguided devotion to aesthetics, such lunatic set-dressing is certainly possible. Mrs Cameron is forever making extravagant gestures in the cause of Art and Friendship, both with capital letters. She is a bohemian (at the very word Dodgson shudders), with sisters of exceptional beauty and rich husbands. She hails from Calcutta, and burns incense. While Dodgson takes pictures only of gentlemen (and gentlemen's children), Mrs Cameron poses shop-boys and servants for her dreamy Pre-Raphaelite conceits. In short, in terms of exotic personality, she is quite off Dodgson's map. He has heard that she will sometimes run out of the house, Indian shawls trailing, stirring a cup of tea on its saucer! Out of doors! If in London, she will do this in the street! And sometimes, she gives away the photographs she takes, the act of a madwoman!

'You will be visiting Mrs Cameron, sir?' the carter at Yarmouth asked Dodgson that morning, recognizing photographic gear as he loaded it aboard, straight from the mainland ferry.

'Oh no,' replied Dodgson. He glanced around nervously, to check that this terrifying woman was not in sight; was not actually bearing down on him with a cup of tea and a spoon.

'Not for w-w-w—'

The word refused to come.

'Watering cans?' suggested the carter.

Dodgson shook his head, and made circular gestures with his hands.

'Weather-vanes?'

A strangling noise came from Dodgson's throat. This was always happening.

'Windmills?'

'Worlds,' Dodgson managed, at last.

'Very wise, sir,' said the carter, and said no more.

* * *

At Farringford, Emily Tennyson sorted her

husband's post. Thin and beady-eyed in her shiny black dress, she had the look of a blackbird picking through worms. She spotted immediately the handwriting of Tennyson's most insistent anonymous detractor (known to the poet as 'Yours in aversion') and swiftly tucked it into her pocket. Alfred was absurdly sensitive to criticism, and she had discovered that the secret of the quiet life was to let him believe what he wanted to believe—viz, that the world adored him without the faintest reservation or quibble. To this comfortable illusion of her husband's, in fact, she was steadily sacrificing her life.

Take 'Yours in aversion'. Since this correspondent first wrote to him, he had become one of Tennyson's favourite self-referential stories ('The skulking fellow actually signed himself *Yours in aversion*!'), but Alfred didn't know the half of it; he had no idea the skulker had continued to write. Emily had a large drawer of unopened 'Yours in aversion' letters in her bureau upstairs. She would never let Alfred know of their existence—not while there was breath in her body, anyway. Afterwards, very well, he could find out then. It was only fitting that after her death he would discover the lengths to which she had gone in the wifely defence of his equanimity.

In general, however, the illusion that everybody loved Alfred Tennyson and found no fault in his poetry was quite easy to sustain day by day. It just meant narrowing one's circle of friends to a small, scarcely visible dot, cancelling the literary reviews, and living in a neo-Gothic bunker in the farthest corner of the Isle of Wight. If people still insisted on visiting (and they did; it was astonishing),

Emily's terrible hospitality soon put a stop to that. One of her favourite ruses was to make a note of all who fidgeted during the two-and-a-half-hour readings of Alfred's beloved *Maud*, and then deliberately tell them the wrong time for breakfast. When that gallant hero of the Risorgimento, Garibaldi, had visited Farringford in the spring, he obligingly planted a tree in the garden while the household sheltered indoors; but was he asked to stay for tea or dinner afterwards? He was not. Ironically in the circumstances, he was not offered so much as a biscuit.

Thus was Alfred, the greatest, touchiest and dirtiest living poet, protected from the unnecessary hurt of point-raisers, and family life sealed off from interruption. Luckily, Alfred's eyesight was so execrable that he missed all sorts of nuances in everyday intercourse, including the yawning and snoozing of his Farringford guests. In fact, he could read *Maud* to a library full of empty sofas. It made little difference to him, actually.

Emily tore up some review magazines helpfully forwarded by Tennyson's old Cambridge chums, and made a neat pile of the pieces. A maid would dispose of them later. But talking of maids, what had become of Sophia? Emily frowned. Sophia had been sent to Dimbola Lodge three hours ago. Had she never returned? Emily was just reaching to ring the bell when she saw the maid run through the garden, worriedly plucking flowers from her hair and followed by a small boy carrying a dark wooden box, clearly of Indian origin. Emily signalled to her through the window, and the maid—still pinning her hair into place—raced indoors.

'Oh, Sophia, Sophia, I am disappointed.'

'I do apologize, madam.'

'Did Mrs Cameron make you pose again? What was it this time? Flora? Ophelia?'

'Titania, madam.'

'Titania!'

'We tried to do the ass head with some dusters and wire, but we gave up in the end, although the butcher's lad seemed happy enough to wear them.'

'The butcher's lad!'

'He came by with some chops, and Mrs Cameron said—'

'Don't tell me.'

Emily sighed. Sophia looked wretched. The boy rubbed his ear.

'Are you the butcher's lad?' Emily asked the question quite kindly.

'I am.' The boy looked hopeful, suspecting a tip.

'Well, what am I supposed to do with you?' she snapped. 'Isn't life complicated enough?'

Emily needed some good news, but she had a feeling she wasn't going to get any. She sat down in preparation.

'Did Mrs Cameron accept my gift of the writing paper?'

'No, madam,' said Sophia. 'She said it was far too good, and that you must keep it.'

'And this box, Sophia? Dare I ask?'

'It is for you, madam—'

Emily groaned.

'—She had it only yesterday, shipped all the way from Mr Cameron's estates in Ceylon. She said it would look perfection on the new sideboard.'

'What new sideboard?'

Sophia bit her lip.

'The one which will follow shortly,' she admitted.

Emily slumped back in her chair, and dismissed the maid. She was not a well woman, and the bombardment of presents from Mrs Cameron made her weaker than ever. Last week Julia had sent—admittedly on different days—a leg of Welsh mutton, an embroidered jacket, a child's violet poncho, and six rolls of bright blue wallpaper decorated with a frieze of the Elgin Marbles. This level of generosity was intolerable, more than her frame could stand. Emily reached for the box and sniffed it. Just a day it had spent at Dimbola, and already it smelled so strongly of photographic chemicals that it might have been blown up the road by an explosion.

Inside the box was a long and unnecessary missive from Julia, written in her usual breathless style—full of praise for poetry and beauty and exclamation marks—and ending with her regular plea that Alfred should sit for a photograph. Emily sighed at this. Alfred would refuse, of course; it was a point of principle never to give anything of himself away.

Every day brought requests of some sort, and Emily shook her head at the stupidity of them all, especially the ones requesting money. Did these people know nothing of the world? And what was this? The Reverend C. L. Dodgson had written from Oxford, in his usual tiresomely pompous prose, mentioning a 'small favour' he wished to ask. Emily laughed rather nastily at his letter, and put it in her pocket with 'Yours in aversion'. She would deal with it later. But a 'small favour'? Dodgson was not a man to trust with a favour of any dimensions; experience had taught her that.

She must keep him away from Alfred, she resolved. Alfred's new volume *Enoch Arden* had just been published, and it would make or break his reputation. And sadly, it was not one of Alfred's best. Parodies were bound to ensue. Mr Dodgson was a gifted parodist, albeit an anonymous one, like the rest of the vile cowardly breed. Just two weeks ago, *Punch* had shockingly included a parody of Alfred's *In Memoriam*, and Emily was so surprised by its appearance that she tore out the page at the breakfast table, panicked what to do next, then stuffed it into her mouth, chewed it, and swallowed it.

Alfred had seemed perplexed, as well he might.

'Why did you do that, my dear?' he asked. 'Why are you masticating a page from *Punch*?'

'I don't know,' she said lamely. She thought quickly. 'Perhaps my anaemia craves the minerals in the ink!'

So to sum up, Emily was jumpy. The last thing she needed was this treacherous Oxford stammerer hanging about. The only favour the Tennysons had ever asked of Dodgson—that he keep to himself a photograph of Alfred taken in the Lake District—he had ignored. The photograph subsequently appeared as a popular *carte de visite*, published by a studio in Regent Street. Alfred was outraged. 'Whose picture was it?' he barked at everybody. And when they didn't know what to say, 'It was *mine*,' he answered. 'Quite obviously, it was *mine*.'

Today was Wednesday. Alfred would return this afternoon from London, and Emily was glad. She was very proud of Alfred, despite his touchiness, insensitivity and meanness, and despite even his tragic standards of personal hygiene, which were remarked by almost everyone they met. Truly Alfred Tennyson was the dirtiest laureate that ever lived. But there was more to a man than a washed neck or clean fingernails. That her lord was unacquainted with the soap and flannel did not make him a lesser poet or a lesser husband. As he once cleverly blurted to a fellow who had impudently criticized a dirty collar, 'I dare say yours would not be as clean as mine if *you* had worn it a fortnight!'

Emily folded her hands and smiled. 'There's glory for you,' she thought. She was pleased to reflect that she was well prepared for Alfred. As a matter of routine, he would ask three questions as he whirled dramatically through the door in his black cloak and sombrero, to which his wife's dutiful answers must always be the same.

'Did you check the boys for signs of madness, Emily?'

'*Yes, dear. I did.*'

'Is there an apple pie baked for my dinner?'

'*Yes. Cook has seen to it.*'

'Is anyone after my head?'

'*No, dear, nobody. As I have told you before, Alfred, that's all in your imagination.*'

* * *

Back at Dimbola, a clattering of pans and a smell of lobster curry issued from the kitchen, and from Mrs Cameron's glass house an occasional steam-whistle shriek marked the success or failure of the latest coating of a photographic plate.

'You nudged my elbow!'

'No I didn't!'

Dodgson's curiosity could resist the commotion no longer. Removing the boater, he pushed his head into the briar to see what on earth was happening. And there he saw a beautiful garden, in which maids and boys were slopping white paint onto red roses as fast as they possibly could. To someone who had only recently completed *Alice's Adventures in Wonderland*, this scene came as a bit of a shock, obviously.

Nobody noticed him, with his head poking through the hedge. Of course they didn't. They were absorbed in their strange work. Even when the door of Mrs Cameron's studio opened suddenly and a glass plate came skimming out, breaking against the trunk of a tree, the unflappable rose-painters paid no heed.

'Oh, dear,' piped a small voice near to Dodgson—too near to the hedge for him to see the body it came from. What was this? A little girl? At an educated guess, somewhere between eight years old, and eight and two months? With a dear little fluting voice? Dodgson pushed himself closer, despite tell-tale cracking and snapping.

'Oh dear,' repeated the little girl, disconsolate, 'I do believe I've quite forgotten.' Seeing more clearly into the sun-filled garden of Dimbola Lodge, Dodgson discovered a sight so pleasant to his eager spying eye that for a giddy moment he wished he might push his head right through the flowery bank (though of course without his shoulders, his head wouldn't be much use). A leggy barefoot girl of eight, her thick hair flowing, her skirt pinned up, and heavy angel wings of swan feather attached to her tiny shoulders, stood just two yards before him, staring uncertainly at a rose bush dripping white paint to the earth. And there she pouted, confused—an irresistible image of innocence and poultry cunningly blent.

'Mary Ann!' she cried, at last. Her wings flapped a bit, which was so nice to see that Dodgson whimpered in the hedge.

No answer.

'Can you remember? Are we painting red roses white, or white roses red? Mary Ann!' she shouted. 'I want Mary Ann!'

'Now what's all this?' snapped an older girl, an Irish servant of about sixteen in a dull dress and white apron. She looked quite severe, with her dark hair pinned tight against her head, as if it had deserved punishment by restraint.

'As you well know, Miss Daisy, Mary Ann will be in the mistress's glass house at this minute—why, isn't she there all day every day? And like as not she's pretending to be Mary Madonna, or a Hangel, or anybody else from the blessed Bible who never got their hands dirty doing her fair share of chores around the house.' Mary Ann's modelling duties were clearly rather unpopular with the Irish girl.

'But I say good luck to her,' she continued. 'Oh yes I do. Her with her moony long white face, not that I'd take that face off her if it was offered, even with the neck and the hair and the arms thrown in—'

'But what about the *roses*, Mary Ryan?' interrupted the little girl.

Mary Ryan smiled.

'Well, you're a goose, so you are. Is it really so difficult? What colour do you have there in your little pot?'

'Oh,' said the girl in a small voice, suddenly downcast. (Like all children, she hated to be told off.) 'White.'

The girl pouted again and changed the subject. 'Does Mrs Cameron ask *you* to be Mary Madonna sometimes, Mary Ryan?'

Clearly this was not the right thing to ask. Mary Ryan pursed her lips and emptied her paint pot over the honeysuckle. She probably wasn't supposed to do that, but at least she didn't dump it over Dodgson.

'Does she?' urged the child. 'She took *my* picture! Can I see pictures of you, Mary Ryan—'

'No you can not!' spat out Mary Ryan. 'And you just be careful with those wings, Miss Daisy Bradley, that's all. The mistress ordered them all the way from Mortlake, and if you'll not be crushing them feathers all this time, I don't know what you *are* doing.'

At which the little girl, sensing that the fun was over, ran indoors.

Mary Ryan, left alone, wiped her eyes with her apron and let out a little scream. 'Mary Ann this! Mary Ann that! How I *love* thee, Mary Ann!'

And picking up her pinafore, she turned on her heel. Unabashed at his eavesdropping, Dodgson stepped back from the scene, brushed his clothes for dust and twigs, and re-assured himself there was nobody about. He was never embarrassed when people betrayed private emotions in front of him; having no emotions himself (or none to speak of), he was just very, very intrigued. Sometimes he made notes for use later on. He had no idea why one maid should begrudge another maid her chance to star in Mrs Cameron's photographs—

especially when, in his own opinion, the photographs were dreadful, too big, and shockingly out of focus. Glancing up at the windows of Dimbola, he caught the eye of a white-bearded old man smiling from ear to ear—Mr Cameron, presumably. The old man waved in a jolly sort of way, as though deranged. Dodgson studiously ignored him; you never knew where that sort of thing might lead.

'But I must contrive to meet this Daisy,' he decided, and produced his small notebook again. He wrote down her name. He also wrote it in letters down the page—D-A-I-S-Y—B-R-A-D-L-E-Y—ready for an instant acrostic poem, which he could sometimes complete in five minutes or less. Twelve letters! Excellent! Three stanzas of four! Two stanzas of six! What a charming child, to have such a convenient name, numerologically speaking! With several days planned at Freshwater Bay, there was plenty of time to make friends with the little girls, and get their addresses, and campaign for their photographs, and send them love poems. But he had discovered it was a great advantage to know names in advance, without asking.

'I love my love with a D because she is D-D—Daring,' he mused. 'I hate her because she is Demanding. I took her to the sign of the Dr—Dromedary, and treated her with Dumplings, Dis-sss—temper and D-D—Desire. Her name is Daisy and she lives—'

Indeed, he was just envisaging the scene on the gusty beach—the little girl paddling with a shrimp net; himself nearby pretending not to notice her, but doing fascinating bunny-rabbit tricks with a pocket handkerchief to ensnare her attention (it never failed)—when he heard the approaching trundle of the Yarmouth cart, and looked up to see Tennyson, the great literary lion of the age, dressed as usual in copious cloak and broad hat, holding a book of his own poems directly in front of his face for better reading, but evidently catching a vague myopic passing blur of Dodgson nevertheless.

There was no time to hide, no time to frame a polite greeting before—'Allingham!' boomed the laureate, as the cart passed Dodgson (pretty closely). Dodgson jumped.

Allingham? He glanced behind him, but could see nobody.

'Allingham, we dine tomorrow at six! Come afterwards—not before, there's a good fellow—and I shall read my *Enoch Arden*, and explain it to you, line by line! We shall confound the critics!'

And before Dodgson could voice a word of protest, the poet had passed by. The rush of air pulled Dodgson's boater from his head and left it dusty in the road.

This was not the welcome Dodgson had anticipated. He didn't know whether to laugh or cry. How could he make a visit now? He picked up his hat again, and touched his head carefully with each hand in turn. Still there, still there; still Dodgson, not Allingham. He looked up at the old man, who now appeared (no, surely not) to be dancing with glee.

On the breeze, Dodgson smelled the ozone from the sea, the scent of roses, fresh lead paint, hot buttered toast and potassium cyanide, all mixed together with the lobster curry. He looked up the lane towards Tennyson's home, and then back to the blue sizzling bay, where children would soon be packing their shrimp nets. Salty and sandy, and with their hair in pretty rat-tails, they would head home for tea at the nearby hotels.

Absently, he flicked through his manuscript.

Dear oh dear, how late it's getting . . .

Mary Ann, Mary Ann, fetch me a pair of gloves . . .

I shall sit here, on and off, for days . . .

You? Who are you?

As he pondered Mrs Cameron's interesting corner of the Isle of Wight, another glass plate whizzed across her garden and broke with a shattering sound like someone falling into a cucumber frame. At Freshwater Bay, he reflected, whichever direction you went in, the people were mad.

'Which way?' he said quietly to himself. 'Wh-Wh—Which way?'

Two

When Lorenzo Fowler woke on Thursday morning to the sound of waves and seagulls, and the scream of a maddened beach dragged down by the wave, he had trouble initially guessing where he was. He normally woke to the sound of London traffic and coster boys. Freshwater Bay had been an impulsive decision, prompted by little Jessie complaining of the fug of Ludgate Circus ('Pa, this *heat*!') and accomplished with a spirit of 'What are we waiting for?' that had 'yankee' written all over it.

Lorenzo as a caring father needed no other incitement than his little daughter's cry. She was a pale, freckly child with orange ringlets, and he still felt guilty at transplanting her to England—such a backward land in terms of diet, clean water and fresh air. So at her first complaint, he shoved a few heads in boxes, packed his charts and silk blindfold in violet tissue, selected some hot, progressive Fowlers & Wells pamphlets (subjects included anti-lacing, temperance, tobacco, octagonal architecture and hydropathic cholera cures) and took the earliest train to the New Forest.

Even in a mercy dash, it seemed, a phrenologist did not travel light. For phrenology was Lorenzo Fowler's lifelong pursuit, and after thirty years he was not so much proud of this highly dodgy profession as still busting the buttons of his fancy satin waistcoat. Some people grow tired of fads, but not Lorenzo Fowler. For him, phrenology was the fad that would not die. Talk to him ignorantly of phrenology as the science of 'bumps' and he might throw back his magnificent head to laugh (baring his excellent white teeth) before genially setting you straight for half an hour, dazzling you with his specialist vocabulary, and at the end of it selling you a special new demountable model of the brain for the knock-down rate of two and nine.

Of course, for practising the craft of head-feeling, all you needed were a pair of hands, a good spatial sense, and a map of the mental organs fixed firmly in your mind. But Lorenzo Niles Fowler was more than a phrenologist. He was also showman and evangelist, whose personal belief was that the market for phrenology had never been so vigorous, not even in its heyday in his native United States. Why, already on this trip to the Isle of Wight he had used a cursory reading to pay the carter from Yarmouth, telling him, 'Such a large Self Esteem you have! And what Amativeness!' Gratified by this mysterious, flattering talk from an exotic foreigner, the normally morose carter had gladly waived the fee when he dropped his passengers at the Albion Hotel, right on the edge of the bay. Lorenzo smiled. It worked every time. Tell people they have abnormally large Amativeness (sexuality by a fancier name) and they are well disposed to phrenology—and phrenologists—for ever after. It's just something they happen to enjoy hearing.

Jessie was awake and dressed already, playing with heads in the chintzy sitting room. She was eight, and precocious, and though the scene might strike an outsider as altogether gruesome, she was happy enough, having known no other dollies in her life save these big bald plaster ones with nothing below the neck. Poor kid. She had no idea how it looked. Not only were there detached heads all over the floor, but she had on a thick dress of red tartan—a tragically bad choice when you consider the ginger hair.

'Pa?' said Jessie. 'Oh there you are, Pa! Ada and I breakfasted already, but we made them save you some brains!'

'My favourite!'

This was the Fowlers' daily joke. It was funny because they were vegetarians as well as phrenologists—and looking on the bright side, at least it was generally dispensed with quite early in the day.

'Brains! Ha ha, ho ho!' laughed Lorenzo, slapping his knees, while the nun-like Ada, their British maid, wordlessly unpacked some pamphlets from a trunk, and tried not to count how many times she'd heard this one before. You have to look at it from Ada's point of view. A family of American freaks that delighted in brain jokes? No, the gods of domestic employment had not exactly smiled upon Ada.

'Test me on the heads, please, Pa! Ada can't do it, she's too silly. She's too *British*!'

'Try not to be rude about Ada, dearest,' said Lorenzo, while he blindfolded his horrid little daughter, as though it was the most natural thing in the world.

'Tight enough? Not too tight? We are guests in this country, Jessie,' he continued, as he secured the strings with a dainty bow at the back of the little girl's well formed head. He was a big man with deft fingers. His hands were always warm.

'We have a duty to behave with the very best of

manners. In particular we should lead the way in courtesy to the lower orders.'

'But what if our hosts are all sillies and nincompoops like Ada?' asked Jessie.

Ada left the room, and slammed the door.

'Well, I agree, dearest,' said Lorenzo. 'That sometimes makes it hard.'

Lorenzo had brought a selection of plaster heads on holiday, the way another man might bring a selection of neck ties. Spreading them on the rug in a semi-circle, he handed them one by one to the blindfolded Jessie, who sat with her legs out straight, bouncing her calves alternately up and down.

'Take your time,' he said, as her little hands swarmed over the polished plaster. But his breath was wasted. Time was something Jessie clearly did not need.

'It's too easy, Pa,' pouted the little girl.

'No, it is not. Phrenology is a high science.'

'Well, this one's the Idiot of Amsterdam, aged twenty-five, I know that.'

'Very well. I take away the Idiot of Amsterdam, aged twenty-five. But first tell me about him. How do you ascertain his idiocy, Oh little clever one?'

'But it's so obvious! The flat, short brow, indicating no reflective or perceptive qualities! A cat could tell you that! I mean, if a cat had the Organ of Language, which of course it doesn't. A cat has a large Organ of Secretiveness!'

Jessie never stopped showing off. It was one of the reasons why she had so few friends. (The other reason was that she never minced words about other people's cranial deficiencies.)

She picked up another head, felt it quickly, and

cast it aloft. 'You can take away the Manchester Idiot, too, Pa, while you are about it.'

Lorenzo caught the head before it fell to the floor. Jessie was getting over-excited.

'Now, now, child,' he said. 'These things cost money.' He handed her another. 'Who's this?'

Jessie whooped. 'It's the Montrose Calculator! Papa, you brought the Montrose Calculator! With the enormous Organ of Number!'

'What's the story we tell about the Montrose Calculator, Jessie?'

'That when asked how he could calculate the number of seconds a person had been alive, he'd say' (and here she assumed a terrible Highlands accent) 'I dinna ken hoo I do't. I *jest* think, and the ainsa comes inta ma heed!'

He patted her shoulder, partly to congratulate her, partly in the hope of slowing her down.

'That's enough for now,' he said, but 'No! One more! One more!' she pleaded, and blindly reached out her chubby arms. How could he resist his darling? Especially when she looked so lovely—so *right*—in that violet blindfold? Lorenzo opened a special, individual box, and handed her a new head.

'Who's this, Pa?' she asked in a lowered tone, her face tilted upwards as she eagerly mothered the head in her lap, like something run mad by grief in a Jacobean tragedy. Lorenzo smiled but said nothing. His ruse had worked; the little girl was intrigued. The original owner of this head was no murderer, or idiot, or cunning boy.

'Is he an *artist*, Papa?'

'He is, you clever child. What makes you say so?'

'He has Constructiveness and Ideality very large. Who is he, Pa?' She stroked the head, as though smoothing away its cares. 'He seems to lack Firmness completely, what a shame. I've got enormously big Firmness, haven't I?'

Lorenzo smiled. It was true. There was no denying it.

'Can we feel my enormously big Firmness later, Pa?'

Jessie removed her blindfold to look at the name on the base.

'Benjamin Robert Hay-don,' she read. She stuck out a lip. 'Haydon. Who's he?'

'Mr Haydon was an English painter of great historical canvases and murals, Jessie, who killed himself before you were born.'

'Killed himself?' She opened her eyes wide. 'Oooooh.'

Lorenzo felt very proud. This kid was such a chip off the old block.

'Was he famous?' she asked.

'Famous, but poor. Artistically, some might have called him rich—but no, I'm lying. To be honest, even artistically Haydon was very, very poor. In other words, a useful case for lecturing purposes! He was also a phrenologist, Jessie—from the earliest days of our great science, when few people believed.'

Jessie was intrigued. Her whole life revolved around the heads of dead people, and mostly odd, sad, idiotic or self-slaughtering ones at that. Any other eight-year-old would have changed the subject to Humpty Dumpty or twinkle-twinkle-little-star, but Jessie wanted the full grisly biography. She knew as well as her father did: this stuff would be dynamite on stage. 'So why did he kill himself ?'

'Indebted. Disappointed. Nobody wanted his paintings, except a back view of Napoleon—'

'Did you bring Napoleon? I love doing Napoleon!'

'—Except a back view of Napoleon on St Helena,' continued her father (whose Organ of Firmness was more than equal to Jessie's), 'which he was obliged to paint again and again, some twenty-three times.'

Jessie tried hard to imagine the disappointment that drove Benjamin Robert Haydon to kill himself. It didn't work. After a short pause, she tried again.

'That's silly,' she said, at last. 'To kill yourself just because you have to keep doing the same thing, again and again.'

'I agree,' said Lorenzo. He had been doing the same thing, again and again, since 1834. He absolutely loved it. He looked out of the window to the deserted morning bay, with its bathing machines drawn up on the sand, its cheerful patriotic flags straining in the stiff breeze. He cracked his knuckles. 'But luckily for us, my darling, there are a lot of very confused and unhappy people out there.'

* * *

As Jessie had said, it was hot in London. Queen Victoria had already quit for Osborne, this being the first and last period of history when the Isle of Wight had a fashionable cachet, and well-appointed people longed—positively *longed*—for an invitation to East Cowes. The centre of London stank, and even in the relatively rural Kensington setting of Little Holland House, it was hot enough to broil lobsters without putting them in pans. On Thursday evening, the renowned, long-bearded painter G. F. Watts and his pretty young wife Ellen were sticky and agitated, and had reached the usual point in their near-to-bedtime arguments when the noted painter pleaded 'Stop being so dramatic!'—which was a reasonable enough entreaty until you considered that the wife in question was that glory of the London stage, the sixty-guineas-a-week juvenile phenomenon, Miss Ellen Terry.

Watts was fed up; Ellen was fed up. He was forty-seven; she was sixteen, so they both had their reasons. But it was a bit rich to call Ellen 'dramatic' in the derogative sense, even so. 'Dramatic' had been a continual reproach from this weary grey-beard husband ever since that overcast day in February when foolishly they wed. Ellen wished 'artistic' carried the same force of accusation, but somehow it didn't. Yelling 'Don't be so artistic!'—though perfectly justified when your dreamy distant husband seriously calls himself 'England's Michelangelo' and affects a skullcap—never sounded quite as cutting.

On the other hand, theatricality was certainly in the air. 'Drrramatic, am I?' demanded Ellen in a deep thrilling voice (the sort of voice for which the word *timbre* was invented). She clutched a tiny butter knife close to her pearly throat, with her body leaned backwards from the waist. It looked terribly uncomfortable, and Watts was at a loss, as usual. He stroked his beard. He adjusted his skullcap. Something was clearly 'up'.

'I only said Mrs Prinsep is very kind!'

Ellen groaned and whinnied, like a pony.

'But she is our host, my patron. Really, Ellen, surely you see how lucky we are to live at Little Holland House! I hope I may live peacefully here for the remainder of my life.'

'Painting huge public walls when they fall available, I suppose?' she snapped. 'For *no money*?'

'Yes, painting walls. What insult can be levelled at the painting of walls? You make it sound trivial, Ellen. Yet when I beat Haydon in the Westminster competition—'

'I know, you told me about Haydon and the Westminster competition, you told me so many times!'

'Well, then you know that the poor man died at his own hand. Painting walls is of significance to some people, my dear. My designs for the Palace of Westminster were preferred to his, and Haydon was shattered, poor man. Walls let him down! Walls collapsed on him!'

Ellen narrowed her eyes.

'But on the main point, my dear,' continued Watts, 'Why—*why*—should I want to earn an independent living from my art when we can abide here quite comfortably at someone else's expense?'

And then Ellen screamed. Loud and ringing from the diaphragm, exactly as Mrs Kean had trained her. Watts ran to the door and locked it. This wayward Shakespearean juvenile was always transforming the scene into some sort of third act climax, butter knife at the ready. (The effect was only slightly ruined by the knife having butter on it, and crumbs.)

Watts collapsed on one of Little Holland House's many scented sofas. He had married this young theatrical phenomenon in all good faith, assured by his snooty patrons that she would thank him for his protection; he had been in love with her profile, her stature—in short, her beauty with a capital B! But within five months he looked back on that marriage with confusion and even horror. This beauty was a real person; she was not an ideal form. She expected things from him that he could not even name, let alone deliver. This regular money argument, for example: it always went the same way. Here they were, comfortably adored and protected, and Ellen had to show off about it.

'If you would let me work, George—' she would say. And then all this sixty guineas nonsense would be rolled out again. Watts did not want sixty sullied guineas a week. He did not want to paint lucrative portraits, either. No, Watts was the sort of chap who loses his invoice book down the back of the piano and doesn't notice for four and a half years. Watts wanted to live with the Prinseps, conceive great moral paintings of an edifying nature, sip water over dinner, and be told with comforting regularity that he was the genius of the age.

The sad thing was that when he married Ellen, he assumed she wanted the same release from her own career. After all, her career was the *theatre*. But he had learned that while you can take the child out of the theatre, it is a more difficult matter to extract the theatre from the child. She still dressed up quite often. She danced in pink tights. A couple of times she had sat next to him at dinner, dressed as a young man, and he had talked to her for two hours without in any way piercing her disguise, or noticing the absence of his wife.

'My dear,' he began, 'If you continue with this, I shall have a headache.' But she drew away from him and took a deep breath, so he gave up. If experience was to be trusted, Ellen would probably forge into a famous speech now, and—ah, here it was. '*Make me a willow cabin.*'

Make ME a weell-ow cabin
(so Ellen began, in the thrilling voice again,
with fabulous diction)
    at yourrr gate!,
    (emphatic, with a little stamp of the foot)
And call-ll-ll
(this bit softly cooed)
    uppon my SOUL
    (a plaintive yowl of longing)
        with-in the HOUSE!
        (no nonsense)

Such a shame it was from *Twelfth Night*, Watts reflected, as the recital progressed. Watts had been rather touchy about *Twelfth Night* ever since he painted a huge allegorical picture for the wall of a railway terminus on the theme 'If music be the food of love' which had too much delighted his critics. A naked Venus with a bib at her neck sat down to a hearty lunch of tabors, fiddles and bagpipes. He still didn't see what was so damned roll-on-the-floor funny about it. The bagpipes—the exact size of an Aberdeen Angus—looked particularly delicious. Venus burped behind her hand. The knife and fork were four feet long.

Meanwhile, Ellen continued:

Writeloyalcantonsofcontemned love
(breathless, fast)
And sing them . . . LOUD!

(long pause)
even in the dead of night
(airy, throwaway)
Hallooooooooo your name to the Rreverrberrrate hills
(welsh R-rolling)
And make the babbling 'gossip' of the air
(an arch curtsey to Mistress Gossip, that rare minx)
Cry out!
(sharp)
'Olivi-aaaaa!'

Watts liked Shakespeare, but only as stuff to read in bed. All this prancing about was too tiring. Acting was the lowest of all arts. Still, he thought Ellen's performance was going rather well, and he had in fact just got his eyes closed, the better for listening to the poetry with, when the emotional undercurrent turned abruptly again and his wife burst into tears. She flung down the butter knife and left the room.

'What's wrong now?' Watts asked, jerked awake. It was all beyond him. Settling back on his sofa, with skullcap pulled over his eyes, he thought hard about what he had just heard from Ellen's lips. Yes, he thought hard. But on the other hand it would be fair to say that the expression 'sub-text' meant even less to Watts than to any other Victorian luminary you could mention. So what preoccupied him now was not the underlying tenor of Ellen's theatrical performance, in particular its expression of tortured young female longing. Instead it was the following: should the 'babbling gossip of the air' wear a hat? Should she sit on a gold-trimmed cloud, to indicate the airiness of her babble? And pondering these important questions Il Signor Michelangelo Watts arranged himself comfortably —though unconsciously—in a well—practised foetal position.

* * *

If it was hard to keep up with Ellen's stormy emotions, it was also impossible to contain them. The temperament of Mrs Watts was alarmingly dissimilar from Watts's own. For his own part, any vexation might be healed by the gentle removal of whatever thorn was temporarily in his paw (usually a big bill for buckets of gouache, which the Prinseps paid with their usual handsomeness); whereas Ellen turned hell-cat when offered assistance, especially in the form of Watts's edifying proverbs. Alas, he was a man who dearly loved a verity. 'Youth's a stuff will not endure,' was the sort of thing. 'Fine words butter no parsnips,' the great allegorical painter now consoled himself, for instance—and was instantly preoccupied conceiving an enormous fresco for Covent Garden Market, of tough root vegetables turning their ungreased backs, perhaps, on a bunch of spouting poets with long hair and big shirts.

Ellen had let her nose go red, which was too bad. Such a ruddy child was quite wrong for the Victorians' popular aesthetic of alabaster flesh. In 'Choosing', his latest portrait of her, Watts had allowed her a certain pinky flush, to reflect the surrounding camellias, but he now believed this a profound mistake, and intended to overpaint with a light green at the earliest chance. Overhearing two grand comic novelists at Little Holland House discussing the flesh tones in the picture, he had been quite wounded by their remarks.

'Know what *she's* been doing,' said one great comic novelist, nudging with his elbow.

'Very good, I must remember that,' said the other. Dickens and Trollope, someone said they were.

Despite its lovely pinkness, then, 'Choosing' had few happy associations for Watts. For one thing, it had been a tremendous bother to get the violets into the picture (in Ellen's awkwardly raised left hand), and in any case the allegory failed. Not since 'Striking a Careless Pose' (in which a tall king cuffed a young servant who had dropped something), had one of G. F.'s notions misfired so badly. Ellen was supposed to be choosing between the big scentless showy camellia and the humble perfumed violet, yet it was quite clear from the composition of the picture that her preference for the camellias was pretty strong already. Meanwhile the humble symbolic violets were so extremely shy and retiring that whatever they represented in the picture (marriage? humility? Watts?) got no look-in whatsoever.

'So she's choosing the big red flowers?' said Watts's devoted fans and perpetual support, Mr and Mrs Prinsep, when they first saw the picture. 'Good for her! Mm, you can smell them, Il Signor, you can, really.'

Watts judiciously stifled his impatience. The relationship between an artist and his patrons is an unequal one, despite the flattery on both sides. The patrons flatter the artist (calling him 'Il Signor', for example) because they can afford to be generous;

the artist flatters the patrons because he likes eating, and lying down in the forenoon.

'Actually,' he said, 'the red flowers are mere ostentation. I abominate red flowers. They should all be painted white. No, Ellen, representing Woman in the Abstract, chooses between the superficiality of the scentless camellia and, ahem, the sincerity of the humble perfumed violets.'

'Does she?' they said, eager to understand. 'Oh. But what violets? Where?'

'There.' He pointed.

'Oh yes. I mean, no. Sorry, I can't quite—'

'There.'

'Oh yes.'

There was a short pause, while the Prinseps conferred *sotto voce*, and Watts looked out of the window at the fields, pretending he couldn't hear.

'Perhaps he should make the violets bigger, what do you think?'

'Dare one suggest it?'

They looked at each other, and then at Watts, who was now biting his nails. They decided against.

'It is a *stupendous* picture, Il Signor!' Mrs Prinsep exclaimed, making Watts smile broadly with relief. 'A great success! You are a genius, and we are privileged to sit at your feet. Come! Let us dine from the best fowl the capital can provide, and you our master shall taste the liver wing!' But this was all a month ago, and from Sara's adulation Watts must return bathetically to the present scene, in which the returned Ellen sank to her knees, clutching his trousers like a waif. His artistic reverie had changed nothing, apparently. Here was all the trouble with marriage, in a tiny shell: when you got back from your mental wanderings, the little wife was invariably *still there*.

'Are you still acting?' he whispered, at last.

'How could I choose Viola?' she whimpered. 'Of all the heroines!'

He didn't know what to say.

'But the pose was quite lovely, nevertheless. You have a decided talent, my dear. And the moral of that is, waste not want not, for tomorrow I will sketch you in that exact position for my projected masterpiece, "Fortitude Overcome by Grace in the Absence of Hope".'

Ellen sniffed.

'Ah,' he continued, warming up at once (he loved talking about art). 'You make no remark? Of course. But think, if you will, of the supreme challenge of depicting the *Absence* of Hope! For you see, if I merely *leave Hope out*, it won't do at all! Critics will argue with justice that my picture equally well represents "Fortitude Overcome by Grace in the Absence of Railway Carriages" or "Fortitude Overcome by Grace in the Absence of Soup"!'

Ellen nodded to show she understood, though secretly she thought the absence of hope was a challenge to everybody, and Watts was the usual cause of it.

She rallied a little. 'I don't know why, Viola just came out,' she snivelled. 'But the point was, I wanted to do Lady Macbeth or Lady Ann or something. I want you to take me seriously! I want it dreadful bad!'

'I see. And the moral of that is—?'

'That I want you to take me *seriously*. I'm your wife and I love you.'

'And Viola won't do?'

'No. Because she's too much like me. Viola loves an older man, and he doesn't see her for what she is.'

'I know. The Duke Orsino. And the moral of that is—?'

'Whereas, you see, I don't want to watch and wait like Viola. I am not patience on a monument. George, we have been married *five months*.'

'Ah.' Watts winced at the use of his name. 'Could you not call me Il Signor? The Prinseps call me that.'

She seemed calmer now, and Watts took her hand. He was a kind man by inclination, but unfortunately if an allegorical picture of G. F. Watts were to be considered, it would show 'Inclination Untutored by Practice and Doomed to Disappointment', for he had spent his first forty-seven years unmarried, depending largely on the generosity of patrons, and letting other people pay for the luxury of his high-mindedness. In short, he had never been made to care. His most vivid emotional engagement had been, in childhood, with a small caged cockney sparrow, which he tragically murdered by trapping its head in a door.

Watts never recovered from the guilt or the grief of that accident. His emotion on the subject of that little squashed bird made Alfred Tennyson's great *In Memoriam* look like nothing. It had hindered him for years; disqualified him from happiness. This complex of emotions had now stretched a dead hand into his marriage, too. For whenever he thought about touching his wife in a marital way, the ghost of poor wronged Haydon (for whose suicide Watts was really not responsible) rose up and cried, 'Remember Westminster!' thereby throwing him completely off his stride.

'Let's go to Freshwater,' said his wife brightly, as if she had just thought of it (she hadn't). 'I want to leave London dreadful bad. Let's go tomorrow. I could pose for you there, and for your friend Mrs Cameron, who is beginning to like me a little, I think. You know how well I pose. You know how well I embody an abstract when I set my mind to it. Mrs Cameron needs sitters for her photography. The summer is too hot for London, especially considering your headaches.'

Watts looked unconvinced, so Ellen continued with her list of reasons, realizing she needed to butter him a little.

'You could paint Mr Tennyson again—it must be *months* since the last time—and then Mrs Cameron could take your photograph, making you look so very handsome, my dear! You have such excellent temples, George! And then we can all pose for each other and never stop having fun and larks!'

Ellen was accustomed to getting her own way. Her drop-dead prettiness had a miraculous effect on men of all ages, turning princes and politicians into fawning servants at the merest wiggle of her prominent but tip-tilted nose. This quality was to be her great salvation in life: that a childhood spent portraying Shakespearean nobility had led her to expect slavish devotion as her due. She need only turn the full force of her ingénue good looks on Il Signor, and like all other mortal men he felt privileged to kiss the hem of her gown, or carry her picnic hamper that extra mile up Box Hill. Beauty has power but no responsibility. It is terribly unfair, but there you go.

'Would you?' was generally Ellen's way of saying

'thank you'. 'Would you really?' she said, as she strode ahead of her puffing volunteer minion. Once at Little Holland House, the First Lord of the Treasury pointed out that the wheel of Ellen's carriage was running badly. 'Oh please don't feel you have to do anything about it,' she had assured the astonished prime minister, and although everybody else laughed like rills down a mountainside, Ellen was puzzled. She was quite sure she hadn't meant it to be funny.

How could Watts deny her a trip to the Isle of Wight? What was good enough for the Queen must be good enough for his princess. 'I don't know about the larks,' he said, 'but I agree it is a good plan. What a shame Mrs Prinsep cannot accompany us, she would love to see Julia. I have never known sisters so fond and close.'

'Except mine,' objected Ellen.

'What? Oh yes, well, *the Terrys*,' said Watts, in a tone that suggested the emotional closeness of Terrys did not count.

'Yes,' he continued, 'it will be refreshing to see Mrs Cameron, and she is bound to make us welcome. You know how Mrs Cameron loves to give, give, give!' ('Which is fortunate,' thought Ellen, 'when you prefer to take, take, take.')

'Such selfless generosity,' he continued, as though reading her mind, 'is not within the means of all of us. Poor men must rely on the currency of talent to buy their friends. And I am a very poor man, Ellen, I never misled you about that. *A very poor man*. Yet I esteem Generosity above all other human traits, above Faith and Hope and Discretion and Fortitude and Purpose—'

'George,' said Ellen quietly. 'You're doing

it again.'

'I apologize, my dear. Ah, 'tis love, 'tis love that makes the world go round!'

He slapped his knees and stood up, his wife's emotional outburst now forgotten.

'Do you know, I feel quite restored already. Where's that new bucket of gouache? I believe I can feel an allegory coming on!'

Three

'I don't suppose they've hung that lovely wallpaper at Farringford yet,' said Julia aloud.

It was Friday midday at Dimbola, and Julia Margaret Cameron was having her 'quiet time'—a daily hour by the clock when she eschewed all household duties (including photography) and sat at her westward-facing bedroom window scanning the chalk downs for a sight of Alfred. Ah, Alfred, Alfred! She could hardly wait to see his reaction when he found all her roses had been painted white. The servants had assumed it was one of her artistic whims ('Mr Il Signor Flipping Watts is behind this!'), but it was a valentine to Alfred, of course. A white rose means 'I am worthy of you'. And if Alfred didn't know that, then at least he would recognize the reference to the flower garden scene in *Maud*.

The red rose cries, 'She is near, she is near;'
And the white rose weeps, 'She is late;'
The larkspur listens, 'I hear, I hear;'
And the lily whispers, 'I wait.'

Julia loved *Maud*. She had bought copies for everyone. She had posted them indiscriminately to people she hadn't even met. When she saw Watts's 'Choosing' picture of his wife for the first time, she recognized at once that Ellen's attire was an exact replica of Maud's in the poem:

Queen rose of the rosebud garden of girls,
Come hither, the dances are done,
In gloss of satin and glimmer of pearls,
Queen lily and rose in one;
Shine out, little head, sunning over with curls,
To the flowers, and be their sun.

It was not surprising that silly little Ellen had not endeared herself to Mrs Cameron, when everyone fell at her feet in this nauseating way, and geniuses painted her in the exact guise of Alfred's ideal woman. Julia did most things precipitately; and thus she had rushed into a decision about Ellen—that she was a spoiled child, hopelessly unserious, whose background was not only common, but very possibly Irish.

As she sat in her bedroom now, all around were testimonials to her impulses. The house itself had been bought on a whim—two houses, in fact, joined together with a castellated tower, and all overgrown with ivies and roses. She had bought it, obviously, to be nearby to Tennyson in case he ever needed a leg of mutton in a hurry, or a loan of a violet poncho. The small window in which she sat was not a natural bay, but had been flung out one night when the fancy took her, and had ever since rested on stilts. In her room were intricate Indian pelmets to remind her of life in Calcutta. Yes, the sound of sawing never really left off at Dimbola Lodge, and the god of Carpentry smiled on Julia Margaret Cameron just as broadly as the gods of Art and Friendship.

Moreover, on her back this morning she wore half a cherry-red shawl, having given the other half to a shopkeeper at Yarmouth two days ago who happened to admire it. 'What a lovely X,' was the wrong thing to say to Julia Margaret Cameron, as her friends had long since recognized. In fact visitors to Dimbola were now careful not to exclaim over any object that was not actually bolted to the walls or holding up the ceiling.

At her feet, primly knitting a length of chain-mail with outsize needles, sat Mary Ann Hillier, the local girl (employed on impulse, of course) who posed so well in religious mufti, with her face tilted up to a sublime, framing light. Mary Ann had an unvaryingly stupid countenance, unfortunately, which properly captioned would be 'What?' or 'Huh?' Yet Mrs Cameron discovered great spiritual depth in Mary Ann's vacant, open-mouthed expression, and appended all sorts of poetic tags to it. One of her latest shimmering Mary Ann pictures was called 'The Nonpareil of Beauty', which had been such a hit with the other servants that below stairs Mary Ann was now known as the nail-paring.

Mary Ann ignored their jibes; she knew she was invaluable. Where would Julia's photography be without Mary Ann? Mrs Cameron could hardly rely on Farringford to provide decent photographic subjects—it was the general talk of Dimbola that Emily drove all the Carlyles and Ruskins away with her terrible meals; if not, Tennyson sent them scarpering for the ferry soon afterwards by guzzling all the port, blowing smoke in their faces, and reciting *Maud* till they fell off their chairs.

A railway had been mooted, to bring more people to Freshwater, and Tennyson opposed it with every inch of his body. A visitor once averred in his hearing that a railway link would be 'dandy', but Tennyson dismissed this as the opinion of an ignoramus.

'That man clearly has no idea how one thing leads to another,' he declared. It was Charles Darwin.

Mrs Cameron had a wistful fleeting vision of a carriage-load of celebrities descending on Freshwater, and then regained control of herself. She grabbed a piece of paper and made a note for more photographic subjects featuring those only constant and reliable resources: Mary Ann, a pool of light, a lily and a cheesecloth shift.

'The Angel at the Sepulchre' (she wrote),

'The Angel Just Outside the Sepulchre',

'The Angel on Top of the Sepulchre, Looking Down',

'The Angel at the Sepulchre Saying Move Along Now Please, There's Nothing to See.'

She put a line through the last one on grounds of blasphemy, but was generally satisfied. The important thing when there were no lions around was to *make do*.

Up in London, of course, her sister Sara Prinsep had lions galore. Little Holland House abounded in lions. It even had a resident lion (*couchant*, of course) in the person of the eminent painter G. F. Watts. Sara knew how to tame these large-bearded luminaries. You had to flatter them senseless, and then give them big slabs of meat for their dinner. She was a great success, the hostess with the mostest. In fact it was the mark of a very poor day if the amiable Thoby Prinsep inquired over his teatime bread and butter, 'Who's for dinner tonight?' and his wife replied, 'Oh, just some Rossettis, you know, left over.'

The trouble, as Julia saw it, was that whereas Sara only knew how to feed these lions, Julia could lend them immortality. Life could be terribly unfair. But as Julia was always telling that wretched Irish servant Mary Ryan when she whined about not being photographed as much as the favoured Mary Ann, 'The beautiful are dearer to God's heart, that's all, Mary. We who are not beautiful have an obligation to serve, and to receive the charcoaled end of the joss-stick.' At which the actually not bad-looking Mary Ryan would turn away with her eyes narrowed like letter boxes, and hum 'Oh God our help in ages past'.

Julia rested her hand on Mary Ann's head, and the girl looked up beatifically—light from the window striking her features in that thrilling Bellini-ish way that it always did. It was quite a knack the girl had, and it did not go unrewarded with privilege. While the other servants were expected to wear their hair tidy and pinned, Mary Ann wore hers free and flowing. Its tresses, shining gold and silver mixed, spilled over her shoulders like a stream in torrent. And right now, the stupid girl was steadily knitting it into the chain-mail while it was still attached to her head.

'I fear Alfred does not come today, Mary Ann. He is late! He is late!' said Julia. Mary Ann said nothing. She was wondering whether to unpick three inches of chain-mail. She tugged at the attached hair, but the stitches merely tightened, holding her more securely in place. Still she held her tongue. She had learned from experience that when she opened her mouth and spoke, her Isle of Wight accent rather ruined the Pre-Raphaelite effect. When you owned a profile suggestive of angels and madonnas, it was daft to undermine it with 'Our keerter went to Cowes wi' a load o' straa.'

*   *   *

Meanwhile, on the train to Brockenhurst, a single lion was on its way. G. F. Watts had fallen asleep over his old pocket edition of Tennyson's poetry and was warmly dreaming, his great domed forehead resting lightly against the window glass and his tired eyelids pressed gently on tired eyes. All around (interestingly) the languid air did swoon. Ellen studied him from the seat opposite, and folded her arms. She found it odd to be married to a man so attached to the horizontal, when her own body sang with energy, vigour and bounce. She had heard many times that Julia and Sara's father was 'the biggest liar in India'. How peculiar, she reflected, that these women were now so fond of the biggest lie-er-down in England.

On his lap, the Tennyson lay open at *The Lotos-Eaters*, a poem that endlessly delighted Watts and infuriated Mrs Cameron—concerned as it was with becalmed sailors succumbing to a lifetime of postprandial snooze, 'propt on beds of amaranth and moly' (whatever that was).

Let us alone. What pleasure can we have
To war with evil? Is there any peace
In ever climbing up the climbing wave?
All things have rest, and ripen toward the grave
In silence; ripen, fall and cease:
Give us long rest or death, dark death, or dreamful
ease.

It was the line about ever climbing up the climbing wave that particularly appealed to Il Signor. He felt he knew the sensation, and that he had learned to ride waves not fight them. Also, 'There is no joy but calm' had always been his personal motto until Little Miss Act Five Scene Two Terry had kicked the ottoman from under him. *The Lotos-Eaters* was a great poem, all right. Besides which, on train journeys it always helped lull him to sleep.

In his dream, however, things were less reassuring. He was still in a railway carriage, but Ellen was dressed prettily in a red coat and feathered hat like the child in John Everett Millais's painting 'My First Sermon'. This seemed perfectly natural. Outside the window, the landscape (which should have been Hampshire) was all cliffs and wind and wild flowers, alternating with long stretches of blue coastal sea. Another of the passengers was the dead painter Benjamin Robert Haydon, who studied Watts through the wrong end of a telescope and whispered 'Remember Westminster'. It was very unsettling. Meanwhile the sound of the carriage wheels was saying, over and over, a passage from *Maud*:

'Rosy is the West, Rosy is the South,
Roses are her cheeks, And a rose her mouth.'
'Rosy is the West, Rosy is the South,
Roses are her cheeks, And a rose her mouth.'

Ellen watched him as he twitched in his seat, merely remarking to herself that it was the most animated she had seen him in a considerable time. She returned to her own reading matter, but could not concentrate. Watts had given her a book of proverbs to digest on the journey, bought at Waterloo for the knockdown price of threepence. Watts did not notice that a knockdown present gave his wife very little gratification; he always loved to tell her how little his presents had cost. It was another area in which they would never see entirely eye to eye.

She flicked through the book of proverbs idly.

'It is a silly fish that is caught twice by the same bait.'

'Northamptonshire stands on other men's legs.'

'Cheese digests everything but itself.'

So many picture opportunities for her dear husband! How *would* he manage Northamptonshire's borrowed legs, she wondered. The section on Gratitude included the interesting commandment, 'Throw no gift again at the giver's head'—which was a precept which came just in time for Ellen, since the ungrateful young woman was just about to hurl this ghastly book straight at her nodding spouse.

What is the point of a book without pictures or conversation? Ellen tried to read Tennyson's latest poem *Enoch Arden* (Watts knew better than to turn up at Freshwater without it). But she had trouble with that as well. Its story was the usual cheerless Tennyson stuff, but with slightly more event than one had learned to expect. It concerned a fisherman who undertakes a voyage, leaving his family, and stays away for umpteen years because shipwrecked on a desert island. Back at home, his wife waits and waits (years pass), and keeps putting off another suitor, but finally concedes that Arden will not return. And then, what do you know?

Arden is rescued! He comes home, learns that his wife has remarried, and dies in grief alone. But he makes a friendly landlady promise to tell the whole story after his death, so that everybody can feel really guilty and morbid, including the kiddies.

Ellen huffed, and put the book back in her bag. The whole thing seemed bizarre to her. If she were shipwrecked abroad and returned to find George remarried, she would dance the sailor's hornpipe and set up house with a parrot. Ellen was the least morbid person who ever lived. Those pink tights, for instance. She thought Watts had found her verve attractive; she hoped that was why he had asked her to marry him. But then as his first act as a married man he had asked her to pose for 'Choosing' and she was forced to realize the extent of his self-deception. Given the choice between the big showy camellia and the humble scented violet, Ellen had a decided floral preference, and the violets were in the bin. 'Choosing' was a blatant case of authorial wish-fulfilment. It was so funny it was almost sad.

She looked at Watts. In his dream, he was trying to talk to Haydon as though there was nothing between them, but Haydon was pale and accusing, with a long white finger and a jagged crimson slash at his neck. Ellen kicked him lightly on the shin. Her husband only frowned. Haydon was talking about gouache costing a thousand pounds a pint. Ellen decided on the ungrateful course proscribed by proverb, and with some force threw the book again at the giver's head. Nothing.

In his dream, the railway carriage bucked in the air as though jumping a river. And at that point, Watts felt a terrible wrench to his face, as though someone were trying to pull his head off. He jerked, he saw an ungraspable vision of the absence of hope; and woke to discover that for some reason Ellen had fallen against him and grabbed his beard to steady herself.

*   *   *

Half an hour to go, and still no Alfred. Julia's daily letters had been written (a servant chased the post-boy up the road), so the rest of the time was hers. But it went against the grain, this quiet time. She had promised her dear husband that she would sometimes take things easy, but temperamentally it was quite beyond her. Besides—as she often pointed out to him, as he lay in his bed with his beard spread across the counterpane, a volume of Greek verse under his hand—dear old Cameron took things quite easily enough for both of them.

'Why do you write so many letters, Julia?' Alfred had once inquired. 'I would as soon kill a pig as write a letter. You write to your sisters every day. Do they reciprocate? I can't believe they do.'

'I write to my sisters because they are beautiful; ever since our childhood, I felt I owed it to them.'

'Nonsense,' said Alfred.

Emily had intervened at this point.

'All Alfred's family are mad or morbid, or morbidly mad; isn't that right, Alfred?'

'Barking, the lot of them,' boomed her lord. 'That's why we lost our inheritance, and I'm so beastly poor.'

Nobody said anything. Tennyson's belief in his own crushing poverty was a sacrosanct delusion. 'So we feel it better to remove ourselves as much as possible,' continued Emily sweetly. 'For the boys' sake.'

Alfred had a thought.

'Did you check the boys for signs of madness this morning Emily?'

'I did, my dear.'

'Any signs of black blood at all? Gloom, or anything?'

'None, dear. Nobody's mad in our house. As I will never tire of saying.'

'Well, *you're* not mad, Emily.'

'I never said I was.'

There was a pause.

'Will you pose for me, Alfred?' asked Julia.

'No, I won't,' he replied.

Just then, Mary Ryan knocked and came in. Mary Ann tried to put down her knitting, but unfortunately she was more tangled up in it than ever. When she let go of it, it still hung in the air in front of her face.

'Mrs Tennyson has sent back the Indian box, madam,' said Mary Ryan. 'She says she cannot accept it.'

Julia was astounded. 'Cannot? But it's a very beautiful box. I felt sure she would treasure it.'

'There is a letter, too.'

Julia jumped to her feet, took the letter, and shooed Mary Ryan out of the room.

'Do you know what this letter says, Mary Ann?' she said at last, with passion in her voice.

Mary Ann said nothing.

'It says that the box is too good for them. Well, I shall not give up. Too good, indeed.'

She continued to read.

'Gracious!' she exclaimed, and sat down. 'Mrs

Tennyson also informs me that C. L. Dodgson of Christ Church will be visiting Freshwater this week, that he may even have arrived already. Do you know what this means?'

Mary Ann looked blank. Admittedly, it was her forte. Shrugging mutely, she gave up the tussle with the knitting, and with a pair of shears, cut herself free.

'What do it mean then, ma'am?' she said at last.

'It means that he will get Alfred's photograph again, Mary! And why not? He's got everybody else! The man has already photographed Faraday, Rossetti, he's even got the *Archbishop of Canterbury*! So he'll get my Alfred. How does he do it? He has no connections, no reputation, no sisters in useful houses, and his pictures are flat, small and boring, and have no *Art*.'

Julia paced. 'I can't bear to think of it. I wait here, day after day, week after week, year after year, hoping that Alfred will give me something, *anything*! He does not even come to see the roses! I would give *anything*! And now they are sending back my presents! Oh, Mary! If he would only pose for me, Mary—' She sobbed and sat down. With the letter crumpled in her hand, she looked like a woman in a Victorian melodrama with sobering news from the landlord. 'Oh Mary, if he would only pose for *me*!'

* * *

'And how was your morning on the beach, my dear? Did you make any little child friends?' asked Lorenzo, trimming his beard at a mirror.

Jessie took off her pink bonnet (pink! for a redhead!), plonked it on the Manchester Idiot, and burst out laughing.

'What would I want with little child friends?' she asked. 'They're all such sillies.'

'As you like, dear,' said Lorenzo. He was an easy-going chap. He had recently located the Organ of Human Nature, and discovered—by happy accident—that on his own head it was massive.

'Well, except a girl called Daisy, she was all right, quite clever. Quite arresting to look at, and good fun. She said she could borrow some wings for me, if I wanted, but I can't see the point. Perhaps I'll ask her to tea. Her father is a clever man, but do you know, she'd never heard of phrenology or vegetarianism or the perfectibility of the human brain through the exercise of memory. So I told her, if he hasn't taught you any of *that*, he obviously hasn't taught you *much*.'

'Not everyone's as clever as you, Jessie. Actually, I sometimes think I'm not as clever as you. How old are you again?'

'I'm eight.'

'Good heavens.'

Jessie poured some tea, and handed it to him.

'Would you like me to help you with your grooming, Pa? That's your best suit, isn't it? Where are we going?'

'I must visit the hall I have booked for tonight. You remember the carter from Yarmouth?'

'Pa! It was only two days ago!'

'Well, he has already told everyone arriving from the mainland that I'm here. Interest is growing. News travels fast. I may have to send to Ludgate Hill for more merchandise. You can return to the beach with Ada this afternoon.'

Jessie pouted. While Lorenzo went scouting the venue, the Infant Phrenologist would be left at home again, to re-read *Hereditary Descent: its Laws and Facts Applied to Human Improvement, Familiar Lessons on Phrenology for the Use of Children in Schools and Families* by Lydia F. Fowler (her mother). Jessie sighed. She hated it when Lorenzo left her alone with Ada. Ada was quiet and broody, and unnaturally sensitive to childish insult. Also, Jessie hadn't even the consolation of other Victorian children, that if her father wasn't at home, at least he would be indulging gross unnatural vices, such as smoking and drinking, or tightening himself in a lady's corset.

'Oh Papa, there was something I needed to tell you. Did you know the poet Albert Tennyson lives in Freshwater?'

'I did.' (Lorenzo did not correct her on the 'Albert'. The tantrum could last for hours.)

'I asked everybody on the beach what his head was like, but of course nobody knew how to describe it. They said he usually wears a hat! But apparently he's got big puffs under his eyes, indicating the Organ of Language. Of course, I had to tell them about Language; they only knew about the eye-bags. Oh, and they also said, if you drop in at the house, don't expect tea. Wasn't that an odd thing to say? One of the boys, called Lionel—I think he's the poet's son—did a comic impression of him, rubbing his hands together. And he kept moaning, 'I am a very poor man! I am a very poor man!' Everybody laughed. There's another boy called Hallam, apparently, but he's very shy. Also there was a clergyman sitting on the wall, who looked surprised and made a note. I don't miss much, do I?'

'Jessie, it sounds as though the seaside entertainment was endless.'

'Don't patronize me, Pa.'

'I'm sorry.' Lorenzo patted her on the head, which he knew she loathed.

'And what of this clergyman? What sort of head did he have?'

'Massive, Papa, I meant to say! All number and logic at the front; all love of children at the back. I've never seen a head like it! It seems he's here to photograph little girls, like me, just my age. He sat on the wall doing corny tricks with a pocket handkerchief, and I have to tell you, it was quite shocking how quickly Daisy and the others were swarming around him, giving him their personal details, and letting him pin up their skirts.'

Lorenzo stopped preening. He needed to hear that last bit again.

'He pinned up their skirts? With what?'

'With some safety pins he *just happened to have with him*. I know what you're thinking, Pa. That's what I thought, too. Perhaps he is one of those fiendish pedagogues! Is that what I mean?'

'Not quite.'

'Well, whatever it's called, perhaps you should lecture on the dangers of it while we are here. These people need us, Papa. They need us badly.'

* * *

Meanwhile, at Dimbola Lodge, what an effort it was to sit still! Even with a lovely garden to look at, with stark white roses weeping for love and worthiness beneath, Mrs Cameron wondered how people achieved this stillness, the way she frequently commanded them. Reining in all this energy was enough to make your brain ache, yet others seemed to take to it. Mary Ann was virtually a human statue, of course, but then she was also pretty gormless. Charles Hay Cameron, the beauteous old husband in the next bedroom (a student of the sublime in younger days), not only lay perfectly still for hour after hour, but also smiled all the while, even when asleep.

Such a smile the old man had! It was quite remarkable. In fact it delighted his wife sometimes to reflect that whereas *many* people have seen a man without a smile, only the highly privileged have seen a smile without a man.

Alfred was something else entirely—a vigorous walker with fine stout calves, who strode on the cliff despite being dangerously shortsighted. On the days when he chose to visit, he would burst through Mrs Cameron's Gothic garden gate (installed specifically for the purpose), full of new poetry composed on his bracing cliff walk, or fulminating at some anonymous critic or parodist, or banging on about the railway, blinking against the sun and shouting hellos to whoever was about, and getting their names wrong. Mrs Cameron lived for these moments. She would glimpse his hat, and the sun came out. And if he was accompanied by his wife Emily—pushing that devout fragile lady in an invalid perambulator—Mrs Cameron found it easy to mask her disappointment by raining presents and compliments on the poor saint until she grew so exhausted she had to be wheeled home, limp like a broken puppet.

From the bottom of her soul Mrs Cameron loved

and admired Emily Tennyson, but somehow this did not stop her entertaining treacherous mental visions of clifftop disaster. In fact she rehearsed the happy scene in her mind quite frequently. It went like this: Alfred paused on his blustery walk to hurl himself to the ground and examine a tiny wild orchid, leaving Emily's perambulator temporarily brakeless and rudderless. The wheels began to turn. No! Yes! The black carriage gently trundled off ('Alfred!'), gathering bumpy and unstoppable speed (*'Alfred!'*), lucklessly veering cliffwards to a perpendicular drop. Yes! Yes! Yes! 'Hoorah!' yelled Julia, involuntarily.

Alfred wasn't coming today. Perhaps (some hope) he had gone home to supervise the hanging of the wallpaper. Perhaps Queen Victoria had dropped in, as Alfred often remarked she had promised to do. Having once been summoned to Osborne, Alfred entertained a vain hope that the visit would be returned, since Her Majesty had expressed a wish to hear *In Memoriam* recited by its author; and Emily even kept a plumcake ready, in case, and a pile of laundered handkerchiefs for the inevitable royal blub. When Julia invited Alfred to dinner, he often made the excuse, 'But what if Her Majesty called while I was out?' It was funny the first time, but by now it was wearing thin.

Julia consulted her clock. Ten minutes to go. She dismissed Mary Ann, and told her to get into her cheesecloth as soon as possible—she could feel a photograph coming on. 'Don't forget the lily,' she barked after. 'Think some religious thoughts!' And then, folding her hands, and closing her eyes, Julia Margaret Cameron completed her hour of inactivity by reciting from Tennyson's *Mariana*.

'She only said, "My life is dreary,
He cometh not," she said;
She said, "I am aweary, aweary,
I would that I were dead!"'

For some reason not unconnected with Victorian morbidity, this recitation always made her feel much better.

Four

'Have some more tea,' said Tennyson airily, by way of distracted greeting, not glancing up from his book.

Looking around, Ellen was delighted by the idea of refreshment after such a long and dusty journey, but then kicked herself for falling for this terrible old chestnut. It was the usual thing. How could you take *more* tea, if you had taken no tea already? Yes, the Tennyson table was set for an outdoor repast, with plates and cups and knives, but drat their black-blooded meanness, it was just for show: there was nothing on the board save tableware. Not a sausage for a tired and thirsty theatrical phenomenon to wrap her excellent tonsils around.

Nothing will come of nothing, as any true-bred Shakespearean juvenile will tell you. As she crossed the dappled lawn behind Watts, and surveyed the view of ancient downs beyond, Ellen wanted to jump on the table and render some funny bits from *A Midsummer Night's Dream*; it was a marvellous setting for theatricals. But instead she made her formal salutes to the older ladies and Mr Tennyson (who squinted at her rather horribly) and turned her thoughts inward, where at least they were safe.

Yes, nothing will come of nothing; nothing will come of nothing. Wasn't that a mathematical principle as well? Hadn't a kindly mathematician once explained it to her? Yes, he had. That was in the days when she was adored, of course; when members of her audience threw flowers at the stage, and 'came behind' after. When her face glowed in limelight; when people looked right *at* her, instead of politely askance. This mathematician —it was all coming back—she had met after her very first performance. As the infant Mamilius in *A Winter's Tale*, at the age of only eight.

It all seemed so long ago now, and what was the point of the reminiscence? Oh yes, the mathematician. By means of some pretty, nonsensical example, this Mr Dodgson (for yes, it was he) had proved to her that whichever way you did the sum, the answer was nothing, nothing, nothing, every time.

Ah, Mr Dodgson! Where was he now? If she had chosen to remain on stage, all London would be hers to command, and she would moreover pocket sixty guineas a week to spend independently on food and lodgings and full-priced books without proverbs in them. How mad of her to quit the stage for Old Greybeard here, with his borrowed home and empty flat pockets. And how cruel to her public. Mr Dodgson, for one, would be repining in the aisles. She looked at Watts, and gave him an encouraging smile, but her heart wasn't in it. For thirty years among patrons and well-wishers this husband of hers had soaked up endless quantities of love, money, praise and time, yet still had none to give in return; did the multiply-by-nothingness principle apply to marriage, too? If it did, her continued love for him was like one of his terrible pictures: the triumph of hope over mathematics.

It was a curious fact, remarked on by many visitors to Farringford, that whatever time you arrived for dinner, you'd missed it. The same, it now appeared, applied to tea. Emily Tennyson had long ago adopted the 'every other day' principle of home economics, and found that it suited well. Pragmatically, the poet's boys hung around other people's houses at teatime, eyeing the jam tarts—proof enough, surely, that they were *not* mad. Dimbola Lodge was a good spot for cadging food, which was why the boys were at Dimbola now, in all probability—sucking up to Mary Ann, and telling her how lovely she looked as 'The Star in the East' or 'Maud is Not Seventeen, But She is Tall and Stately'. Hallam and Lionel (but particularly Lionel) had learned quickly that Mrs Cameron rewarded good looks with sweets, so the Tennyson boys spent much of their time away from home, carelessly showing off their charming profiles in her garden, and flicking their girly locks. Lionel was an absolute stunner.

Mrs Cameron was however at Farringford this afternoon, to greet Watts and Ellen in a flurry of shawls and funny smells, and fervent greeting.

'Il Signor! Il Signor!'

Watts loved this kind of devotion, of course, and acknowledged it with a bow. He felt no obligation to return it.

Though the Wattses were guests at Dimbola, Mrs Cameron had conceived this pleasant notion of meeting them at Farringford after their journey. For one thing, in the garden at Farringford the roses were not all half-dead (and dangerously flammable) from the recent application of paint. Also, Watts and Tennyson were mutual admirers, with matching temples and pontiff beards, and Mrs Cameron loved to witness their hirsute solemn greetings for the aesthetic buzz alone. 'The brains do not lie in the beard' was an adage with which she had always argued. And beyond all this was a more pragmatic reason for the Farringford rendezvous: it was an excuse to see Alfred in the afternoon, when he had somehow forgotten to come in the morning.

Chairs from the banqueting hall had been arranged around a table on the wide green lawn, in the shade of the ilex, and if the furniture was a peculiar assortment, this only reflected the odd people sitting in it—Mrs Tennyson silent and gaunt in black, her beady eye alert for gentlemen of the *Edinburgh Review* lurking in the shrubbery, Watts already asleep with his head on the table, Mrs Cameron hatching benevolent schemes and waving her arms about, and Tennyson preoccupied, in his big hat, speaking in riddles.

Ellen took off her own hat, patted her golden hair and sat down gingerly in a sort of throne at the head of the table. Her real impulse was to kick off her shoes, let her hair down and shout, '*Bring* me some tea, then,' but in the company of this particular set of grown-ups, who often scolded and belittled her, she found herself too often at fault. They even disapproved of pink tights: she was clueless how to please them. So, her throat rasping for want of refreshment, she played a game of onesided polite conversation she had recently taught herself from a traveller's handbook left by Mr Ruskin at Little Holland House. And nobody took the slightest notice.

'My portmanteau has gone directly to Dimbola Lodge,' she announced (with perfect diction, as though speaking a foreign language). 'My husband and I will travel there later also. It is only a short walk. My parasol is adequate although the sun is strong. Are you familiar with the Dordogne? Our journey from London was comfortable and very quick.'

No one said anything. Not a breath stirred. In the far distance, childish voices on the beach could be heard mingled with the crash of waves, piping like little birds in a storm. Watts emitted a snore, like a hamster.

'The bay looks delightful this afternoon,' she continued. 'I hope there will not be rain. The Isle of Wight has the great advantage of being near yet far, far yet near. Rainbows are not worth writing odes to.'

Nothing. Bees hummed in the shrubbery, and Watts made a noise in his throat, as though preparing to say something.

At this stirring from the dormant male, Mrs Cameron signalled at Ellen to hush her prattling.

'Speak, speak, Il Signor!' urged Mrs Cameron, grandly.

But Watts did not speak, as such. Rather, he intoned. 'An American gentleman on the boat to Leghorn,' he said, 'lent me without being asked *eight pounds*.'

He resumed his slumber, and Mrs Cameron nodded shrewdly as though a great pronouncement had been made. Tennyson continued to read his own poetry silently, with occasional bird-like tippings of the head, to indicate deep thought.

'At what time do we arrive at the terminus?' Ellen persisted, her voice rising a fraction. 'I have the correct money for the watering can. You dance very well, do you know any quadrilles? No heavy fish is unkind to children. Will you help me with this portmanteau, it is heavy. I require a view with southerly light. Please iron my theatrical costumes. This gammon is still alive. Northamptonshire stands on other men's legs. Phrenology is a fashionable science. Would you like to feel my bumps?'

It was at this point, when Ellen was just beginning to think she would not survive in this atmosphere for another instant, that she spotted a dapper figure in a dark coat and boater dodge nervously between some trees in the garden. Behind him ran a little girl in a pinafore.

'That man is behaving very curiously,' she said aloud. But since this exclamation might have been just a further instalment of her phrasebook speech, no one glanced to see what she was talking about. Ellen, however, burned with curiosity.

Tennyson looked up from his book, but luckily did not notice the intruder. So wary was he of fans and tourists ('cockneys') that he had once run away from a flock of sheep in the belief they were intent on acquiring his autograph. In fact, even after the mistake was pointed out, he still maintained that they might have been.

'George Gilfillan should not have said I was not a great poet,' he finally announced, in an injured tone.

Emily sighed. She didn't know who George Gilfillan was—indeed *nobody* knew who George Gilfillan was—but she had heard this complaint a hundred times. Gilfillan's opinions of Tennyson's poetry had somehow eluded her vigilance. Meanwhile, a hundred yards away, between the trees, the curious man had frozen to the spot, gazing at a pocket watch.

Emily tried to recruit Julia to her cause.

'Really, Alfred, you must forget Mr Gilfillan, he is of no consequence. And besides, to repeat bad criticism of yourself shows no wisdom. Yet you do it perpetually. What of the many fine words written in your praise? What of the kindness and approbation of the monarch? It is too vexing. The Chinese say that the wise forget insults as the ungrateful a kindness.'

Julia murmured her approval. 'And apart from all that, you should be a man, Alfred, big fellow like you,' she said. 'People will say there's no smoke without fire, if the cap fits!'

She tried to think of more suitable clichés. Watts beat her to it.

He opened one eye. 'The more you tramp on a turd, the broader it grows,' he remarked.

Julia patted his hand. 'Thank you for that, Il Signor,' she said. 'There never was a man more apt with a vivid precept. We shall have dinner at Dimbola later,' she added, in a comforting whisper. 'With food.'

'Kill not the goose that lays the golden egg,' he said, and closed his eye again.

To Tennyson in full flow, however, all this talk of broadened turds was mere interruption.

'He should not have said I am not a great poet,' he continued. 'And I shall prove it to you. Listen to this:

With blackest moss the flower-plots
[note the way "moss" and "plots" suggest the rhyme; a lovely effect, do you think you could do it?]
Were thickly crusted, one and all:

["crusted" is a fine word here]
The rusted nails fell from the knots
["knots" rhymes with "plots", you see; "crusted" with "rusted"]
That held the pear to the garden wall—

'Peach,' interjected Mrs Cameron, dreamily.

'I beg your pardon.'

'Did I speak? Yes, I do apologize, Alfred, I did speak without meaning to. It's just that the line is, *That held the peach to the garden wall.*'

'No, it isn't.'

'I ought to know, Alfred! It's your *Mariana*. I recite your *Mariana* to myself every day of my life! I make a point of it!'

'You do?' asked Emily, quickly. Julia gulped. She suddenly realized what she'd said.

'Well, perhaps not every day,' she laughed, hoping to make light of it. 'And not because it means anything, of course.'

Tennyson huffed. He wanted to press on with the recital. But Emily was not to be put off.

'But that's very curious, Julia. Why do you recite *Mariana*? I can hardly think of anybody less like Alfred's Mariana than yourself, my dear. She is all passivity and tranquillity. You do not die for love, surely, Julia? For whom do *you* wait, aweary, aweary, wishing you were dead? It is quite the antithesis of your lively character!'

Julia pulled a shawl tighter, and stirred a cup furiously, which was an odd thing to do, because there was nothing in it.

'Well—' she began, but Alfred huffed again. He had no idea what was going on.

'She recites *Mariana*, my dear, because it's a very

fine poem, of course! What an absurdly simple question! I am surprised you could not guess it!'

And he flung himself back in his chair, quite satisfied.

'Now, where was I?' he said, and resumed his book.

'At *peach*,' insisted Julia, spiritedly.

'Pear,' he rejoined.

'Peach.'

'Pear.'

'Peach.'

'Stop!' snapped Emily. 'You must explain yourself, Alfred.'

Tennyson shut the book.

'You are right, Julia. The word was "peach". I changed it.'

'You did? When?'

'I don't know. Recently. "Pear" sounds better, as I think you will agree.'

Emily silently practised peach-pear-peach-pear, and then pear-peach-pear-peach.

'But you wrote *Mariana* in 1830, Alfred,' exclaimed Julia. 'That's thirty-four years ago. Why don't you leave it alone? Thousands of people have learned it as "peach".'

'She's right,' mumbled Watts, his contribution so unexpected that the others jumped. Tennyson blinked in confusion and looked behind him. He clearly had no idea where the noise had come from.

'It is still my poem, Julia. I can do what I like. You might say that I like what I do, and I do what I like.'

'But you gave *Mariana* to the world—'

'I did no such thing.'

'You published it, Alfred.'

'That's quite different.'

Tennyson scowled, and changed the subject. He looked away from the table altogether.

'And as for Ruskin,' he continued, tiresomely, 'that foolish man, when he read my *Maud*, objected to the lines, "For her feet have touched the meadows / And left the daisies rosy", representing me most unjustly as a subscriber to the pathetic fallacy. Ha! The pathetic fallacy? Me? Such stupidity is enough to make the heavens weep!'

Nothing agitated or excited Tennyson more than adverse criticism. *Enoch Arden* was already in the shops. The title poem ends with the lines, 'So passed the strong heroic soul away / And when they buried him that little port / Had seldom seen a costlier funeral.' No wonder he was getting punchy.

'But what lack of understanding,' he continued (he was still banging on about Ruskin). 'Daisies *do* go rosy when trodden on. *Ask any botanist*. I have every intention of sending Mr Ruskin a real daisy one of these days, without comment, to show him that the under-petals are pink.'

Mrs Cameron, still reeling from the news of the peach, felt she could make no further comment on poetic licence today, but the saintly Emily chipped in—and with surprising—vehemence.

'For the last time, Alfred!' she shouted, 'We all agree with you about the daisy!'

'I know, but—'

'It was years ago! You know more about daisies than Ruskin does! It is understood! You are right and he is wrong! The man has a brain the size of St Paul's Cathedral, but he does not understand that daisies can be rosy! That's enough!'

'But—'

'All right! *Send* him a daisy, then! Here's one!' Emily leaned over the arm of her chair and ripped a daisy from the grass. 'Here's two!' She did it again. 'Here's a *whole bunch*!'

Tennyson narrowed his eyes. The normally placid Emily seemed to have lost her grip.

'I will,' he said, gravely.

'Go on, then.'

'Don't think I won't, because I will.'

'I dare you.'

Ellen shrugged. These grown-up literary discussions were beyond her; perhaps because of her extreme youth. Looking on the bright side, however, she calculated that nobody would miss her if she slipped away, to investigate the curious man.

Instead, she met Lionel Tennyson skulking behind a camellia bush. From the state of his cheeks, smeared with red, he seemed to have scored rather well with the Dimbola jam tarts this afternoon.

'Lionel? It's Mrs Watts. Do you remember me? We played at Indians.'

'Shh,' said Lionel. 'Keep down, won't you?'

Assuming this was a new game, Ellen joined him in hiding behind the bush.

'I thought I saw a man in a straw hat,' she whispered. 'Is he a friend of yours?'

'That's who we're hiding from,' said Lionel. 'It's a Mr Dodgson from Oxford. Mother doesn't like him, so I'm making sure he doesn't reach the house. Nobody knows he's here except me. Not even Hallam. Did you see the way he was lurking? Mother says—' Lionel looked around before finishing the sentence.

'What does she say?' asked Ellen, in an excellent stage whisper, which could be heard for a hundred yards in all directions.

'Shh,' said Lionel. 'Mother says *he's not a gentleman*.'

'Indeed?' said Ellen. 'How dreadful.'

'He takes people's photographs without asking.'

'But that's not possible,' objected Ellen. Lionel's handsome little face assumed a contemptuous expression.

'You agree that photographs are taken?'

'Well yes, but—'

'Have you ever heard of anyone giving a photograph?'

'I suppose not.'

'So.'

Just then, Dodgson appeared in a glade twenty yards away. He seemed to be having trouble shaking off the little girl.

'Go away,' he pleaded. (Dodgson had no stammer or ceremony when he talked with children.)

'But you said you loved your love with a D,' said the child, who was holding a sheet of paper with writing on it. 'Doesn't that mean you want to run away and get married?'

Dodgson closed his eyes. 'Please, please,' he said. 'Hop it.'

'But I love you too, Mr Dodgson. I love my love with a D because he is Dapper. Come to the beach and tell me a story.'

'Daisy. I am here to see a man about a book. I have come to make a magnificent gesture; a priceless gift, the fruit of my genius. You wouldn't understand.'

'If you come to the beach, I'll let you do the thing with the safety pins.'

Dodgson considered. He looked at his watch again.

Daisy rested her hands on her hips.

'If you *don't* come to the beach, I'll tell Mama about the thing with the safety pins.'

'You wouldn't.' He gasped.

'I would though.'

He groaned and capitulated. He took her little hand and turned back.

'I suppose it *is* a bit late to call now,' he said. 'They seem to have company, too.'

Ellen and Lionel watched him out of sight. For some reason, his retreat filled Ellen with a sense of loss, and she had an urge to wave a handkerchief. As he disappeared from sight, they heard him say, 'But apart from making my excellent gift, I would dearly love to talk to Mr Tennyson about the railway. It sounds such a splendid proposal . . .'

Ellen looked at Lionel. 'What a strange man,' she said. 'What did she mean about safety pins?'

'I have no idea. But I happen to know a secret. Mr Dodgson writes parodies of Father's poems. I'm not supposed to know, because if Father finds out, Mother says he'll froth at the mouth.'

'Why is your father so sensitive to other people's opinions? Is he mad? Surely he knows he is a great, great man?'

Lionel did not answer at once. He was seriously considering the 'mad' part of Ellen's question, like the true black-blooded Tennyson that he was.

'*Is* he mad? Is *he* mad? Is he *mad*?'

He tried it all three ways. The exercise was not particularly helpful.

'Well,' he said, 'He's not exactly Mister Stable of the Isle of Wight. Let's just say it's a bit rich the way he checks *us* for madness every day.'

Lionel straightened up.

'He's gone,' he said. 'Shall we go down to the sea?'

'Yes, please. Where's Hallam?'

'Oh, Hallam stays indoors a lot. He's such a girly.'

Ellen smiled. 'I see.'

'Are you coming, then?'

'But won't we see Mr Dodgson there too?'

'Oh yes, but we'll ignore him. I'm terribly good at that. I'll teach you, if you like.'

* * *

Freshwater Bay was very popular this afternoon, and Dodgson was the most popular thing about it. On all his summer seaside holidays, four o'clock was his regular story-time with children on the beach, and by the time Ellen and Lionel located him, he was seated on a rock (conveniently low) telling the story of the Gryphon and the Mock Turtle to a group of six children, all so enthralled by the underwater curriculum that they were currently practising reeling, writhing, drawling, stretching and (best of all) fainting in coils. Daisy made sure that when she fainted in coils, she made contact with Mr Dodgson's boots, which made him extremely uncomfortable.

Ellen's heart leapt when she saw him more closely; for this (as she had hoped) was her very own dear Mr Dodgson, who had adored her once! But she was afraid to disturb the story, so she waited beside a barnacled breakwater with Lionel, just listening to his words, and catching the sun on her face. Waves lapped and seagulls flew; maids giggled behind bathing machines. Ellen watched the bright faces of Dodgson's eight-year-old admirers. They were entranced.

'How many hours a day did you do lessons?' said Alice.
'Ten hours the first day, nine the next, and so on,' said the Mock Turtle.
'What a curious plan!'
'That's the reason they're called lessons,' the Gryphon remarked.
'Because they lessen from day to day.'

The children groaned, and Lionel laughed before he could stop himself.

'It's very funny, this,' Ellen said, suddenly performing a little pirouette. 'Don't you think he might write it down? It would make a splendid entertainment for Dimbola Lodge. I would play little Alice, of course. In fact, that would be rather fitting, because my first name is Alice, did you know that?'

Lionel clearly wasn't interested.

'Isn't it fun eavesdropping?' she said, 'Like something out of Shakespeare. Do you know those children?'

'I know *of* them,' conceded Lionel. 'I wouldn't count them as friends.'

Without much grace, he pointed them out. They included Daisy and her cousin Annie (both enraptured); and on the end of the line, sitting up straight, and trying not to look interested in the story except from a scientific point of view, was Jessie Fowler.

'Oh, I ought to have told you!' said Lionel, prompted by the sight of Jessie. 'Tonight the great Lorenzo Fowler gives a demonstration of phrenology in the parish hall. The carter told me. It was arranged terribly quickly. Father says we children can't attend, of course; but Mrs Cameron's Mary Ann will be going, and Mary Ryan too, and our gardener, and the coachman. I've asked them to tell me all about it. I wish I could go. Will you be allowed to go, Mrs Watts?'

'I don't suppose so.'

It was alarming to realize that even though he called her Mrs Watts, he lumped her in with the children.

'Is he famous, this Lorenzo Fowler?'

'Jessie says he's the most famous phrenologist that ever lived. That's Jessie with the orange hair. She's a phrenologist, too. She's very stuck up, and disapproves of everything, including ham-and-egg pies and narrow waists. She's awful. I hate women who talk too much about what they know. What do you think?'

Ellen perused the child.

'Well, she shouldn't wear yellow.'

'But on the other hand,' added Lionel. 'She seems to like me, so she can't be all bad. She told me this morning that she helps in her father's demonstrations, but I don't believe her. She just wants me to find her fascinating because I'm so fantastically good-looking.'

Jessie, who had been all this time pretending not to be eight, suddenly gave way to a childish impulse. At the sight of the truly gorgeous Lionel behind Dodgson's back, she smiled and waved, flapping her hand furiously, as if it was something stuck to her, and she wanted to shake it off.

'Lionel!' she yelled.

At which, of course, Dodgson looked round. And seeing both Lionel and Ellen, stopped his story abruptly, in mid-sentence.

'L-L—Lionel, my dear friend!' he exclaimed. (Lionel groaned.) 'And can this really be Mrs Watts with you? The brightest star of Drury L-L—?'

'It is a pleasure to meet you again, Mr Dodgson,' said Ellen, extending her hand. 'I have never forgotten your kindness to me when I made my first appearance on the stage. And now you tell stories about little Alice. I was reminding Lionel that Alice is my first name—you remember that, of course, Mr Dodgson.'

Dodgson made no comment. He was rather overcome.

'You are very brave to return to Freshwater,' Ellen continued, her self-esteem swelling as she felt herself adored. She could be very grown-up and condescending when it came to talking with fans, and she was a finely made young woman. Like Maud in the poem, she was not seventeen, but she was tall and stately.

'B—brave?' queried Dodgson.

'Yes. Lionel told me as we walked from Farringford that he once offered to strike your head with a croquet mallet.'

'Oh! Ha ha,' said Dodgson uncomfortably, patting Lionel on the shoulder. 'He didn't mean it, I'm s—sure.'

'I did, though,' said Lionel, pulling a face.

'Ha ha! Youth, youth.'

They all looked at the sand for a moment.

'But Miss Terry,' he began again. 'I am so very pleased to see a fr-fr—' He rolled his eyes, and tried again. 'Fr-fr—'

'Frog?' suggested Lionel.

Dodgson waved away the very idea. He pointed at the children. 'Fr—' he continued.

'Phrenologist?' Lionel tried again.

'Fracas?' said Ellen.

'Frigate?'

'I know! I know!' said Ellen, getting carried away. 'Fretful porpentine!'

Dodgson took an exaggeratedly deep breath, mainly to shut them up.

'Friend,' he blurted, at last.

Ellen looked abashed. He had called her Miss Terry; he had called her a friend. She couldn't remember the last time anyone had been so nice to her.

Dodgson caught his own mistake.

'But I apologize. I must call you Mrs W-W—'

Lionel let him wallow.

'Mrs W-W—'

'Miss Terry will suffice, I think,' interjected Ellen, 'just between ourselves. I know from my own experience that the other title is sometimes hard to say.' She looked at the little girls on the beach—particularly Daisy, who was studying Dodgson with big round purposeful eyes—and felt suddenly overcome with sadness.

'I have been fancying myself little Miss Terry all afternoon, Mr Dodgson—at about the same age as these pretty girls here, in fact. And I can barely express how much pleasure it has given me.'

Five

While all this childish excitement was taking place at the bay, Ellen's husband was engaged in a far more serious and elevated pursuit. In a small circle of light in a darkened shed, he sat stiff-backed on an upturned tea-chest, trying very hard not to move. His whole body ached from the effort, and it was a strange way to spend a Friday afternoon. His hair was brushed from his face, to reveal his excellent temples. He had been most emphatic on this point.

'Can you see my excellent temples, Julia?'

'They are displayed to great advantage, Mr Watts!'

Taking photographs by the fashionable wet-collodion process was a tricky, smelly, neck-straining business, and took an unconscionable amount of time, especially the way Julia preferred to do it, with dim light and slow exposures. Watts's beard was spread dramatically over the bodice of a grubby white muslin shift, belted at the waist. He sat completely still, with an expression fixed and glassy. Underneath his tunic, where realistically he should have sported bare legs and sandals, he wore tweed trews and thick boots. They made him very hot.

'These trews, Julia—' he had begun.

'Forget them!' she said. 'They will not be visible in the picture!'

'Oh. I see. Oh, very well.'

Not only was it stifling in this makeshift studio, but there was a strong smell from the fresh seaweed coiled round his neck, yet Watts was a fairly happy man. How charming to see someone else slaving for art, for once. How pleasant, too, to slip away from the tiresome child-wife, who had been in a peculiar mood ever since leaving London. The last time he saw her she was skipping off like a little girl through the garden at Farringford, without a thought for the etiquette of tea with one's elders. The trouble with Ellen, he reflected, was that she could be so many different sizes in the course of a single day.

'Forty-two, forty-three, forty-four, hm?' barked Mrs Cameron, nodding to him encouragingly, as she walked briskly up and down in her red velvet dress (such energy she had, she was the sort of woman who seemed to run at breakneck speed just to stand still). Watts could feel the sweat starting from his brow. Also, was he imagining it, or could he really remember mentioning a turd at teatime to Mrs Tennyson?

'Forty-five, forty-six!'

Watts had been in Freshwater just three hours, and already Mrs Cameron had dressed him up and got him to work, photographically speaking. Mrs Cameron was deeply fond of Watts, and the reason was not hard to find. Here was a man who knew how to accept her presents, to repay hospitality with humble thanks and words of praise for her kindness. This was a simple matter to Watts, for early in life he had learned the confoundedly simple social lesson that 'How can I ever repay you?' released you from any obligation to cough up ninepence. Amazing, but true. *Throw no gift again at the giver's head* was a foolproof precept for a cheap life in good company. And of course he would sit for Julia. Did it cost him anything? No.

She sneezed. He reacted, but recovered himself.

'Ignore me!' she said. 'Just the chemicals, you know! Don't move! Hm? Stay still! Observe your map, George, with conflicting emotions! Big eyes! Big eyes!'

Watts complied with all this barked advice (delivered in a loud voice, as if sitting still had made him deaf), but he was convinced his crown was slipping, and that the picture would be ruined by the silvery ghost of his locomotive hat. But summoning up the required conflicting emotions of the old Ulysses was not too difficult, he found. On his knee was a crude outline of the Aegean, drawn on a pillow case. 'Why? How? What? When? Where?' he therefore asked himself with genuine confusion.

He had no idea why Julia chose him for Ulysses. After all, he was hardly the heroic nautical type. One minute he'd been snoozing pleasantly in Tennyson's garden, the next he was planning one final heroic voyage toward death in a blacked-out chicken shed. But despite his shortcomings in the Greek hero line, he saw nothing inherently ridiculous in the situation. Where lesser aesthetes, for example, might have queried the choice of implement in his right hand—a small, three-pronged toasting fork, representing ten long years of epic maritime adventure—Watts thought it rather ingenious, and made a mental note.

'A hundred and one, a hundred and two, a hundred and three.' The painter did not move his head—after all, he had his conflicting emotions to attend to, and he had selected a daring combination, comprising pensive and sublime in the upper cranial regions, with a bit of melancholy in the cheek-bone area, and poetic firmness about the mouth. Knowing the action to be permissible, he blinked every thirty seconds. Mrs Cameron allowed her sitters to blink, partly because she grudgingly accepted the necessity, but mainly because she had found the effect of blinks on the final picture artistically desirable. Blinking added a spiritual opaqueness to the eyes, which in turn added to the general air of sublimity. Her latest picture of Mary Ann—'Can I but relive in sadness?'—had the eyes so filmy and opaque that truly it made people yawn and stretch their arms just to look at it.

'A hundred and forty-nine, hm? A hundred and fifty.'

Watts had no idea how long this would go on (it could go as high as five hundred if the exposure was seven or eight minutes), but he was already tired. He resolved that for his next sitting he would choose his own hero, and select a dead one. The corpse of Hector, perhaps; or the Morte d'Arthur—anything that would entail lying prone on cushions. Or he could embody that superb short sentence, 'Homer sometimes nods.' Now his arm ached; the occasional whiff of ether snatched at his tonsils, and at his side, not improving matters in the least, that uppity Irish servant girl recited Tennyson's *Ulysses*, presumably to get him in the mood.

Such a lot of Tennyson one must endure suddenly! He gave her his attention for a moment. She had just reached the bit that went, 'Tis not too late to seek a newer world.'

'Oh, dear,' thought Watts. 'More dreary exhorting stuff. A chap who is capable of *The Lotos-Eaters*, too. Why does Ulysses not remain at home with his charming wife? It has taken him such a long time to get there, after all.'

'A hundred and sixty, a hundred and sixty-one,' continued Mrs Cameron, nodding at him with her hands steepled together, praying him to be still. 'A hundred and sixty-two—Don't move!' Watts could feel the crown sliding, and his emotions conflicted even more. His thoughts turned to Ellen again—before they left London she had casually mentioned the phrase 'Patience on a monument', an absolutely splendid notion for a high-but-extremely-narrow wall he'd heard mentioned in the Clerkenwell area.

'*It may be that the gulfs will wash us down*,' said the girl, unheard by Watts. 'Oh, this part is so *grand*,' she said, breaking off. 'Do you not think so, madam? Is it not the grandest thing?'

'It is by Alfred Tennyson, Mary,' said Mrs Cameron.

'I know, madam. We learned it in the schoolroom—your sons and I, when you very kindly educated me above my station for no purpose. I know it word for word. In fact I feel that I know it as well as Mr Tennyson does himself.'

'I wouldn't count on it,' muttered Mrs Cameron (the treachery of Mariana's peach was still fresh in her mind).

And so the girl continued, from memory, closing the book.

'It may be that the gulfs will wash us down:

It may be we shall touch the Happy Isles,
And see the great Achilles, whom we knew.
Tho' much is taken, much abides; and tho'
We are not now that strength—'

Mrs Cameron interrupted.

'That last part again, Mary, please. I think I heard you touch on the ideal title for this very wonderful picture of Mr Watts, whose noble brow has never shone to such advantage. But I must respect Il Signor's concentration, which is profound, and is a lesson to us all!' (It was true. Mentally, Watts was no longer in the room.) 'Again, Mary! But quietly. Let me hear the lines once more!'

'It may be that the gulfs will wash us down:
[repeated Mary]
It may be we shall touch the Happy Isles,
And see the great Achilles, whom we knew.
Tho' much is taken, much abides; and—'

Mrs Cameron clapped her hands for joy.

'That's it!' she exclaimed. '*Tho' much is taken much abides!* That's *it*!'

Watts, hearing the cry, was recalled from his reverie.

'It is?' he said thankfully, standing up, and removing his crown. 'Much as I love to labour for the muse, Julia, I am profoundly glad to hear it.'

He looked at her.

'Is something amiss, my dear?'

And Mrs Cameron, her picture ruined, watched him with her eyes like saucers, all aghast.

*   *   *

Several minutes after the Ulysses disaster, Mrs Cameron had prepared another plate by coating it with collodion (gun cotton dissolved in ether), washing it in water, and then sensitizing it in a bath of silver nitrate and glacial acetic acid. This chemical stuff had been a bugger to learn, as you can imagine. She removed the plate carefully between two blackened fingers, peered closely, remarked, 'Perfectly satisfactory, just a few hairs and scratches,' and then sneezed on it violently. She threw it out of the door.

The next plate was ruined when it cracked and broke being taken out of the camera; the next when the door to the chicken house flew open unexpectedly during the exposure; the third reached its required seven minutes without mishap, but Mr Watts was found to have moved some inches, due to falling asleep; another plate was dropped on the floor during another tricky process involving pyrogallic acid. The worst hold-up of all, however, was not technical but artistic, when Mary recommenced her reading of *Ulysses*, and mentioned that the king sat 'among these barren crags'—an optional point, thought Watts; but Mrs Cameron, who groaned and smacked her forehead when she heard it, felt bound to represent the rocks, and sent the gardener to find a craggy-looking sack of garden rubbish for Mr Watts to stand on. Watts begged to be excused: he could not stand on a bag of rubbish. And so she had him lolling—which suited him more—and finally, a plate was exposed, developed and fixed.

At which point, with the picture printing on to

coated paper in the late afternoon sunshine outside, the accumulated stress overcame Mrs Cameron and she began to cry out, 'Oh! Oh!', shaking her hand and running on the spot.

'What is the matter, Julia?' asked Watts. 'Have you pricked your finger?'

'I haven't pricked it *yet*. But I soon shall, George, it is only a matter of time, and then potassium cyanide will pass into the cut and course through my bloodstream and then I shall die! Oh! Oh! And nobody will miss me—least of all Alfred Tennyson, the biggest ingrate who ever lived! Oh! Oh!'

'You mean you may give your life for your art, Julia?' asked Watts, patting her hand. 'But wouldn't that be a splendid thing to do? I think so often these days of poor old Haydon, you know.'

'Haydon? Why?'

'I'm not completely sure. But he haunts my dreams with a telescope, Julia; he never quite leaves me alone. He seems to blame me for having a patron and a comfortable life, when he struggled alone in the hard, hard world of bills and debt and children. But that's not my fault, is it? He even begrudges me Ellen—although I'd better not go into that.'

'Oh the dear talentless man,' agreed Mrs Cameron. Kind-hearted soul that she was, she immediately forgot her own troubles, thinking of someone else's. 'Of course we bought his sensational journals when they were published after his death. Charles and I read them in the evenings aloud, and cried a great deal, especially the bits about his brain being too big and driving him mad.'

'I know,' agreed Watts morosely. 'Those journals

were a cracking read.'

'Yes, but Alfred must never know I read them, George! You know how he disapproves of morbid curiosity—which is odd in him, really,' she reflected, 'when he has done so much to make morbid his own middle name.'

And at the thought of dear old Alfred 'Morbid' Tennyson, Mrs Cameron sighed and slumped, and stared at his special gate with eyes forlorn.

'Julia?'

'Yes, George.'

'You don't suppose it *was* my fault, do you? That Haydon took his life? It wasn't because I was getting all the decent walls?'

Mrs Cameron was amazed by the question.

'I am sure he never blamed you, George. But I think it shows the greatness of your heart that you think in such terms.'

She paused. A thought had struck her.

'Are there not plenty of walls to go round?'

'Alas, no, Julia. A good public wall is worth a thousand pounds a foot. And before Haydon made a point of demanding some, there were virtually no walls at all.'

'No walls at all? I see. Well, no wonder he was such a champion of the Elgin Marbles—there's walls for you. Speaking of which, you didn't see whether the Tennysons had hung that exquisite wallpaper I gave them? I've asked so many times now, I can't—'

She trailed off. Watts looked nonplussed. He was not a man on whom wallpaper made an impression.

'As for Haydon, however,' continued Mrs Cameron, 'it was the American midget that killed him, George, metaphorically speaking. Everyone knows that. He could not endure it that all the visitors to his terrible last exhibition preferred to go next door and see that yankee short person, what was his name—?'

'Colonel Tom Thumb.'

'—Yes, that's him. Losing out to a freak, it was so undignified, for a man of his high artistic aims.'

Watts considered. He supposed this must be true. The indignity must have been frightful.

'Actually, I heard the freak was good,' he said at last.

'He was. We went twice.'

'Oh.'

'We bought the book.'

'And Haydon's pictures were bad?'

'They stank, George. They reeked. His talent was never close to yours, whatever you may think. You are England's Michelangelo! Haydon was just a dauber on a very large scale. People only kept asking for his "Napoleon on St Helena" because it was a back view, you know, and because they felt sorry for him. And another thing. Despite all his devout talk and perpetual prayer, it must never be forgotten that Haydon used his own face as a model for the countenance of Our Lord. I fear I can never forgive him for that.'

'It was a bit presumptuous, I suppose—'

Mrs Cameron snorted.

'—But perhaps no other head was available, Julia.'

Mrs Cameron considered the argument for a moment and rejected it.

'There is always a head available, George. We both know that.'

* * *

Back at the Albion Hotel, Jessie folded her arms and assumed an expression which in an older person might have been deemed murderous. It had been a horrible day. Those nincompoops Daisy and Annie had mooned around Mr Dodgson, letting him write them poems and draw funny pictures on the sand with a stick. Daisy had even let Mr Dodgson pin up her skirt again, pretending that she had no safety pins of her own. (She had lots, in fact. Jessie had seen them. Jessie had even equipped her with a dozen of her own.)

Her face was nearly purple with emotion. If Watts had seen her, he would have been prompted to pronounce that old infallible dictum, 'Short folk are soon angry.'

'I love my love with a D!' said Jessie, spitting out the words. 'Because he is a Darling Doggie Dumb-Dumb Dodo! Argh! Pah! Pooh!'

Jessie had expected a bit more attention for herself, that was the sum of it. Dodgson had been absorbed elsewhere, and although she disapproved of him, the rejection stung her. She had yet to learn the sad fiscal lesson of the plain female, that if you don't pay compliments to the male gender, you don't get any back. Lionel Tennyson had virtually ignored her, preferring to chat with a pretty woman fully double her age (Ellen, who was indeed sixteen). To cap it all, Ada had abandoned her, disappearing behind the bathing machines in a sneaking manner the moment Lionel turned up. Ada ought to be a bit more grateful to Pa and me, Jessie thought. We picked her up when she was virtually destitute, and we can just as easily drop her again.

She kicked a table leg.

'The trouble with everybody,' said Jessie aloud, 'Is that they've got no Organ of Gratitude.'

She pursed her lips, pulled her folded arms more tightly to her chest, and let the words revolve in her mind.

Ha! No Organ of Gratitude at all, some people; What some people need sharpening up is their Organ of Gratitude.

Hardly knowing what she was doing, she started to feel her own head, to check that her own Organ of Gratitude was of decent size and health. But she stopped again. Hold on a minute, she thought, where is the Organ of Gratitude? She knew where Benevolence was. Also Acquisitiveness, which in her own case was substantial. But Gratitude? Where ought it to fit in? Was it a higher emotion, or a baser one? Animals were supposed to feel gratitude. But wasn't it a cornerstone of human relations? Weren't good people benevolent so that others could be grateful? Puzzled, she ran to Lorenzo's charts and scanned them for an answer.

It wasn't there.

Jessie took several deep breaths and searched again.

It still wasn't.

'Christopher Columbus!' she whispered. For suddenly it was as plain as day: Nobody had yet discovered the Organ of Gratitude! Phrenology had been going for seventy years, and nobody had located one of the most fundamental organs. And then, one day, a small lisping infant asked the question, 'Where ith gwatitood Daddy?' and revolutionized science.

It sounded like a great myth; she could already visualize the pamphlet. 'How Jessie Fowler located the Organ of Gratitude, Unaided by a Grown-up—Chapter One: Out of the Mouths of Babes.'

As you may see, the scientific implications of this breakthrough were not lost on Jessie. In phrenological terms, her discovery on this Friday afternoon in Freshwater Bay was a landmark. It was like being the first person ever to say, 'Yes, this River Nile is all very well, and yes it's got some very snappy crocodiles in it, but *where does it come from, then*? Don't you think somebody ought to head up country in a pith helmet and find out?'

*   *   *

Back at Dimbola, Mr Watts was invited to remove his smock and see the first signs of the finished picture entitled 'Tho' Much is Taken, Much Abides'. He was quite glad to get the smock off. Its last inhabitant had been an artisan involved in cleaning mackerel (representing King Lear), and if his nose did not deceive him, it had not been washed in between.

Shadows crept across the lawn, and Mrs Cameron moved the printing frame progressively nearer to the house, to keep it in the light. The process of printing was like hatching an egg, she explained to Watts. You had to keep it warm for hours and hours. In fact, the paper had been coated in albumen, which was egg-white, funnily enough, and—

'So you think Haydon did not hold me directly responsible?' said Watts. He was still harping on, apparently.

'If he did, he was even sillier than everybody thought,' said Julia. 'But what's brought all this on, George? He killed himself eighteen years ago.'

'Is it as long as that?'

'Yes, it is.'

Watts had no explanation, but Haydon had haunted his dreams ('Remember Westminster!') only since the marriage to Ellen. Sometimes he showed Watts a tumbling heap of unpaid dress-making bills, and gestured with an unambiguous neck-sawing motion.

'Shall we place the apparatus on the garden wall, perhaps?' Watts suggested. 'If it would be secure, it would catch the last of the warm sun.'

'You are a genius, Il Signor. I have always said as much. We will place it above Alfred's gate, for he never calls at this time. There is no breath of wind, hm? Another hour and the print is made.'

And so Mary Ryan took the precious delicate plate in its printing press, and placed it above the Tennyson gate to catch the last hot rays from the west. Mrs Cameron squeezed Il Signor's hand.

'Thank you,' she said. She should have said it earlier, but she could say it now.

'My dear Julia,' said Watts, with dignity. 'It was the least I could do.'

They went inside.

'I do apologize for my outburst earlier, George, when I said that Alfred wouldn't care if I died from potassium cyanide poisoning. It was unjust.'

Watts was puzzled by the reference.

'Consider it forgotten,' he said, carefully.

'I have been contemplating a picture of "The Absence of Hope",' she said. 'Perhaps that explains my unusually sombre mood.'

'"The Absence of Hope"?' said Watts. 'My own dearest project, Julia! I long to show it to the world. Haydon felt it, I am sure. It is like an undercurrent dragging pebbles down the beach, the sound of a wire snapping, Eurydice dragged back to Hades, or a door slamming at the edge of your hearing.'

'But how to show it?'

'Indeed.'

'Indeed.'

They sat together in glum silence, with Absence of Hope written all over them.

'Despair is not the same, of course,' said Watts.

'Oh no.'

'Haydon, you know, sketched his own children in their death-throes, such was his dedication to his art.'

'Do you think we could stop talking about Haydon now, George?'

'Julia, of course.'

'Would a cup of tea be acceptable, George?'

'I would worship you for the rest of my life.'

Julia laughed. How pleasant it was to hear real gratitude, for once. 'You know what Cameron would say if I asked him that? He would say, "If it makes you happy, Julia".'

Watts considered it. 'He's got a point, I suppose.'

Julia spluttered.

'But George, it is the most infuriating reply! It suggests that I perform kind deeds merely for my own satisfaction. I can't tell you how dispiriting that is.'

This was too deep for Watts, who had never performed a kind deed. But he smiled sympathetically, being keen to smooth the path to the teapot.

'Don't concern yourself about Haydon—' Julia began. But as they made their way to the drawing room, a faint but unmistakable slam and a crash reached their ears. They looked at each other. The sound came from the far end of the garden. On their joint countenance, the Absence of Hope made a long and fruitful visit.

'George!' yelled Ellen, as she capered into the house, showing her petticoats.

'Hello?'

She appeared at the door with shards of glass in her hands. 'Was this important?' she said excitedly, holding out a corner of plate negative.

'I just came in through the gate, and the next thing I knew, well—all the king's horses and all the king's men!' She paused, but only for breath. 'I was lucky it didn't fall on my head, actually.'

Mrs Cameron, who had remained unusually silent, spoke up.

'Oh, I don't know about that, Mrs Watts.' And with a muffled 'Excuse me,' retired upstairs, at an undignified half-run.

'What have I done *now*?' said Ellen.

'You should take more care,' snapped Old Greybeard.

'Why?'

He gave her an accusing look. 'We shan't have tea now.'

'I don't know what you're talking about,' said the girl. 'Why does everybody expect so much of me, without telling me what it is? But I wish you would listen, George. I have discovered a very charming clergyman on the beach who has written a book all about me. Isn't that perfect? This is the first time anyone has written a book about me, George! You should be pleased. And best news of all, tonight there will be a demonstration of phrenology at the parish hall. I knew we would have fun here if we made the effort. Phrenology, George! As Mr Kean used to say so beautifully, *So much for Buckingham! Off with his head!*'

Watts harumphed, and reached his hand towards her face. But it was not a gesture of tenderness; he adjusted her collar, which had come up.

She knew what he was going to say. He said it.

'The phrenologist will manage without us, Ellen, as you well know. Phrenology! At the parish hall! You might as well express the wish to see the Gymnastic Feats of Mr Reynoldson, the Celebrated Cripple!'

'Why, is he on too?'

'Ellen!'

'Well, honestly!'

'Ellen, tonight we must stay with our hosts, of course, and try to repair some of the damage you have done.'

Unquelled, indeed not even listening, she examined the shards of glass and peered at the fractured, ghostly image of Watts. It looked like a real hoot. Was that a toasting fork? Surely not. She tried to pull a long face, indicative of regret.

'What was it called, George—this lovely picture I have ruined?'

'"Tho' Much is Taken, Much Abides", if you must know.'

She brightened. 'Well, not much of it abiding now,' she said, and ran upstairs to prepare herself for an evening of adventure.

Six

That evening, at Plumbley's Hotel, Dodgson made notes in his diary about the children he'd met on the seashore. He was attempting to keep his spirits up. Next to the name 'Daisy' he made a large emphatic cross, and then, after a pause, added a thoughtful question mark. There was certainly something very attractive about the child, even though her forwardness terrified him. Perhaps it was the image of her in the garden with the wings. For some deep reason, Victorians always liked to picture small girls as figuring somewhere between a corpse and a chicken. Next to 'Annie' he wrote 'A triumph, pic soon' and next to 'Jessie' he wrote 'Needs work. Unimpressed by bunny tricks. Poss not child at all, but imposter midget?'

What a life for a grown man with a huge intellect: sucking up to kiddies on their holidays. Yet every day he recorded the names of the new conquests, and calculated whether their parents would let him share them for a couple of hours. Sharing was Dodgson's life, really. The way he looked at it, other people seemed to have lives not so much full to the brim as wastefully overflowing; they generated left-overs of all sorts; it seemed therefore an offence against the Almighty not to cream off some of the surplus. Great trees are good for nothing but shade, as the saying is. So Dodgson shared other people's fame when he took their pictures. He shared other people's poems when he made a parody. He shared other people's teatimes when he dropped by at six. And the little girls? Well, he would never have one of his own.

He stood up and made a decision. He would attend the phrenology lecture. In Oxford or London, he would not have risked the impropriety, but here in the Isle of Wight he could mingle with the artisans and housemaids, and pay his tuppence for the privilege. He always loved a show, as long as there was no harm in it; and to be honest, the social opportunities of Freshwater had been a bit of a disappointment thus far. No response to his letter from Farringford yet; and as for Dimbola Lodge, he was so anxious about being hauled in to pose for Mrs Cameron as Beowulf with a coal scuttle on his head that he had started going past on all fours.

Even from the photographic view, he had got nowhere in Freshwater. Both evenings since his arrival he had stayed in his hotel, alone, writing little letters to child-friends, closing his eyes to picture them with not much on, and polishing his equipment vigorously with a rag.

And why should he not attend the lecture? From all that the dear, pretty Ellen had told him, none of the resident geniuses of Freshwater would stoop to the level of Lorenzo Fowler ('Old Watts will never let *me* go,' she said), so Dodgson felt safe from recognition if he joined the throng. No, the biggest worry was the possibility of audience participation. The great Lorenzo would require heads to practise on; what if Fowler called Dodgson on stage? Phrenologized him in front of a hall full of people? Pulled the secrets out of his head like a magician producing a coloured scarf from a nose? Dodgson reached for a hat and tugged it firmly on his head.

He placed another on top of it. And then the boater.

Dodgson had been phrenologized once before, and had hated it utterly. Even years later, the thought of it made him feel nauseous. That another person should touch one's head, even in a private consulting room in Edinburgh—the intimacy was outrageous, horrifying. And then one must endure the diagnosis, too. Dodgson's outstandingly logical mind had been deduced in Edinburgh; also his abnormally large love of children. But 'Emulous' this insolent Scotsman had called him, to Dodgson's indignance. *Emulous*? Why, he was no more emulous than any other distinguished man of letters writing in England today, if he might include himself in that company (and he thought, on the whole, he might).

Dodgson resolved to stand firm against Mr Fowler if the question of volunteers arose. He wished only to watch the phrenologizing of the lesser orders. If asked to participate, he must simply say no in the firmest possible way.

He practised it now.

'You are very k-k—' he began.

'Thank you but n-n—'

'I f-f—feel I must decl-cl—'

As usual with the Reverend C. L. Dodgson, the firm words needed work.

It was eight o'clock when he left the hotel, and the sun had almost disappeared behind the western downs, but the bay beneath glowed sapphire as though lit from within, the surf danced, and Dodgson felt a surge of happiness. His skin still burned from the day, and he shivered in the sea breeze, but he decided not to return for a scarf, even though he had prudently packed a nice woollen one when leaving Oxford. Life for Dodgson was a succession of resisted urges—as he walked up the lane to Dimbola (it was on the way), he wanted to turn up his collar; he wanted also to break into a frantic run; he fancied snorting like a buffalo, or striking an Anglo-Saxon attitude. But he resisted all of these things, and hardly admitted them even to himself. No wonder he didn't want a scientist poking at the assorted giveaway offal inside his head.

All the rooms at Dimbola Lodge were lit this evening (a typical extravagance of the Cameron woman) and since the curtains were open, he saw as he approached that all sorts of merry larks were taking place inside, including the table and sideboards set for a fashionable dinner *à la russe*—a wasteful method of dining, in Dodgson's opinion. Heaps of fruit, there were, too; and Mrs Cameron darted from room to room with a dripping photographic print in her hands, letting chemicals fall on the table linen as well as on the bare heads of her guests. Dodgson noted that Mr Watts, the painter, was taking an enthusiastic interest in Mrs Cameron's efforts, while pocketing some biscuits for later, and that Miss Terry was nowhere to be seen.

Dodgson clucked at the mess Mrs Cameron made; it was quite unnecessary. In all his years photographing, Dodgson had never sustained the smallest mark or abrasion from his hobby, yet Mrs Cameron ran around with fingers blackened by the chemicals to the state of rotten bananas. 'This is not dirt, but art!' she exclaimed. But the story was told that the great Garibaldi, visiting Tennyson to plant that tree in the garden, had sent her packing, assuming she was a gypsy. He gave her sixpence, apparently, and warned her in Italian that God's eye was upon us all.

This sea breeze was surprisingly nippy. Dodgson sheltered beside Dimbola's briar to readjust his sleeves and cuffs, and was pleased that he had done so, for straightaway from the house came two maids, evidently heading in the same direction as himself.

He let them pass. They didn't see him. One he recognized to be the Irish Mary Ryan; the other must be the famously photogenic Mary Ann. And as if reading his thoughts, the unknown girl threw back her head to observe the first stars, and a beam of silver light picked out her chiselled profile, illuminating her with a kind of halo. It was quite a spooky gift this girl had, actually—even a religious chap like Dodgson had to acknowledge it.

Luckily Mary Ryan noticed what she was doing.

'Will you stop that!' she snapped.

Mary Ann lowered her face and stuck out her tongue, and the sublime patina fled.

Dodgson was just about to move when a door slammed at Dimbola again, and another figure came hurrying past—one of Mrs Cameron's sons, perhaps?—a slim young man in a peaked cap who muttered to himself as he walked. There was nothing very remarkable in that, of course; a man may mutter. No, it was *what* he muttered that intrigued Dodgson.

'My name is, er, um, Herbert Pocket,' he said, in a squeaky and then a gruff tone.

Dodgson wrinkled his nose. What? *My name is, er, um, Herbert Pocket*? Why would the young chap be telling himself his own name? Also, why wasn't he completely sure what it was?

'Yes sir, Herbert's my name, sir,' Mr Pocket continued, 'Down from Lunnon; don't know nobody in the districk—'

Dodgson followed quietly behind. Herbert's stride was lengthening, and he was beginning to stick out his elbows like the ears on a pitcher. What on earth was going on? Herbert poked some loose hair up into the hat, impatiently. He seemed to have a thin waist and ample chest, too; there was a suggestion of hips, moreover. Dodgson would have said 'Curiouser and curiouser', but true to his instincts, resisted it. He knew it might take him all evening to get it out.

* * *

Jessie Fowler had known no other life than this. A hundred times she had heard her father announce to a complete stranger, 'Now, I don't know you from a side of sole leather, is that correct, sir?' And a hundred times the subject had grimaced and shrugged that he supposed the case was so.

The useful thing about phrenology, from the showmanship point of view, was that it really worked. There was no need of trickery. What made one phrenologist better than another were presentation, entertainment, and the quantity of easily affordable products available for sale at the exit. Lorenzo had made and squandered a personal fortune from phrenology, mostly out of selling pamphlets at a penny a go. Getting the character analysis correct was merely the first, easy stage; Lorenzo honestly thought nothing of it. Back in

America, where he hit the sawdust trail thirty years before with his big brother Orson, the Phrenological Fowlers were know to be infallible. Imposters they exposed, murderers they accused, the secrets of human distress they diagnosed with compassion. Almost never had they been run out of town. Those stout fingers could not be fooled. The Fowlers were awesome.

'No Conscientiousness whatsoever!' Orson once exclaimed, his hand flying off a volunteer head as though subjected to a shock of electricity.

'Oh! No Conscientiousness!' repeated the audience with a lot of hissing, as they glanced at one another, wondering exactly what this meant.

Orson bit his lip. Cautiously (as though the head might explode if he pushed it in the wrong place) he continued his search for clues of depravity. The audience held its breath. He lifted a handful of hair and peeked beneath. 'No Approbativeness!' he cried (the audience recoiled). 'No Shame!' He backed away from the head, and begged the audience to tell him what this man had done. He killed a female slave, they said. Orson shook his own head and drooped his shoulders, as though all the strength had been taken from him by the evil of this man. The Fowlers sold out all their pamphlets that famous night in Virginia, even the dog-eared unsaleable ones about the modern miracle of the broad bean and the cause of female suffrage.

Jessie's role on these English tours was to pick out the volunteers, and also to help with the heads and charts at the beginning of the show. Lorenzo always began slowly with a history of the science and a quick run-down of the 'congeries of organs' that comprised the brain. 'Three storeys and a skylight,' was how he genially explained cranial organization—with the base instincts such as sexuality (Amativeness) in the cerebellum, then reflective and perceptive qualities as you moved further upstairs ('You can see more from the top floor!'); and finally Veneration and Hope and Benevolence with the best view of all. You could always tell an archbishop or theologian from the high cathedral dome of his head, Lorenzo explained. And it's true, when you think about it. People who have been dropped head-first on a stone floor in infancy almost never make it into the higher echelons of the church.

During the lecture, Jessie kept her eye on the audience, and smoothed her special stage frock. It was a misguided shade of coral. She would pay particular attention to the people who surreptitiously removed their hats and ran their hands over their Self Esteem. As she looked out now, she could see several people she recognized from the beach, including Mr Dodgson (that pedagogue), who was currently poking his Amativeness with a small pencil. She would have *him*, she resolved quickly, if only to pay him back for all the 'I love my love with a D' business. She also alighted on the Irish maid from Mrs Cameron's house, who had a broad space between her eyebrows—a quality Lorenzo always admired in a woman, since it betokened Individuality.

Jessie listened to the lecture, though she had heard it all before—the pygmies and Napoleon and the Idiot of Amsterdam (aged twenty-five). Lorenzo gave her the Montrose Calculator and she indicated the enormous Organ of Number beside his eyes while mugging in Scots. She watched

Dodgson reach up and touch his own head again. Dodgson had Number and Causality so obvious that Lorenzo would instantly guess he was a logician. In phrenological terms Dodgson was a *gift*; she could hardly wait to give him to her pa.

But tonight Lorenzo was not to be rushed; he was making his public wait and wait. He was displaying Benjamin Robert Haydon now, showing his lack of Firmness but also his—Individuality.

'Persons who have this organ large,' he said, 'are apt to personify abstractions.' Jessie noticed that when he said this, a slim young lad in the audience frowned under his peaked cap as though deeply interested.

Jessie was very proud of her father sometimes. These people were ripe for the picking. By the time she finally raided the stalls for volunteers, she would be knocked down in the commotion.

* * *

'And now,' said Lorenzo, 'My daughter Jessie will ask some of you to join me on this little stage. At no extra cost I will conduct a personal analysis. Please do not resist the call; do not insult me by refusing. Our time is short enough.'

Jessie tugged at his sleeve, as though excited.

'Yes, my dear,' he commanded her grandly. 'Find me a head!'

Dodgson watched with astonishment the downright eagerness of the paying public to be made laughing stocks. Every time Jessie plunged into the audience, he resolved to leave the hall before she did it again—yet something (let's call it prurience) repeatedly prevented him. Up they went, one after another, to be told that their Ideality was superior to their Adhesiveness, each nodding gravely as if making a mental note, and feeling in their pockets for change (charts and explanations were on sale after). One volunteer had Approbativeness out of all proportion—'An intense need for approval, ladies and gentlemen!'—and then proved the diagnosis, rather neatly, by asking nervously 'But I do hope that's *a good thing*?'

Dodgson watched enthralled, horrified, especially in that portion of the evening devoted to Mary Ryan, who spoke up well under questioning, was found to have a good mind and strong character, and even agreed to be hypnotized.

'In this experiment,' said Lorenzo, 'I will demonstrate the power of Phreno-Magnetism.'

'Oooh,' said the audience.

'Phreno-Magnetism is the very latest development, and luckily for you Freshwater folks I am its principal exponent. By hypnosis we may cure the diseases of the brain, direct the mind to purity. For we all strive for perfection, do we not?'

The audience, who had perhaps never looked at itself in quite such a flattering light before, cheerfully agreed that perfection was all it lived for.

'By hypnotizing this young lady I can not only indicate the organs of her brain, but obtain direct access to them. Prepare to be amazed. Simply by touching the Organ of Self Esteem, for example, I will alter this young woman's demeanour.'

Mary, in her trance, sat staring forward at the audience, looking slightly disgruntled as she always did.

'Mary, I will now excite your Organ of Self

Esteem,' said Lorenzo, and with his beautiful hands smoothing and swarming over her head, he exerted pressure with his thumbs on a back section of her skull. Dodgson was astonished at her reaction. Mary Ryan sat up straight, held her nose in the air, and gave a look of such confidence that some of the audience started to titter.

'Please do not laugh,' commanded Lorenzo. 'Self Esteem is a very serious matter. Mary, tell us what you do from day to day.'

The hall fell silent. Mary spoke quietly, but they all heard.

'I do work that is beneath me.'

Mary Ann leaned forward.

'Why do you continue with it?' asked Lorenzo.

'Because I am indebted to my mistress.'

'Indebted? I see. You mean you are grateful to her?'

'No, that's different.'

'You are proud, Mary!'

'Not proud, but I know my worth. I may not be beautiful but I am educated. I am not seventeen, but I am tall and stately. I will marry well.'

'You will?'

'I know it.'

Mary Ann Hillier guffawed, and stopped herself. The audience was agog, but Dodgson shifted in his seat. He hated seeing someone so vulnerable and off-guard. He also hated to hear the lower orders getting above themselves.

'So much for Self Esteem,' said Lorenzo, releasing his grip. 'I must explain that if I asked anybody those questions they would reply in the same surprising way. Our true estimation of ourselves may be masked by daily convenience, but the self esteem remains intact, waiting its moment. It is a flame that is never snuffed out.'

'Tho much is taken, much abides?' said Mary, still in her trance.

'Precisely,' said Lorenzo, pleasantly surprised. 'I will now excite your Organ of Mirthfulness, Mary.' And as he pressed her temples with his fingers Mary started to laugh so cheerfully that the audience laughed with her, and Lorenzo brought her gently out of her trance. Finding herself laughing and joyful, she grasped his hand and would not let go until Jessie grabbed at her skirt and pulled it.

'Thank you, sir,' she said to Lorenzo, wiping her eyes. 'I don't know what you did to me, sir, but don't I feel a whole lot better for it?'

All this was very intriguing for Dodgson, but he never forgot his original resolve to leave while someone else was on stage. The last thing he wanted was to be trapped by his own curiosity. A couple of times he changed seats, to encourage his own false perception that he was invisible. He vowed that during the next demonstration he would definitely slip away—and yet, when the next sitter proved to be the mysterious young er-um-Herbert from Dimbola Lodge, he found himself lingering dangerously. There was something very familiar about the young fellow; he made Dodgson think of *Twelfth Night* for some reason, in which he had once seen Miss Terry play Viola.

Herbert was on stage already, but refusing absolutely to remove his cap. And the audience jeered at him, to take it off.

'Come now,' said Lorenzo, 'You must be reasonable.'

'Either read me with my cap on, or not at all,' said the fellow in his gruff breathless voice.

Lorenzo acquiesced, saying he had never done such a thing before, in thirty years as a practical phrenologist. But when he started to feel the youth's head, he stopped grumbling, because he soon found several things to intrigue him.

'I find that you have large Amativeness, combined with large Hope and small Caution. This will tend to warp your judgement in matters of love, and blind you to obvious failings in the object of your affections.'

The boy looked up at him in amazement. 'It doesn't say all that, does it?' he said.

'Ah, I see I have hit on a truth,' said Lorenzo.

The boy denied it, but looked glum. Down in the audience, Mary Ann nudged Mary Ryan; she liked the look of this boy.

'I think I have never felt a Caution as small as this, sir,' continued Lorenzo. 'It will lead you to many rash deeds. You must remember never to confuse Courage with Carelessness, Firmness with Foolhardiness. You would make a fine actor, sir, incidentally.'

'Oh good,' squeaked Herbert faintly, and tried to rise from his chair. It was clear he would like to step down, but Lorenzo was enjoying himself too much. In all his years of phrenology, he had never encountered a transvestite before—not even on the island of Manhattan! Yet here was one, amazingly, in this little place at the back end of the Isle of Wight.

He ran his fingers across Herbert's fine white neck, making him shudder. 'You have a large Organ of Marvellousness, too—which means you love novelty and adventure,' he announced to the hall, and then he leaned forward and whispered in Herbert's ear. 'Luckily I have Marvellousness large as well. Perhaps we should get together.'

He placed his big hands on Herbert's narrow shoulders. And then he let him go.

'I must explain something now,' said Lorenzo. 'This boy seems sad when I tell him what I read in his head. But I think he should be grateful. He is much too young to have made a bad marriage. There is no sign of a beard on his cheek. The motto of the Fowlers is *Self Made or Never Made*, and I stand by it, young sir. The findings of phrenology are lessons, not prescriptions. Man can, and must, overcome any failing in his nature. How else will he ever be perfect? Now that you know yourself, sir, you must never allow yourself to marry in the hope of being able to work a reform after marriage. You are lucky to receive this warning. It is a lesson many people wish they had been taught!' But Dodgson noticed how the boy still looked glum, even while the hall cheered and laughed Lorenzo for his wisdom.

Lorenzo turned again to his people, and pressed his hands together. 'When you leave here tonight, I want you to write your own epitaph in legible characters on a slip of paper. Make these epitaphs as flattering and eulogistic as possible. Then spend the remainder of your lives endeavouring not only to reach the standard you have raised, but to go far beyond it.'

Jessie looked up at him in admiration as the crowd threw hats in the air. She felt a lump in her throat. What a man!

'And now!' said Lorenzo. The audience held its

breath, while Jessie stood on tiptoe and whispered in his ear. Lorenzo grinned, and looked directly at Dodgson in the back row.

'And now!' he repeated, 'We have time for the last, but most special, demonstration of the evening.' He pointed at Dodgson. 'Would you come forward, please, sir? It has not escaped my daughter Jessie's attention how closely you have followed proceedings this evening!'

Dodgson felt his body jerk with the shock. Trapped and sick, he wanted to shut up like a telescope. Jessie ran straight to the back row and pointed to him and the audience turned round to look. 'Go wan then!' they heckled. 'Wouldn't you guess it ud be an overner tho?' (They were disappointed. The star turn was someone from the mainland.)

Should he run? Should he shout 'Fire'? Miserably Dodgson stumbled to the front and took his seat in a chair beside Lorenzo. Up close, he could see that the man wore a small amount of theatrical make-up. His big pliable hands smelled of sandalwood and other people's hair oil. Dodgson realized he had at last discovered something other people had that he did not wish to share.

'If I may ask your forbearance, ladies and gentlemen, I will ask my assistant Jessie to tell you her first impressions of our friend's head here. For at this point it is my great pleasure to ask Jessie Fowler—the Infant Phrenologist!—to take her very first public reading!'

Dodgson blinked in horror as the crowd cheered.

'May I ask your name, sir?'

Dodgson clenched his fists, swallowed hard and got it out. 'Dodgson,' he said.

'Mr Dodgson,' said Jessie, stepping forward with a big threatening smile. (She got a round of applause.) 'I thought we might start with the base of your cranium, where I perceive, ladies and gentlemen, that the Organ of Philoprogenitiveness is considerably enlarged.'

She said 'Organ of Philoprogenitiveness' as if it was 'Bread and butter'. Which in a way, of course, it was.

Dodgson fought for breath. 'We ought to explain, Jessie,' added Lorenzo, 'that Philoprogenitiveness is the love of children.'

'It is, father. It is a great addition in a parent, and I have always been glad to know that you have it substantial, Pa.'

The audience laughed at the cute, pre-rehearsed joke, but Dodgson felt weightless in his distress. Jessie had climbed on a stool behind his chair. He could feel her breath on his ear. He could smell her clothes. And then, gently, Jessie laid her small warm fingers on the back of Dodgson's skull and massaged it. The unprecedented intimacy of this contact with an eight-year-old girl—in front of a hundred people—made Dodgson want to scream like a railway engine.

'Mr Dodgson, may I ask if you have any children of your own?' began Jessie. But he heard it only as in a dream. Jessie, who had been all set to ask what the name 'Daisy' meant to him, had already lost her first client, as Dodgson's conscious psyche simply snapped under the strain. His body twitched and whiplashed beneath her hands.

'Pa!' she cried in horror, and Lorenzo leapt

forward to assure the audience everything was under control. But the good people of Freshwater stood up and gasped, with their hands to their mouths, as Dodgson reeled and writhed in his chair. No one had ever seen anything like it. Dodgson reeled and writhed, he stretched and drawled; and finally—some might say inevitably—he fainted in coils.

Part Two

Hats Off

Seven

Freshwater Bay is easily located on a map of the Isle of Wight. Imagine the island as a pair of pursed lips—the kiss-me mouth of Lillian Gish comes to mind—and Freshwater is on the bottom lip, to the far left, a small imperfection in an otherwise smooth line of high chalk cliff. There is an apocryphal story told of a Russian tsar, asked by his engineers to indicate on a map where a major railway track should be plotted. With a loud exclamation of 'Do I have to do *everything*?', he took a ruler and drew a straight line—through hills, forests, churches, whatever. And so the railway was built exactly as he drew it, but where his fingers accidentally overlapped the ruler's edge, there came two kinks, which the engineers faithfully replicated. Freshwater Bay is like the kink of a tsar's fingertip. For no observable reason, the chalk dips dramatically for the tiny bay, and then quickly rises up again to lordly heights, as if embarrassed about the lapse.

It is named Freshwater because the River Yar rises here, not far from the sea, and flows perversely in the other direction, across flat land, to the northern coast at (of course) Yarmouth. If the sea defences were knocked down at Freshwater Bay, the waters would merge, and the West Wight become a tiny island of its own, as perhaps it once was. But in 1864 a small isthmus keeps the Isle of Wight in one piece, and that highly insular poet

Tennyson is obliged to put up with it, here at the quiet limit of the world. From his windows at Farringford, he can survey the Afton Down, which he says dates back four hundred million years. From the top of his cliff, he can look to the Needles, stately in their lucid mist. He appreciates grand views. It has been shrewdly observed by modern critics that in Tennyson's poetry, there is no middle distance—things are either big and far, or small and near. Had Victorian ophthalmology been more advanced, the history of English poetry might have been quite other.

*   *   *

Three days after the phrenology lecture, at half past three on Monday, Ellen stood on Tennyson's cliff and watched the laureate point his face at the warm wind and the sea's horizon, his big heavy eyes closed thoughtfully as though he were listening to what the waves were saying six hundred feet below. She recognized the posture and expression from Watts, of course, who had a knack of falling into such a reverie without warning, usually in the middle of a railway terminus. It was whisper-of-the-Muse time—all very worthwhile and pretty on a clifftop with a poem coming on; not so useful if you were racing for an express.

Perhaps she should tweak the laureate's nose, while stamping on his foot and shouting, 'Wake up'. (It usually worked for Watts.) But no, she could just imagine all the tiresome recriminations afterwards, if he fell off the cliff and she trailed home without him, carrying his hat. 'Where's Alfred?' they would ask. And she would sit down in a huff, 'Don't *start*.'

The grass up here was tough and springy, and it mingled with abundant tiny flowers—blue orchids which took the modest course of choosing survival over display. 'They must have Caution pretty huge,' she said to herself, and twiddled with one, attempting to pull it out. She would like an orchid, and Alfred was unlikely to offer her any. If she just took one while he had his eyes closed, he would never be the wiser.

Tennyson leaned into the wind. The thing about this man, she realized as she watched his cloak furl and crack behind him like a flag, was that he was rather like a cliff himself. His large white face looked hewn and shaped by centuries of rain and landslip; and all his life (even when it was quite unnecessary) he seemed to defy a gale, staunch on his stocky Lincolnshire legs, with his chest puffed out. Here was a man who would never discover a sheltered place in the world and then relax in it. Tennyson was a walking personification of the verb 'to buffet'. When Watts was cut up by a review, Ellen had observed that he would mend again by teatime. But Tennyson went all to tatters, and displayed his wounds perpetually, even to people who strenuously desired not to see them. Perhaps his Approbativeness needs looking at, thought Ellen (who was now fully up to speed in phrenological jargon). Tennyson's Approbativeness must be the size of a baby gnat.

Watts had been asked to come, but had declined. You would never get Watts up here, so far from anything upholstered. Though he loved the elements, he preferred to paint them indoors, out of his own head, and since he started visiting

Freshwater he had tried the cliff walk only twice. The first time he was sick, and the second time his hat blew off. (How Tennyson kept his big hat on, incidentally, while striding through gales on his daily walk, was a marvel to all who knew him.)

But Ellen was glad Watts stayed at home. It gave her time to reflect on the phrenology lecture, and her little adventure as Herbert. Appreciating for the first time the variety in the shapes and sizes of the human head, she suddenly understood why hatters went mad. As for her own head, large Hope and small Caution, that was Ellen's destiny—and she thought (as obviously she was destined to) that this was excellent news. And hang the consequences. Watts was always posing her as Hope in some grisly picture or other ('Hope is a Good Breakfast but a Bad Supper'; 'There is Hope from the Mouth of the Sea, but None from the Mouth of the Grave'). What a lark that he had been right all along.

But in other ways her adventure in male disguise had back-fired horribly. For one thing, Lorenzo had guessed at once the game she was playing (the young Herbert's hat stuffed with luxuriant hair); and for another, she had felt terribly discouraged by Lorenzo's other pronouncement, about her tendency to love blind. 'Do not expect to reform your spouse's character after marriage,' Lorenzo had said. Too late, too late for that.

Reappearing at Dimbola—having used the commotion of Dodgson's collapse as a cover for flight—she found she had not been missed, least of all by her husband. A cup of tea had been poured for her, in fact. So she drank it cold, and listened to Mrs Cameron announcing her latest plan for a theatrical evening in the garden, a selection of tableaux vivants, possibly from *Twelfth Night*. It was curious how Mrs Cameron did not seek Ellen's professional advice on theatrical matters. A less resilient person might suspect that Mrs Cameron didn't like her.

'Oh, there is nothing like *Twelfth Night* for tableaux vivants,' sighed Julia, leaning back in her chair.

'I would have thought *A Midsummer Night's Dream* more apt,' said Ellen.

'I didn't say there was nothing more apt,' snapped Julia, 'I said there was nothing like it.'

Watts snoozed over a volume of verse, and when he woke to find his wife sitting beside him, he said happily, 'Ellen. Oh yes. Do you know, I was just telling Julia. When I resided with Lord and Lady Holland in Italy, you know they refused to allow me the merest personal expense? "You are our *guest*, Il Signor," they insisted, "Take some more soup, you eat like a little bird," they said. "And no more talk of such nonsense. Your purse is nothing to the matter here." Julia agreed with me, such generous sentiments are very fine. Between friends, *especially where one is very poor*, there should never be talk of money.'

Ellen rolled her eyes. She noticed that Watts was wearing a new velvet skullcap—a present, no doubt, from Julia, who had noticed that George was balding, his Organ of Veneration quite naked to the elements.

'Sixpence a pint!' boomed Alfred, unexpectedly.

Ellen turned to find him smiling. Amazingly, his clifftop reverie had finished before hers.

'This air,' he explained, gesticulating with his

cloak. 'Worth sixpence a pint!' And playfully he scooped armfuls of it towards her, as though he would knock her flat with the force. Ellen laughed. A game at last! She pretended to gather the sixpenny pints in her skirt, weighing the material in her hands, as though loaded with heavy logs. 'That's at least five shillings' worth! Ten shillings! A guinea!' she said gaily, staggering.

But Alfred stopped when she said that.

'Oh,' he frowned, suddenly serious. He bit his lip. 'In that case, my dear, I think I'll ask for some of it back.'

* * *

News of the sensational phrenology lecture had been quick to disseminate, especially since the bewildered and whimpering Dodgson had been wheeled through the village on a grocer's hand-cart and left at Dimbola for Mrs Cameron to deal with. No sooner had Ellen set down her teacup, in fact, and recovered her breath from the quick change, than the whole household was in uproar, with Dodgson dropped on a sofa in the drawing room, and Lorenzo Fowler presenting calling-cards to everybody in the *mêlée*, and Mrs Cameron flapping the prone logician with an Indian shawl.

'Tempt him with a dry biscuit!' she told her girls, who ran off efficiently for bandages and camphor and everything else the crisis suggested.

Privately, in a whisper behind the drawing room door, Mary Ann apologized for bringing him. She knew Mrs Cameron's feelings towards the Reverend Dodgson.

'No, child, you were quite right,' Mrs Cameron

declared. 'He is a rival, as you know; and also a very pompous man, and I believe an opponent of my good friend Jowett in Oxford. But a rival and bore in distress is another matter. Poor fellow, what can we do for him?' She ran back into the room and shook her hands as though drying them. 'I would give *anything*. How did it happen, Mr Fowler? Tell us that.'

Lorenzo shook his head. The room waited.

'Speak, speak,' urged Julia.

He looked very grave.

'I believe he was overcome by the size of his own organs, ma'am.'

Dodgson's eyes opened and he saw Mrs Cameron quite normally, surrounded by her friends in the drawing room of Dimbola. But then something rather odd happened. With her face horribly enlarged, she leaned towards him and said directly in his ear, 'I dare say you're wondering why I don't put my arm around your waist?'

He stiffened with alarm, but she continued, 'I'm doubtful about the temper of your flamingo.'

Dodgson squealed and pressed his body into the sofa. Mrs Cameron gripped Lorenzo's wrist. 'What have you done to him? He seems to be out of his wits.'

Indeed he did. Inside his head, Dodgson was currently attending a game of croquet organized by the Queen of Hearts; and an ugly Duchess was stealing her arm around his middle towards the flamingo he was using as a croquet mallet. Not surprisingly, Mrs Cameron had not the faintest notion that this was going on.

'My dear man,' she said, and patted his hand.

'He might bite!' warned Dodgson, and flashed

his eye-whites. (He meant the flamingo.)

Without a trace of annoyance, Mrs Cameron told the girls to make a bed for Mr Dodgson and send at once for his belongings at Plumbley's Hotel. This man needed nursing, nourishment, and battering with gifts, so much was clear.

'Mustard isn't a bird,' said Dodgson, rather feebly, as he was lifted from the sofa and helped upstairs. 'It's a mineral, I *think*.'

'That's right,' said Mrs Cameron, following behind.

'There's a large mustard mine near here,' he continued. 'And the moral of that is—The more there is of mine, the less there is of yours.'

'I quite agree with you.'

Watts and Ellen heard him continue until he was out of sight.

'Never appear to be otherwise,' he said, 'than what it might appear to others that what you were or might have been was not otherwise—'

Watts and Ellen stood in the Dimbola hallway watching Dodgson's progress upstairs. Ellen felt very sorry for him; but she couldn't help noticing how the shock had cured his stammer.

'Well, it's an ill wind, George—' she began, but stopped. She never got Watts started on a wall if she could help it.

She took Watts's hand and turned to him, her eyes still blazing from the thrill of the escapade. Should she tell him about her Organ of Hope? His happy Italian reminiscences seemed to have lifted his spirits so much. For once, he was looking positively animated.

Taking his hand to the top of her head, she began, 'Did you know, George—', but he pulled it away and interrupted. He put his arm around her shoulder instead. It was the most intimate thing that had happened in weeks.

'Oh George,' she said. 'Are you concerned for Mr Dodgson?' He put his lips to her ear. She thrilled. This holiday was already doing them both *such* good.

'Ellen,' he confided in an excited whisper. 'In all the commotion—'

'Yes, George?'

'—Somebody dropped a florin. Look.'

She looked down and saw the coin in his hand. Nudging her in the ribs, he slipped the coin in his pocket and patted it there.

*　　*　　*

From the commercial point of view, Lorenzo's phrenological evening had been a fiasco.

'But you were magnificent, Pa,' Jessie was still saying after the weekend, 'everybody said it.'

She hated it when he was unhappy. She had already fed him some breakfast ('No brains for *you*, Pa! Ha ha!') and soothed his brow with a damp handkerchief; now she volunteered to polish the heads as well, even though they didn't need it.

'Ada did them yesterday,' he objected.

'Then I'll do them again. She doesn't know how to do them anyhow. Ada said I had red hair, Pa. Red hair! When all the world can see I am strawberry blonde!'

Lorenzo looked beyond his child to Ada, whose air of condescension was beginning to get on his nerves. Behind Jessie's back, this difficult maid was now working some scissors in thin air—as though practising for cutting something thick—and all the while frowning menacingly at the back of Jessie's head.

Jessie was oblivious. She shook her horrid curls. She was dressed today in orange.

'Look how shiny I'm getting Mr Haydon. I bet nobody ever did this to him in real life. That's probably why he killed himself. Oh, cheer up, Pa! Think of your Organ of Firmness.'

But Lorenzo refused to be comforted. He ran his powerful fingers through his own iron-grey locks. 'I had them in the palm of my hand,' he kept repeating. 'The palm of my hand.'

It was no wonder Lorenzo was downhearted, however. Generating mass hysteria takes a lot of effort, and Lorenzo had reached the time in life when he only expended in energy what he bargained to recoup in cash. Freshwater on Friday had been a three-guinea crowd. But with Dodgson's dramatic collapse, the guineas had all dispersed, skipping over the usual rush for merchandise; and if Lorenzo now had a considerable *succès d'estime* on his hands, he also had two hundred pamphlets he had expected to sell at the door.

He kicked a demountable brain which Jessie had just cleaned and assembled on the carpet.

'Pa!' she objected, as the labelled bits of grey plaster cerebrum exploded across the room. Secretiveness skittered under a bureau; Amativeness flew high in the air; only Inhabitiveness stayed put. Ada was commissioned to gather them up. She whistled between her teeth.

'Look,' Jessie said, 'I wasn't going to tell you this, but has it ever occurred to you that there is an organ missing from this model?'

'More organs are discovered every day, Jessie. The year alone saw the location of Graveness, Gayness and Awe.'

She patted him encouragingly. 'And where would we be without *them*?' she agreed.

They were on their hands and knees, fitting the pieces together with automatic efficiency—it was a job they could do with their eyes closed. Jessie had never seen a conventional child's puzzle; her earliest memories were of assembling bits of brain.

Should she tell Lorenzo about Gratitude? What if he didn't say thanks? Part of her still wanted to keep her discovery to herself, but she had gone too far to turn back now: she knew she would have to share it.

'But what about Gratitude, Pa?' she blurted. 'Where's that?'

'Gratitude?' He had replaced the final piece in the demountable brain, and sat back on his heels to look at it. Gratitude? Just as Jessie had done before, he considered where Gratitude ought to come in the scheme of human feelings. Was it a fine emotion or a base one? Didn't the lion feel grateful to Androclus? On the other hand, didn't children have to be trained to thank?

'I think we should look for it, Pa,' said Jessie, firmly. 'I've been thinking about it. And I believe it says more about a person than anything.'

'Nonsense.'

'But you remember the Irish one on Friday night? She said she was indebted, not grateful, and you were shocked.'

'Mm.' Lorenzo stroked his beard.

She tried another angle.

'Even if it doesn't really mean anything—if nobody ever feels it—people would want to know they had a big organ of it, wouldn't they? And what's the point of Benevolence without it?'

Lorenzo said nothing. He was not convinced. So the child chose another tactic.

'I just thought you'd be pleased to beat Uncle Orson to something. But don't worry, Pa. I'll write to him in Boston, he's sure to do it.'

'No, don't do that!' said her pa.

'No, Uncle Orson will polish it off in no time—'

'Give me a minute, Jessie, please.'

He thought quickly. He pictured the pamphlet. *A Million Thank Yous. How Lorenzo Niles Fowler discovered the Organ of—Gratitude, Unaided by his Know-all Brother Orson*. It sounded good.

Also, he had to admit he was rather stuck at the moment. Thanks to Dodgson's spectacular breakdown, the Phrenological Fowlers would need to stay in Freshwater for a few more days in any case, organizing some other kind of event to pay for the expense of the first one. Why not conduct a little research at the same time?

'Jessie, would you care for a stroll on the shore?' She folded her arms. She hated it when he changed the subject. Was this a yes or a no?

'What would you say if I preferred to stay here?' she said distrustfully, her eyes like slits. 'With Ada,' she added.

'Huh,' said Ada, and left the room.

'I'd say your Organ of Gratitude is probably very, very small.'

Jessie jumped into his arms and kissed him.

'Oh, Pa!'

* * *

At the bay, Daisy sat alone in the lee of a bathing machine and unfolded a dog-eared paper. It was Mr Dodgson's 'I love my love with a D', and it filled her with pleasure. She had known this man—this genius—less than a week, but already he was desperately in love with her. He had asked her to pose for a photograph called 'The Elopement', standing on the sill of an upstairs casement, with a packed bag in her hand. It could mean only one thing.

The stupid Jessie Fowler had told her to refuse the safety pins, so nah-nah to Jessie Fowler now. Mr Dodgson did not love his love with a J, because she was Jealous. When Daisy ran away with Mr Dodgson and got married, she would send Jessie Know-All Fowler a whole cartload of safety pins along with a copy of Mr Dodgson's delightful book, illustrated with photographs of herself.

'*Daisy's Adventures in Wonderland*,' she said to herself.

Daisy was a very determined little girl. A man did not meddle with her precocious femininity without reaping the consequences.

* * *

Back on the cliff, Ellen had just finished telling the laureate about the new guest at Dimbola, careful not to mention his name. She remembered what Lionel told her, that Tennyson loathed Dodgson; if she spoiled this pleasant walk by making her companion angry, she was bound to get into trouble later on. Tennyson would not inquire for details, anyway. He was notorious for his lack of interest in other people. But on this occasion he enjoyed Ellen's spirited account of the story so much (she did all the voices, and acted bits out) that he actually wanted more.

'Does he have a profession, this fellow?'

'Oh.' Ellen thought quickly. Better not to mention the Euclid or the photography. 'Well, he is a gentleman and a cleric, of course, sir. And he has written a book for children, which he has been telling the little girls on the beach.'

'A book of morals?'

'No, something quite different. Little Daisy Bradley told Mrs Cameron that his story was very funny and dreamlike—with songs and mad people and animals who take offence. Daisy seems quite taken with Mr Do—' She stopped herself. 'Actually, I saw his manuscript when it was brought from his hotel. I read it.'

Tennyson frowned.

'I hope you did not read it without the author's permission.'

Ellen was obliged to confess. 'Well, to be honest, I did.'

'Without the author's permission *or knowledge*, Mrs Watts?'

'Er, yes.'

She could tell he was shocked. Another telling-off was coming.

'I cannot begin to condone—' he began.

She made a quick decision. 'His name is Lewis Carroll,' she added. 'His book is very good.'

Tennyson snorted. He hated to hear about other people's writing. Especially when it was described as very good.

'What's good about it? What do you mean about animals taking offence?'

'I think you have to read it, sir. It's hard to explain. Alice is always in the wrong, because the rules of behaviour in Wonderland are mad and topsy-turvy. It's supposed to be a fantasy; but personally, I find it extraordinarily true to life.'

'And is he in his right mind now, this Mr Carroll?'

'It's hard to say. This morning he sat up in bed and said, "Mary Ann, what are you doing here? Run home this moment, and fetch me a pair of gloves and a fan!" But when she brought him what he asked for, he seemed to have forgotten all about it. He looked her in the eye and said "You? Who *are* you?" He seems to be quoting his own book. We are thinking of asking Mr Fowler to treat his brain.'

'Mr Fowler was the phrenologizer?'

'Yes, and he was spectacular. Not that I was present, of course.'

'Of course.'

Tennyson fell silent again. They had reached the lower part of his cliff walk, near to the bay and the military fort. He would be taking her down to his special cove, she hoped.

'What about madness?' he said, stopping.

'Oh, I don't think he's mad.'

'No, I meant, can a phrenologizer detect signs of madness—say, in the head of a young boy? Oh, we check Lionel and Hallam every day, we make a point of it. What with the, you know—'

'Black blood of the Tennysons?'

'That's right. But the trouble is—' he lowered his voice '—we are not exactly sure what we are looking for.'

Ellen didn't know what to say.

'I think I will approach the fellow—although Emily must not know. She thinks I worry too much about the boys' melancholic inheritance. "You're just being morbid like the rest of your family, Alfred!" she says. Which, as I tell her, is precisely the point I'm making!'

And he strode off into the wind again, while Ellen skipped along to keep up, her hand still gripping tight the little blue orchids—a dozen or so—that Alfred Tennyson had not given her.

* * *

Below stairs at Dimbola, Mary Ann was having a bad time wringing clothes. Her hair kept getting caught in the mangle. It was a funny life, being the Mother of God yet fated to such humble pastimes. She wondered how the original Mary, mother of Jesus, had managed to bring herself down to earth when it came to cleaning out the stable and such. Education had not been the main focus of Mary Ann Hillier's upbringing.

'So what be aall this tork o marryin?' she asked Mary Ryan, who had just returned from shooing Lionel Tennyson out of the pantry. (The servants had a rota for this job.)

'Marrying?'

Mary Ann spluttered in disbelief.

'Be you forgooat?' she exclaimed. 'When old me nabs ketch'd you in yon traance, zee what you zed o ticin a townser!'

Mary Ryan looked perplexed, as well she might.

'What do you say, Mary? Can we start again at

"marrying"?' she suggested, without facetiousness.

But Mary Ann had started to enjoy herself, repeating the story of Mary Ryan's wiggled Self Esteem, in a dialect so impenetrable that alas for the consequences, it left the exact contents to be guessed at only vaguely.

Mary Ryan picked up only that she had discussed her marriage prospects with Lorenzo Fowler in front of a room full of people. But why? Had he predicted she would marry well? Why couldn't she remember?

Meanwhile Mary Ann kept jabbering and mangling, with considerable gusto. It was not often she spoke her thoughts aloud, which was just as well. It was like hearing the Rokeby Venus speak in the accents of a Tyneside shipbuilder.

'Thee wast querken like a wold zow then, bwoy!' she said. 'The whole show wudn't nowhere near what twas puted to be, but "I know my worth" zes shee. If thee gits vound out, there'll be a pretty piece o work! An I dooan't gee noohow. Them towner rantipikes be no count at all anyways, swap me bob.'

Mary Ryan recognized the last bit. 'Swap me bob' meant 'So help me God', but goodness knew what the other stuff entailed. Rantipike? What was a rantipike? But one thing was certain. She must consult Lorenzo Fowler as soon as possible.

Mary Ann had changed the subject. 'Have ye zid the wold cappender about y'ere lately? A was here yes'day smaamen over the back door wi tar but I han't zid nothen on en zunce.'

Mrs Cameron put her head round the door. 'Is all well?' she asked.

'Mary Ann has caught her hair in the mangle

again, madam,' said Mary Ryan. 'Shall I cut it all off to save us the trouble every day of saving it?'

Mrs Cameron looked shocked, and then burst out laughing. Mary Ann, temporarily unable to raise her neck from waist-height, gaped with astonishment.

'You are a bad girl, Mary Ryan,' said Mrs Cameron.

Mary Ann tried to extricate herself but couldn't.

'Swap me bob!' she said.

* * *

Ellen and Tennyson continued their walk on the cliff.

'Does your husband work on any canvases here in Freshwater?'

'I am sure he will ask you to pose again, sir,' said Ellen. 'Otherwise, I have high hopes for "Take Care of the Pence and the Pounds Will Take Care of Themselves", a new painting in which coins of small denomination are tucked up in Crimean hospital beds, while bank notes exercise in the fresh air, with a set of Indian clubs.'

Tennyson tried to picture it.

'I was joking,' added Ellen quickly.

'Oh,' said Tennyson gravely. 'A joke. But not a disrespectful one, I hope? It sounded slightly disrespectful. Watts is a very fine painter, my dear, even if sometimes a little misguided by his enthusiasm for simple verities.'

She didn't argue. But she had to admit that this walk was putting her right off Tennyson. He'd told her to say 'luncheon' instead of 'lunch', and was fiercely emphatic about it, even though London fashion had now swung quite the other way. Why were people always telling her off? Surely she made it clear often enough that she didn't like it.

They walked on.

'Will you take me down to your special cove today?' she said.

'I will if you desire it. But it's a steep climb, my dear. Do you think you can manage?'

'Of course, sir, lead the way,' she said. But then she remembered the modest size of her Caution, and wondered whether she was muddling foolhardiness with firmness again.

'My only fear, sir,' she added, 'is that, were I to slip, I would knock you down ahead of me.'

Alfred frowned, and then had an idea.

'Then you shall go first!' he said.

Eight

Unluckily for her friends, Mrs Cameron never stopped to consider why she gave presents all the time; why she flattered, helped, donated and worshipped to such an embarrassing degree. Perhaps she spent her whole life compensating for being the only unattractive sister in a family of beauties. While Tennyson's family were all mad, and Ellen's all flighty, and Dodgson's all boring, Julia's were all knockdown dazzlers who caused breaches of the peace in London shopping districts. It wasn't easy being nicknamed 'Talent' in these circumstances. To be called 'Talent' when your sisters include 'Beauty', 'Dash' and 'Eyebrows' sounds a bit like a codeword for 'Ugly'.

Whatever the cause, however, Julia might reasonably have asked, 'What's so *wrong* with giving presents?' In fact, she asked it repeatedly, because her benevolence was treated like an impediment or a club foot. Why weren't people just grateful? But when anyone said 'You shouldn't have!' to Julia Margaret Cameron, they usually meant it. On receiving a prayer book from her, Thomas Carlyle is supposed to have said, 'Either the devil or Julia Cameron has sent this!' Such bad grace bewildered and hurt her, but did not put her off. When she met with rebuff, she deduced that the present was at fault, and conceived a better one. Thus was she caught in an ever-tightening spiral, requiring more and more profligate ingenuity.

For Julia would not learn. She had Benevolence so enormous that her lace cap wouldn't fit her head properly and was always falling off. Items were returned with polite demurrals; high-quality wallpaper was *not* hung; she was rhetorically lumped together with the father of lies; and worst of all, those inferior persons who were objects of her charity simply forgot their debt and took their luck for granted. She just couldn't understand it. If an allegorical picture of Mrs Cameron were attempted, she often thought it would have to depict 'More Kicks than Ha'pence'.

Look at the ungrateful Mary Ryan, snatched from poverty (and a dirty gypsy mother) on Putney Heath, and reared by Mrs Cameron at her own personal expense. 'You are too good, Julia,' friends said. 'The girl is inexpressibly fortunate.' Yet the girl herself was blind to the claims of charity. She was sullen, she refused to be beautiful in any useful photographic way, and she whined about her position in the household—was she a maid or a daughter? Why had she been educated if she was meant only for housework? Why was that dullard Mary Ann given all the nice jobs? Mrs Cameron was exasperated by such ungrateful talk. Mary Ryan was now joking about cutting off Mary Ann's lovely hair!

'Doesn't she realize that without my intervention, she might be dead of neglect?' Mrs Cameron railed bad-temperedly at Mary Ann, in her quiet time. Mary Ann, instead of speaking, tilted her very best 'Eve Repentant' profile, knowing how well a picture of feminine humility broke Mrs Cameron's heart. She was looking particularly soulful these days, because she was in love. Ever since the lecture, she had dreamed of young Herbert—such an exotic young creature, with such an unusual figure!

Julia's old white-beard husband kept aloof from such upsets, although he pitied her when she stormed into his bedroom, her cheeks wet with tears. 'Thrown back in my face,' she would cry, pacing up and down. 'Thrown back in my face.' Generally supportive in a wry, ironic, bedridden kind of way, he would nevertheless gently warn her when he thought she expected too much from Mary Ryan, or when her grand, unlikely presents overstepped the mark. The Elgin Marbles wallpaper for Farringford was a case in point.

'Perhaps you went too far, my dear, although acting as always from the best intentions?' her husband suggested. 'And the mutton was a lovely idea, Julia, except that the Farringford estate is over-run with sheep. See the white fluffy things on the downs?'

She sat on his bed, and slumped, helpless.

'I shall knit you a muffler, Charles,' she said.

'If it gives you pleasure, Julia.'

This was non-committal without being rude, and was his usual, well-practised response. As Julia had complained to Mr Watts, it avoided saying thank you and thereby implying an obligation.

'See, Charles, I have converted the vegetable plot into a lawn overnight! You said you wished we had more grass!' Julia would declare.

Or, 'While you were asleep I redecorated your bedroom! You said you preferred a darker shade!'

And rather than discouraging her by saying, 'You're mad, Julia,' he would smile. 'If it makes you happy, my dear.'

But what *was* the problem with this Elgin Marbles wallpaper, you ask? Well, obviously, it had the Elgin Marbles on it. As with so many of Julia's presents, the wallpaper was a gift inadequately thought through. Where would it hang at Farringford? Did it accord with the Tennysons' usual taste? What did it say about how Julia perceived her friends?

'She thinks we belong in the British Museum,' said Emily.

Yet Julia had such a powerful vision of Alfred's pleasure on receiving this imaginative gift ('Julia, what a kind person you are') that she had been unable to resist it. She had little idea what discord it would sow between Alfred and Emily, who were now scarcely on speaking terms. Lord Elgin and his wallpaper were now touchy subjects at Farringford. Lionel Tennyson had noticed (with delight) that even if you dropped the words 'Parthenon' or 'Great Russell Street' fairly innocently into a conversation, you would get some very sour looks.

'Let's burn the damn stuff,' Alfred had said.

'But how would Julia feel? She is such a good friend, Alfred.'

'Would you rather we hung it on the walls and let it look at us?'

'No.'

'Well, then.'

Emily was glad that Julia could not ensnare Alfred's better nature by the gift of a few baubles; but at the same time horrified by the possibility that he simply had no better nature to ensnare.

'It must be frustrating for Julia,' she sympathized, but only half-heartedly. It was quite comical, actually, from Emily's point of view. That Julia openly adored Alfred did not impress him; he regarded it as only natural. That her unreturned attentions made her unhappy was nothing to him. The stream of votive presents were an amusement ('What's it today? A teapot!'); now that Emily had started sending things back, he was puzzled, nothing more.

Emily ordered that the wallpaper be piled at the base of Alfred's little spiral staircase—the special escape route built on the corner of his library so that he could avoid meeting invaders and invited guests. Emily felt he had been passing her the problem and forcing her to solve it; this seemed like a good passive way of handing it back. Every time he ran down his stairs, he would have to vault six rolls of wallpaper.

This was only fair. Emily protected her husband from so much that was unpleasant, she refused to protect him from well-meant gifts as well. Another letter from 'Yours in aversion' had arrived this morning, and she put it in her pocket unopened, as always. She was glad now, anyway, that she never warned Alfred about the imminent arrival of Mr Dodgson. By some unknowable stroke of good fortune, the dreadful fellow had not shown up.

* * *

The great delight at Dimbola Lodge was the discovery that they had a new genius in their midst. To add to the greatest living poet and the greatest living painter, Julia could now lay claim to the greatest living nonsense writer (Edward Lear always gave her the cold shoulder anyhow). So while Dodgson took beef tea in sips and continued to mislay his reason, the manuscript of *Alice's Adventures in Wonderland* was read by everybody, even old Mr Cameron, who particularly approved the Cheshire Cat, and the philosophical discussion between the King, Queen and executioner about whether a head can be beheaded when it is not connected to a neck.

'I could quite happily think about this logical point for a week or more, Julia, if I were not excited with unexpected presents.'

All Mrs Cameron's former dislike of Dodgson—based only on reputation—was now swept away by her enthusiasm for Lewis Carroll. 'I refuse to believe Mr Dodgson was overcome by the size of his own organs,' she said. 'The sheer imaginative effort of writing this book could break the constitution of any man. But I do wish the poor fellow would recover himself,' she added. 'I want to know why a raven is like a writing desk.'

Watts grew cross and grumpy, but Julia barely noticed. All weekend, everything was *Alice* this, and *Alice* that. Il Signor got almost no attention. Julia's behaviour was quite insensitive, and her noisy trilling about *Alice* was causing him a headache. On Sunday he had set up his easel and begun work on the recolouring of Ellen's portrait ('Choosing'), but nobody asked him why the rosy cheeks were turning pale. Every time he sat down to instruct Julia on the Italian masters, too, she would think of some other mad coincidence that brought the world of *Alice* closer to her own existence.

'How extraordinary, George, that I painted my roses on Wednesday! You see, that is the sort of thing that may have *set him off*. As we both know, George, genius must always be treated with delicacy.'

Watts winced.

'In that case, could you call me Il Signor?'

'Of course, George. Just say the word. But I feel sure the way to jolt him out of this state is to bring Alice alive for him in some way—perhaps little Daisy. What do you think? We could do tableaux! Ellen says that before his breakdown, he always stammered, people supplied his words for him. Now he speaks fluently, but nonsense. The human mind is fascinating, hm?'

Watts shrugged and stared out of the window toward the bay, where he saw Ellen approaching with Tennyson, just in time for tea. Ellen really was very beautiful. It was such a shame he couldn't do anything about it.

'Haydon came to me again in the night,' Watts confided.

Julia said, 'Did he, dear?' but she had followed his gaze to Alfred and the pretty girl, and was not really listening. It was truly irritating that Mrs Watts was the living Maud. Julia loved Alfred better than anybody, and he was always rotten to her because she was not young or pretty.

'Yes. The poor dead fellow was shaking his fist at me and pointing to the place where he cut his throat.'

'Don't take it to heart,' she said, still preoccupied. 'It was really not your fault. It was the yankee midget, as I told you before. Live for the present, George.'

'But Julia—'

Ellen and Tennyson arrived at the front door,

and Julia recovered herself with a great effort.

'And what a coincidence that we have a Mary Ann in the house when there is one in *Alice*, too!'

Watts gave in. Was there any profit in pointing out that half the maids in England were called Mary Ann? Probably not.

'Fancy,' he clucked.

'What's that, George?'

'Mary Ann, fancy that. What an uncanny coincidence. Ellen's first name is Alice, too, did you know? Another accident which isn't one really.'

'No?'

'No, she tells me that Dodgson met her and admired her when she was only eight. She has concluded that the child in the book is her.'

'Little Alice is Mrs Watts!' Julia exclaimed in disbelief, as she watched Ellen arrive at the front door and remove her bonnet.

'Oh I don't think so, not Mr Dodgson too,' she muttered. 'That silly girl can't inspire *everybody*.'

* * *

After tea, Ellen was commissioned to sit upstairs with Dodgson for an hour, to see if there was anything she could do. Mary Ann came with her. They found him sitting morose in a high-backed chair beside an open sashed window, dressed in a heavily embroidered Indian shirt and a purple fez, evidently some inappropriate gifts from Julia. His gaze was far out to sea, and he hardly looked around when the others entered. His demeanour reminded Ellen of the mad scenes she had seen in Shakespeare—people are always mad when there is a crashing shore nearby, it seemed. If she dared, she would put her orchids in Dodgson's hair and tousle it a little.

But what really impressed her was that Dodgson, in this big shell of a chair, reminded her of the Mock Turtle on the sand in *Alice*, which she had read again that morning. So she sat on a low stool, quietly, and listened to the distant breaking waves, wondering who would play the Gryphon to complete the picture.

Mary Ann spoke up, with a big effort to sound normal.

'This here young lady,' she said, 'she wants to know your history, she do.'

Dodgson looked at Ellen, and then at the sea again, and then turned back. Demented or not, he certainly looked unhappy—as you would, too, if you were remembering that you were a real turtle once.

'I'll tell it to you,' he said. 'Sit down both of you, and don't speak a word until I've finished.'

Since they were already both sitting down, they did not move. They glanced at each other, and Ellen put her finger to her lips. She had a plan to remind him of his normal self.

'Once,' he said, with a deep sigh, 'I was a real t—'

'Turtle?' Ellen prompted.

Dodgson bit his lip, and looked back out of the window. Biding for time, he wiped a tear with the back of his hand.

'When we were little, we went to school in the sea,' he continued. 'The master was an old turtle. We used to call him T—'

'Tortoise?' she interrupted.

Dodgson sobbed, as though a bone was in his throat, and tried again.

'You may not have lived much under the sea, and perhaps you were never even introduced to a lobster—'

'No, but I would love to see a Lobster Quadrille!' said Ellen.

Dodgson put his hands to his head and closed his eyes. This wasn't supposed to happen. When he opened them again, the little girl was still sitting at his feet, with her chin in her hands, her big childish eyes gazing up at him.

'Alice?' he said. 'Is it you, Alice?'

'Yes, I'm Alice,' she said, quite truthfully. (Well, she was.)

'Alice, a terrible thing has happened. I hardly know how to tell you, my dear. But somehow or other, you have got inside my head.'

* * *

As night fell across the bay, Lorenzo and Jessie finally gave up testing each other for the Organ of Gratitude. After hours of hypnotic tests, expert manipulation, and some fairly brutal heart-searching, they were forced to admit the possibility that neither of them had one.

'Perhaps one of these characters had it, though, Pa,' said Jessie, indicating the heads, piled like a Golgotha in the corner of the room. 'That Haydon was always glad of help, wasn't he?' She went and got Haydon, and set him on the table.

Lorenzo frowned. 'He was always asking for help, certainly, but—'

'Now it seems to me,' she said, 'That the key to

Gratitude is Self Esteem.'

Lorenzo leaned back in his chair and whistled. 'Jessie, how old are you again?'

'I'm eight and you know it.'

'Where in damnation did you learn to be so worldly?'

'Ah, cheese it, Pa,' she declared, but she blushed nevertheless. She loved it when Lorenzo told her she was a brat prodigy.

'But come on, Pa, apply yourself. Say Uncle Orson gave you—'

'Jessie. I am tired of hypotheticals. It keeps turning out that I'm the most ornery ingrate that ever lived. Shouldn't you be in bed? Let me call for Ada.'

'But this is just getting interesting.'

'Well, I honestly think—'

He was just about to tell her what he honestly thought when Ada interrupted.

'There is a young man to see you, sir.' She pulled a face.

'Go on.'

'He says he attended the Freshwater lecture, and would like to purchase a pamphlet. Should I send him away, sir? It's very late. If I were you I'd send him away, but then nobody listens to me of course, because everyone here is so much cleverer than I am.'

Lorenzo ignored the uppity sarcasm. He smiled. It was a visit he had been expecting.

'Jessie, you must go to bed at once. Ada, bring the young man, and ask for some lamps to be brought. Why, we should have had lamps half an hour ago. What were you thinking?'

It was true. While he and Jessie sat talking, they

hardly noticed how the room had darkened, until the only light came reflected from the sea in the moonshine. When the boy came in, the room was still thus dark, even darker, and Lorenzo could hardly see him, but he knew at once who it was.

'Hello, young man. Is it Herbert, am I right?'

'That's right, sir,' came Ellen's disguised gruff voice. 'Herbert it is.'

She edged into the room, where all she could clearly make out was the shape of Lorenzo standing at the window. She began to wish she had not come. Compared to the weedy aesthetes she had grown accustomed to, Lorenzo seemed such a large and manly man; a sixteen-year-old cross-dressed woman alone with such a man was the sort of situation she knew only too well from the stage. It led to all sorts of embarrassing mix-ups. Lorenzo would be suggesting they wrestle soon, and take their tops off.

'I am sorry to disturb you in the evening, sir,' began Herbert. 'But I wondered if I could have the benefit of your advice.'

Lorenzo did not reply at once. Perhaps he was waiting for her eyes to become accustomed to the dark. She heard him sniff the air.

Ellen wished the lamps would be lit, but she thought it was going pretty well until Lorenzo took a step closer and she smelled the sandalwood on his hands.

'May I take your hat?'

'No, thank you.'

'Come now.'

'No. Really.'

'Herbert, would you really want me to kiss you with it *on*?'

'Oh no, sir,' she squeaked.

'So we should take it off, then.'

'Oh, sir, I never meant—'

'You see, I feel attracted to you, Herbert,' he laughed, as he moved towards her again, and reached out to touch the brim of the hat. 'You have the biggest Organ of Hope—But ah, the lamps are come,' he said good-naturedly, as the servants appeared at the door with oil-lamps, apologizing, curtsying, lighting more fixtures with spills. Ellen felt she had never been so glad to see anybody, but when the room brightened, and she could see Lorenzo plainly, smiling at her and indicating a seat at the table, the thrill of danger did not pass. In fact, she felt a jolt of desire.

'So tell me why you've come,' said Lorenzo, not waiting for the room to clear. Ellen coughed and thought. Was it really true she had come here for a *pamphlet*?

* * *

Back at Dimbola, over coffee and muffins, Julia decided it was time to confide in Mr Watts. She had conceived the ultimate present for Alfred, a magnificent present which he would appreciate all his life.

'What sort of present?' asked Il Signor, vaguely interested, picking a buttery muffin from a platter. 'Can you eat it?'

'No, you can't eat it,' Julia said. She seemed to find the question amusing. 'You can't hang it on walls, either.'

Watts had not the energy to guess.

'What is it?'

'George! It's what he wants more than anything in the world. It's something that dear Emily could never give him, either. It is the gift of a true friend.' Her eyes flashed with happy tears. 'You still can't guess?'

Watts shrugged.

'It's a review, George.'

And she poked him in the ribs.

'A review? But where? You can't just write him one, you know.'

'I know that, George. It's in the *Westminster Quarterly*! Alfred will receive it tomorrow. Sister Sara has used her influence with the greatest critic and editor of the age, and *Enoch Arden* is to be accounted Alfred's most accomplished work to date. A proof-sheet arrived yesterday from town. It is a wonderful review. I wrote it myself. Listen to this—!'

She removed a folded sheet of paper from beneath her shawl, and opened it.

'It says there never was such a perfect depiction of absence of hope, George! *Enoch Arden*'s story is relentless in its poignant tragedy. The reviewer says the poem made him feel utterly despondent from beginning to end! Imagine how such words will comfort Alfred. The reviewer quotes thus:

And Enoch bore his weakness cheerfully.
For sure no gladlier does the stranded wreck
See through the gray skirts of a lifting squall
The boat that bears the hope of life approach
To save the life despaired of, than he saw
Death dawning on him, and the close of all.

Despite himself, Watts was impressed. It was the

most miserable thing he'd ever heard. 'There's glory for you,' he said.

'But Alfred will be so happy!' exclaimed Julia. 'You and I both know the wicked sting of the critic, George; but as for the critic's fine words, we take them straight to our bosoms as balm!'

Watts masticated his muffin.

'How will he know it's from you?' he said, with his mouth full.

'George?'

'How will Alfred know this is a present?'

'Oh but he won't! He never will! That's the beauty of it!'

'That's very selfless of you, Julia.'

'I know,' she said, thoughtfully. She still wasn't sure she could cope with this aspect of the thing.

'But now where's your little wife got to?' she asked brightly, changing the mood. 'Shall we ask her to entertain us with a little dance?'

* * *

At this precise moment Ellen scurried back up the lane to Dimbola Lodge, her heart pounding. She ran fast and removed her bothersome hat, so that her golden hair swung loose on her shoulders. She laughed for pleasure. All in all, she was far too preoccupied to notice Mary Ryan standing hooded in the shadows near the hotel, watching her as she passed.

'He *will* love me!' Ellen said to herself in Mary Ryan's hearing. 'He will be unable to resist me.'

Ellen was supremely happy. She flicked her hair in the moonlight as she ran. She had solved the problems of everybody. Lorenzo would visit Mr

Dodgson in the morning; he would consider Alfred's requirements about the mad children, too. And as for her marital problems with George! Well, Lorenzo had promised some practical help in a theatrical extravaganza. No longer would George yell 'Remember Westminster!' at the precise moment any intimacy—threatened.

For the first time since her marriage, she had been able to discuss this peculiar marital plight with another person, and the depth of Lorenzo's compassion had overwhelmed her. Not once had he suggested that the failure was hers. He said she was brave to come. The relief was as though someone had drilled a hole in her head and let out the accumulated pressure of sixteen years.

'Perhaps small Caution is a benefit sometimes,' she had said to him, meaning to make a light joke.

'Oh, it is useful, of course, if you are a hero in a tight spot. But in matters of love it is the source of more trouble than you can imagine,' said Lorenzo. 'I too have small Caution. And I have Amativeness so massive and bulging that I must rest it on the back of my chair, look, just to obtain relief.'

Ellen gulped. She pictured the back of her husband's head. It was flat, like a wall.

'I am very grateful for your kindness this evening,' she said. 'If you will help me with George, help make him love me, help him get over this Westminster thing, I will think well of you for ever.'

Lorenzo shook her hand.

'But do you think gratitude exists, Mrs Watts? Or is it just a name for obligation? If we are truly grateful to somebody, perhaps we must love them, too? Is that what defines real gratitude, a love of the giver for himself and not the gift?'

'I don't understand,' said Ellen, worried. She feared his Organ of Amativeness was nudging into the discussion again. 'But in my experience it is always a good idea to say "That's kind" or "Would you really?", because people set such store by it. It doesn't take long to say. It doesn't mean anything. But it makes people help you again, or give you more things.'

'Well, that's certainly a practical attitude, Mrs Watts,' Lorenzo admitted, as he walked her to the door. 'Perhaps you can show your gratitude to me, by helping me with a little research. If you are *truly* grateful, Mrs Watts, I fear you are going to have to take your hat off to me, sooner or later.'

Outside in the shadows Mary Ryan considered what to do.

Perhaps the hour was too late for a visit to Mr Fowler now, although she still burned to know her marital fate. She looked upstairs to the rooms, for sign of a light. 'He *will* love me,' Mrs Watts had said. She must have meant Mr Fowler.

As Mary Ryan watched the building, Lorenzo opened a window and leaned out. At moments like these he wished he smoked cigars. Watching Ellen run back to Dimbola Lodge, he blew a kiss towards her.

'Ah, Mrs Watts!' he sighed happily. 'God bless my Organ of Marvellousness, but I'm enjoying this.'

Mary Ryan looked up the road at Mrs Watts, and back to the hotel window, where Lorenzo still watched, with a look of enchantment.

Mr Fowler and Mrs Watts? She shook her head and whistled. For once, only the local exclamation would do.

‘Swap me *bob*,’ she whispered.

Nine

Lorenzo Fowler had very much enjoyed his evening of verbal foreplay with young Mr Herbert. As he kept repeating to himself next morning as he dressed at the cheval glass, you hardly expect romantic interest on the Isle of Wight. A man who in another life might have been a top opera singer (with a slightly different cranial arrangement, to include musical ability), he puffed out his chest, stretched out his arms at shoulder level and sang the words as though to a Handel aria—

‘A man!’

‘Hardly!’

‘Expects rrromantic . . . Interest!’

Pause for orchestral diddle-diddles.

‘On the Isle of Wight!’

A positive thinker at all times, Lorenzo now concluded that life was better than ever. At breakfast he found himself saying grace for the first time in many years. He said it with enormous sincerity, too. ‘Thank you with all the juices of our humble mortal excitable bodies, Lord, for the splendid gift of your lovely, lovely plenty!’

‘Did he take his hat off, Pa?’ asked Jessie conversationally, spreading some butter rather badly.

‘Not this time. But I’m sure he will. For me.’

‘How are you supposed to do him properly with his hat on?’

'Jessie, that's exactly what I said.'

'I mean, does he think we've never seen scurf ?'

Lorenzo smiled and helped her with some jam. He remembered how he had just got his fingers on the tweedy brim of that hat when—

'Ada offered me bacon again, did I tell you?'

'No!'

'She said it could be our little secret.'

'I hope you reiterated our position on the consumption of flesh?'

'Oh yes, but she doesn't understand. Ada says that if I don't eat meat I'll grow up a simpleton and dullard. Yet I keep explaining that my farinaceous family is full of alert, energetic people who never miss a trick. Look at Uncle Orson, I said, the most productive brain in the whole United States, and moreover the world's greatest expert on martial love!'

'Marital, Jessie.'

'Yes, marital. Why doesn't she examine the evidence that's right before her eyes?'

'Perhaps because her intelligence is clouded by animal fat.'

Jessie looked puzzled, and then guffawed.

'Can I tell her you said that, Pa? I can't wait to see her face!'

It was quite true that the Fowlers defied the usual dumpy phlegmatic fate of the vegetarian. Somehow their blameless lifestyle—meatless, drinkless, smokeless, and disencumbered by the vile fashion of corsetry—had not only sharpened their wits, but given them an abnormally large appetite for other base, animal activities. Both literally and metaphorically, they were full of beans. Uncle Orson, back in Boston, was the prophet of so many popular health movements that he was on the verge of losing his mind keeping up with them all. He promoted all progressive notions with the same total enthusiasm. When he became consumed by a passion for gardening, for example, he sent packets of seeds (free) to any part of the United States.

As for marital love, Uncle Orson was not so much afroth on this subject as a human egg-white beaten to a stiff meringue. Reportedly, he saw sex in everything. Given the opportunity, he might even have seen it in G. F. Watts.

Intercourse summons all the organs and parts of the system to its love-fest, wrote the lathered Orson. *It compels their attendance, and lashes up their action to the highest possible pitch. The non—participant female . . . is a natural abomination.*

Orson's latest pamphlet—an abstract from his projected hundred-thousand-word book *Creative and Sexual Science*—Lorenzo had read quietly to himself a couple of times (no more) and then hidden in the lid of his portmanteau. True, every so often he retrieved it, to refresh his memory. He particularly liked the expression 'lashes up their action to the highest possible pitch', which made his cheeks warm under the bushy beard. To be strictly honest, he had taken a quick perusal of the pamphlet again in bed last night, after Ellen's visit.

Orson had wanted to send five thousand copies, to be sold from Ludgate Circus at a penny each. But England was not yet ready for all this lashing up, Lorenzo decided. And let's be frank here, the Isle of Wight never would be.

'I have an appointment at Dimbola Lodge this morning, Jessie. Will you come?'

She put down her knife with a clunk.
'To see Mr Dodo? No fear.'
'But Jessie—'
'I only touched his *head*, Pa!'
'I know. But sometimes that's enough, Jessie. Sometimes that's enough.'

*   *   *

At the breakfast table at Farringford, Emily opened a note from Julia and some embroidery silks fell out.
'Alfred,' she said, flatly.
He picked up the silks and poked them in his pocket. He continued reading *Enoch Arden*, his tragic fisherman poem. Although the book was scarcely off the presses, he was already considering emendations. 'Under the palm tree' in line 494 would be yards better as 'Under *a* palm tree', he thought. He practised 'Under the palm, under a palm, under the palm, under a palm,' while tapping time with a spoon.
Emily smoothed her hair and composed herself for the letter, but when she resumed it, she felt all the hope drain again from her body.
'You read it, Alfred. I can't.'
Alfred sighed, put down his book and scanned the letter, holding it three inches in front of his eyes. *Receiving the American phrenologist this morning (Tuesday)*, Julia said; *you are both invited to meet him*. He read the note first upright, then sideways, then upright again. It was important that he keep this news from Emily. He wanted to consult this phrenologist on the urgent matter of the boys' inherited madness. He played for time.

'I wish she wouldn't cross her letters,' he said. 'Her handwriting is bad enough without it.'

'What does she say?'

'Oh. Nothing.'

'Nothing at all?'

'Just will I sit for her. The usual thing. And please accept these lovely silks, bought when last in London. The blue is quite a rare shade, she says.'

Emily felt like a heel.

'Am I wrong to be so agitated, Alfred? I had a dream about the wallpaper last night, in which you were papered all over with it, and wore a big hat made of it, and the boys were *eating* it. And I was being papered to the wall. When I awoke, I could still smell the paste.'

Alfred patted her hand.

'Don't worry, Emily. You're not mad.'

'I didn't say I was.'

'Did you check the children?'

'Yes.'

She opened another envelope. Inside, mysteriously, was a copy of the *Westminster Quarterly*, a publication she had cancelled several years ago. What on earth was going on? Opening it, she found a review of Alfred's new volume. She snapped it shut again, and thought fast.

'Mmm?' said Alfred, noticing a sudden movement.

Emily nearly burst into tears. What could she do? A review! a review! Help! Help! She couldn't eat this one, it was too big. And besides, the minerals in the ink of *Punch* had actually done her frail digestion no good whatsoever. She decided to divert his attention.

'Oh look,' she said, pointing a bony finger at the

window. 'Alfred, who's that? Who's that—at the Garibaldi tree? Can it be—er, who's the other one? Not Garibaldi—you know. Count Cavour!'

It was a wild invention—but it worked. While Alfred leapt to the window, squinting for more uninvited Italians of the Risorgimento invading the tranquillity of his house and garden, she tore out the review, and looked round frantically for a hiding place. It wasn't easy. She didn't have a cleavage, and her pockets were already full of anonymous letters. In desperation—and just as Alfred looked round—she took the lid off the teapot and stuffed the pages inside.

* * *

Breakfast at Dimbola on this Tuesday morning was an altogether more jolly affair. Ellen in particular was in excellent spirits. For some reason she kept patting her husband on the back of the head, and then feeling the back of her own.

'*When that I was and a little tiny boy, With a hey, ho the wind and the rain,*' she trilled, happily contemplating another day of fine blue skies and seagulls over white cliffs. 'Does it *ever* rain in Freshwater?' she asked, not expecting an answer. 'Jove knows I love, but who?' she continued, tweaking her husband's nose in an unseemly manner. 'Lips, do not move! No man must know! Ha! I really can't think why I objected to *Twelfth Night*, you know, George, it is a capital play. Wonderful speeches. *What is your parentage?*'

Watts was taken aback by the question. He exchanged glances with Mrs Cameron. Both of them knew that George's sire was a piano tuner. It was not something to be mentioned over breakfast.

'Don't you know anything, George? If I say "What is your parentage?" you say "Above my fortunes but my state is well." It's very appropriate. You know, in your case.'

'Have you spoken with Mr Dodgson today, Mrs Watts?' asked Julia, trying to slacken the pace.

'I did see him yesterday but he was still Lewis Carroll. He said persons over a mile high should leave the court, so I made an exit, no applause. But I'm sure Mr Fowler will set us all straight. I have such a firm belief in phrenology. It's a science, you know, yet it's about people. Isn't that a marvellous combination? I learned—um, somewhere—that Mr Fowler was the man who discovered Human Nature. And guess where it is located? Above Comparison! Isn't that tidy? Human Nature is above Comparison! There's one for your canvases, George. I'm surprised you never thought of it.'

Only the arrival of devilled kidneys slowed Ellen down. She attacked them as though her last proper meal had been at Christmas.

Julia looked at her and wondered at the unfairness of life. How could Lewis Carroll write a book about this silly girl? How could Watts think of marrying her? And worst of all, how could Alfred prefer her company? What would this girl ever do for Alfred Tennyson? What *could* she do that would compare with the magnificent gesture of the *Westminster* review? She hugged herself to think of Alfred reading it at this very minute.

'I hope your walk with Alfred yesterday was not too tedious, my dear?' asked Julia. (Naturally, she hoped the opposite.)

'Oh no.'

'I expect he drifted off a great deal? He sometimes forgets his companion, I find. Those of us who love him—and know him very, very, very well—learn to forgive him. Much as I admire the man, I must admit that when there is a masterpiece stirring in his brain, he takes no account of the special claims of female company.'

Ellen struggled to understand the tenor of these questions. Surely Julia didn't want to know that Alfred had been boorish? She was his friend, wasn't she?

'Not at all, he was *most* attentive,' she reassured the older woman.

'Really?'

Ellen took a swig of tea.

'Oh yes, most attentive. No drifting off at all. He pointed out cormorants and such, named the flowers, explained geology. Oh, and he took particular pains to teach me to say "luncheon" instead of "lunch".'

'That was well done,' observed Watts.

'And he gave me these,' she added, pointing at the tiny blue orchids. Proud of her booty, she had attached them to her collar with a cunning little silver brooch in the shape of a rose.

Julia peered at the flowers with her mouth open, and then—rather alarmingly—clutched her chest and flailed her legs in the air. Thank goodness she was sitting down at the time. She seemed to be suffering a kind of seizure.

'He *gave* them to you?' she squeaked, 'Alfred? Gave them to you *as a present*?'

Ellen realized she was stretching things a bit here, but it was too late to admit she'd picked them herself.

She shrugged.

'Don't you think they go with my eyes?'

* * *

Dodgson still sat in his upstairs room, staring out of the window. He hated to admit it, but much of his post-traumatic stress had now passed. In a very boring life, this Freshwater episode was, by far, the most interesting thing that ever happened to him. To slip into his own book! A lucky man. But now he was recovered, and the occasional glimpse of a rabbit darting down a hole made him a bit dizzy, nothing more. He could now behold the Dimbola cat without thinking it hailed from Cheshire.

'It has p-p-p—*passed*,' he said, as if to prove it.

It felt rather a shame. While he'd been mad, everyone had been so nice to him. Mrs Cameron had been quite wonderful, bringing him nice drinks and sheets of paper and small oriental ornaments to cheer him up. These knick-knacks he had now packed carefully in his portmanteau, in case she changed her mind. A lacquer box of considerable value was among them; it would stand as a useful prop at home, when he posed little Oxford girls in mandarin pyjamas with parasols and chinoiserie screens.

He sighed. He really ought to get back to his art, even if the unaccustomed hospitality of Dimbola Lodge tempted him to stay. Mrs Watts, too, had been an angel, though he was uncomfortable about her awkward insistence that *Alice's Adventures in Wonderland* bore some immediate relationship to herself.

People will believe anything if it's flattering

enough, he concluded. And he was just about to get dressed and announce himself cured (possibly in time to catch a morning ferry from Yarmouth), when he heard the sound of Tennyson arriving downstairs. Muffled greetings and questionings reached his ears, but he couldn't make out much.

'Any news, Alfred?' asked Julia, happily, only to be bewildered when Alfred rejoined, 'None at all, praise God!' and hurried past her to talk to little Mrs Watts outside the front door.

Upstairs, the arrival of Tennyson set Dodgson in a quandary. It was the nearest he had come to the laureate all week. 'Should I consider remaining an extra day?' he thought. 'If Mr Tennyson felt sorry for me, perhaps he would not only allow the dedication, but offer it himself ?' And so Dodgson finished his breakfast tea in his high-backed chair and gazed at the view again, thinking of his next best move as though puzzling a strategy in chess.

His window stood open, however, which was how he came to hear Tennyson and Mrs Watts conferring in whispers outside, on the sheltered path below. They were discussing the anticipated arrival of Lorenzo and the madness of Tennyson's boys, but Dodgson did not know that. To an outsider, their conversation sounded suspiciously like a tryst.

'My dear! You must pardon me for speaking to you yesterday on such an intimate matter.'

'Not at all,' Ellen assured the great man. 'Your passion commends you.'

There was a significant pause, while Dodgson wondered whether to take notes, but decided to sit very still instead.

At last, Tennyson sighed.

'Should I live in hope?' he asked.

'You must!' said Ellen, rather thrillingly. 'I know I always do!'

'This is such a delicate matter. I would confide in Julia, but she loves Emily so dearly! And Emily must never know about this, Mrs Watts. She already believes I am irrationally obsessed on the subject, simply because—'

He stopped.

'Why?' asked Ellen. Alfred lowered his voice even further. Dodgson craned to hear.

'*—Because I ask her every morning.*'

Dodgson held his breath. But at this moment Mary Ryan entered to clear away his breakfast tray, and heard the same exclamation—'Julia might tell Emily!'—and the gape-mouthed 'Swap me bob' look from the previous night appeared on her features once more.

'What can be done?' Tennyson continued, breathlessly. 'If an organ is to blame for the disorder, perhaps it can be beaten down and vanquished?'

Dodgson winced, but Ellen merely replied, 'Well, possibly. But I wouldn't know. Obviously it's not an organ I've got.'

'I should never have had children, Mrs Watts! I have been selfish!'

At which point Mary Ryan made a decision. She was a very proper girl who did not eavesdrop deliberately. So she closed the window, quite noisily, making Alfred and Ellen look up; and Dodgson subsided in his chair. As the Irish maid left the room with his breakfast tray, Dodgson thought he heard her say to herself, 'Mr Fowler *and* Mr Tennyson in love with Mrs Watts, well swap me bob *twice*!' but it wasn't very likely. What was certain, however, was that the morning ferry would sail without Dodgson today. He realized, as he relaxed his muscles, that he had been sitting in his chair fully six inches above the actual seat.

* * *

While Alfred and Ellen made a pleasant walk in the garden, Julia arrived at Farringford breathless. A mad dash has rarely been madder, but Julia was confused, worried; she had to do something. She had less than half an hour in hand before the phrenologist's arrival, but after dreaming all night of Alfred's wonderful review, her perfect gift seemed to have gone wrong. 'None at all, praise God!' Alfred had said. Yet Julia had sent the *Westminster* by hand this morning, her only copy. And then what did he do? He went into a huddle with the Terry girl, the young pretty woman to whom he had given his *first ever recorded present*. No wonder Julia felt the need to be up and doing. But what, in fact, could be done?

In the gloom and chill at Farringford, she discovered Emily sitting alone in the drawing room, writing. A clock ticked on the mantelpiece. Stepping in from the warm, bright morning, it was like entering the British Museum; the birdsong stopped, and the house smelled of stone. Perhaps, unconsciously, this was why Julia had bought them the Elgin Marbles wallpaper. In her journal Emily mentioned that it was her birthday today, but that 'A' did not concern himself with such anniversaries, so she had not mentioned it to her husband or the boys. She was jolly brave about it, actually. Emily was one of those tough, wiry invalids who outlive their fitter spouses, and give rise to the wise old saying 'A creaking gate hangs longest'.

'My dear!' called Julia.

'My dear!' echoed Emily, with slightly less enthusiasm.

'I'm afraid I come empty-handed,' confessed Julia.

'Oh,' said Emily, and shrugged. Her feelings were mixed.

'But I sent the silks.'

'Of course. Thank you, Julia, I always say that you are kindness itself.'

'Did you like the blue?'

'I have already begun a sampler with it.'

Julia looked around, vaguely hoping for signs of classical Athenian bas-relief on the walls. There was none.

'But there must be something else?' asked Emily.

'Oh yes. I forget myself. Did Alfred receive any good news today?'

'No, I don't think so.'

'I see.'

'What sort of good news?'

'Oh, you know. About the new poem.'

Emily looked shifty. What did Julia know?

She decided to stand her ground.

'No, none at all, praise God!'

There was nothing Julia could add without giving herself away. The two women looked at one another. Emily closed her journal, as though to say her inspiration had fled; her thoughts would not recompose themselves now.

'I'll be off then.'

'Goodbye Julia. It is always a pleasure to see you, for however short a time.'

Julia looked brave, kissed the invalid, and scurried through the house. But as she approached the front door, she saw a pile of torn paper and recognized amid the scraps the cover of the *Westminster*. So the Tennysons had received it, but not even looked at it! She almost collapsed in her dismay. All that effort for nothing? Those Tennysons were the living end. She felt a sudden terrifying urge to torch the house.

But luckily another wild scheme occurred to her at the same time, and before she knew quite what she was doing, she darted up the main staircase. In her pocket she still carried the proof sheet of the *Enoch Arden* review. She could save the day by placing it on Alfred's desk, where he couldn't help but see it!

But two minutes later, she stood indecisive at his library window, the sheet trembling in her hand. It wasn't working. She put the review down on some papers; she picked it up again; she tried tossing it carelessly on the floor, and poking it in his pen holder, screwed up like a shuttlecock. Nothing looked right.

Even in her heightened emotional state, she retained enough good sense to see that. For this most perfect of gifts to find its mark, Alfred must see the review in the *Westminster Quarterly* or nowhere. Resignedly, she folded the sheet and put it back in her pocket. She must return to Dimbola at once! She had a quick, hopeful scan of the walls—what *had* they done with it?—and made for the door.

'Julia! is that you?' The call startled her. Help!

Emily must be coming up! Julia looked round in panic and made a quick decision. Alfred's emergency staircase! The spiral one he used for escaping Americans! She flung open the door and plunged down into the darkness.

And Emily, having struggled half-way up the main stairs, heard the scurry, screwed up her face and said 'Ouch!' in anticipation. Seconds later, a muffled crash and scream confirmed the awful, the inevitable, the fitting end. Julia had located the Elgin Marbles wallpaper.

* * *

Meanwhile Lorenzo had arrived early at Dimbola, and his first sight was Ellen apparently canoodling with Tennyson in the garden. With her hair visible for once, and those orchids on her collar like sapphires, Ellen looked more beautiful as a female than he had dared to imagine. He looked at her; she blushed. She put her hands behind her back. He made her feel terribly self-conscious. Alfred peered into the blur and saw only a large figure in a bright dandy waistcoat, bearing down on him with a big right hand outstretched. But he felt self-conscious too. For once, in fact, he was actually nervous. Nothing touched him more deeply than the mental health of his sons.

So instead of the usual careless greeting, Alfred took some care with his introduction.

'Alfred Tennyson,' he said. 'Poet Laureate.'

Lorenzo shook his hand.

'Lorenzo Niles Fowler,' he announced. He smiled at Alfred and Ellen warmly. 'No head too big!'

*   *   *

'Mr Dodgson?'

Dodgson heard a small voice behind him, and turned round. It was Daisy. He said nothing.

'Mr Dodgson, I have brought you a present, and I hope you will soon be well enough to travel.'

Dodgson watched her suspiciously. How had she got in? More importantly, how could he get out? Was there any escape from her, save through the window to a ten-foot drop?

'I have been thinking about the photograph you want to do. The one where I stand on the windowsill with the packed bag. I think I understand what you mean by it.'

She moved towards him, and reached out her little hand.

'Don't touch my head!' he shrieked.

'I'll leave it here,' she said, placing a slim package on Dodgson's trunk.

'I hope you like it.'

Dodgson shuddered as he watched her go. Less than a week ago, he had thought Daisy an ungraspable vision of loveliness. Now she was like the Eumenides in the *Oresteia*.

He unwrapped the paper. Inside was a photograph of Daisy, which Dodgson guessed (by the novice murk and bad focus) to be the work of Mrs Cameron. It was, however, an extraordinary picture, which quite disarmed him. This was not the usual Victorian photograph of a demure prepubescent. Confidence and determination were the main qualities of this little face with its quizzical stare. Daisy held her right hand dramatically to her throat, as if to say, 'Moi?' And underneath, she had written, 'I am ready for *The Elopement* whenever you are,' and signed it 'D'.

Dodgson heaved an unusually racking sigh, and dropped to his bed.

* * *

Lorenzo, meanwhile, was wilfully neglecting his mission to Dodgson. In fact, when Mary Ryan entered the drawing room with some cups and plates, she heard Lorenzo in full flow, addressing Tennyson and the other luminaries in a kind of makeshift circle. 'What I tell my paying audiences is this,' he said, slapping his knees. 'Go home now, I say, and write on a slip of paper your own obituary. Make it grand, I say; make it flattering. But then live the rest of your lives making it come true.'

He beamed at them all, gauging the appreciation. They were all impressed. They reflected on their own lives. In fact Mrs Cameron—who had already had quite a bad morning running to Farringford and back (and falling down stairs)—gulped and rubbed her shin. 'Oh Alfred,' she said wistfully. 'It is true that we have but one chance to get things right.'

'I know I can't offer you much,' continued Lorenzo, 'except free analysis and advice in absolute privacy and confidence, but I have every hope you will allow me the honour.'

Tennyson coughed. 'Free, did you say?' Things were turning out better than he hoped. To get the children checked over by an expert, who wanted nothing in return! He need only string the fellow along, which was easy enough.

'I did, sir,' said Lorenzo. 'And a Fowler is a man of his word. To examine your heads will be the pinnacle of my professional life. And if I could take a plaster moulding for my own personal use—not for public display, of course, nothing like that—' He noticed a certain amount of dissent and shuffle here '—Well, we will talk of that at another time.'

Tennyson leaned toward Julia and whispered (loudly enough for everyone to hear), 'Perhaps the boot's on the wrong foot here, Julia. Perhaps *he* should be paying *us*! Eh?'

She smiled nervously, and offered Lorenzo more tea.

Sensing his audience slipping a little, Lorenzo regathered it expertly. 'Imagine my position. I have before me the greatest names of the age,' he said, 'and I myself am nothing, nothing. The greatest living poet, sir; the greatest painter, photographer and actress. Such heads. I tell you frankly, my fingers itch to find the secret of that greatness. Science begs on its knees.'

Mrs Cameron interjected. She hated to see a nice man wasting his time. 'I think I can speak for Mr Tennyson here, Mr Fowler. He refuses consistently to sit for me, and I am one of his oldest friends. The simple fact is, he will not allow such an intrusion, it is anathema to his—'

But Alfred interrupted.

'Julia, you are too hasty,' he said.

Julia blinked hard. What?

'But Alfred—'

'I think I may be allowed to do what I like with my own head?'

'But Alfred, my dear—'

'It is quite a different matter from your damned silly photographs, Julia!' he snapped. Agitated, he jumped to his feet and walked up and down, while Julia stared at him. Mr Fowler and the Wattses, suddenly wishing they were invisible, all studied the pattern on the carpet.

'You must come to Farringford this afternoon, Fowler, and meet my boys too,' declared Alfred. And then, deliberately avoiding Julia's hurt expression, he fidgeted for a handkerchief in his pocket, making one of Emily's new embroidery silks fall out. Julia, with a little gasp, saw it fall.

It was the blue one.

She sniffed.

Why was this always happening?

But worse was to come. As he stooped to pick it up, Alfred peered closely at Mrs Watts for the first time and saw the orchids on her collar. Julia watched his face and Ellen's, as he recognized the flowers. Ellen coloured.

'You look remarkably well this morning, Mrs Watts,' he said with a big smile. 'Does she not, gentlemen? Is she not a very beautiful young woman?' The other men agreed loudly. Ellen, glad of the attention, beamed at them all.

All plain women will know how Julia felt at this moment. It is a bit like being hit in the face with a sack of wet sand.

'Alfred!' Julia called to him. He was heading for the door.

'Oh, I meant to mention it, Julia,' he said. 'When I came through my gate this morning, I noticed that your garden has an infernal smell of paint.'

Julia stood up, too, although her legs were shaky. Suddenly, she felt very old. 'I must consult my husband, I do hope you'll excuse me,' she said, and vacated the room before the first sob of anguish escaped her. What a terrible morning! She burst through the back door and ran to her glass house, her heart thumping. In the space of a couple of hours, she had been rejected by Alfred in every way conceivable—as a friend, as a benefactor, as a photographer, as a woman, and lastly (most cruel blow of all) *as an aesthete*.

'What I wouldn't give!' she cried. 'Alfred, I would give *anything*, but I don't know what you want!'

She sat completely still for ten minutes, her face a perfect picture of misery. In fact, had she only prepared a photographic plate in advance, she could have got her 'Absence of Hope' picture right there, on the spot.

While her guests ate warm biscuits in her drawing room, she trailed back to the house, and was met in the hall by Mary Ryan.

'A parcel has come from Mrs Prinsep, madam.' The maid indicated a small box, which had been opened.

'A dozen copies of the *Westminster Quarterly*,' she reported, puzzled.

Mrs Cameron dried her eyes with a corner of shawl. She blew her nose on it too. Such a robust spirit this woman had. Her Hope was not as big as Ellen's, but her Benevolence was prodigious.

'A dozen copies, my dear Mary? Twelve? Then all is not lost, Mary. All is not lost, after all!'

Ten

No phrenology was done that morning, but Lorenzo felt invigorated nevertheless by his meeting with the Dimbolans: as if he had just done the blindfold test and successfully untangled the history of a really tricky head—a wife murderer turned archbishop, say, with a strong aptitude for woodwork and gaming. What he failed to notice, however, was that while he grew sticky with excitement about getting his hands on the heads of these Freshwater people, most of these Freshwater people were pretty keen to get their hands on *him*.

'He is Lancelot!' exclaimed Mrs Cameron to her husband, later. 'I shall pose him with Mary Ann as the Lady of Shalott! Such human passion! Can't you imagine him singing "Tirra Lirra" on the river?'

'I believe I have found a model for Physical Energy, my dear,' confided Watts to his wife. 'Mr Fowler is a magnificent specimen. How do you think he would look with no clothes on?'

'I can't quite define it,' said Ellen less elevatedly (and to herself). 'But I would just like to get my hands on him, that's all.'

Only Tennyson saw no practical application for the phrenologist in his own work. But then he never was a head-hunter; he was always the head hunted. Many years ago, his miserable brother Charles had written a derisive poem about phrenology, which began,

A curious sect's in vogue, who deem the soul
Of man is legible upon his poll.
Give them a squint at yonder doctor's pate,
And they'll soon tell you why he dines on plate.

After such a strikingly bathetic start to the genre of the Phrenology Poem, most Victorian poets agreed the wisdom of conserving their candle for something else.

Once outside in the garden, Lorenzo had run straight into Tennyson.

'I meant it, come to tea with us, Fowler,' he boomed. 'Bring your charming daughter. I suppose she is charming? I mean to say, if she isn't, don't bring her. However, I will insist the boys are present, so that you may conduct your examinations in full view of everybody, as though in a spirit of—well, teatime fun!'

Teatime fun was not something Tennyson had ever experienced; in fact the word 'fun' was so new to his vocabulary that he paused for a moment to repeat it to himself, fun-fun-fun, weighing its poetic value (which was short).

Lorenzo bowed. 'It will be a pleasure. And will we have the delight of meeting your wife?'

Tennyson frowned. 'Emily? Why ever not?' He paused. Here was a point, actually. How was he to break the news to Emily? She had been so nervy in the past few days. A few random memories suddenly converged in his mind. Count Cavour in the shrubbery. Her hand guiltily in the teapot. Eating bits of paper torn from *Punch*.

'But *she's* not mad, you know,' he said.

'I didn't say she was.'

'As sane as anyone in this house.'

'Good.'

'It's the boys I'm worried about.'

'Understood.'

'Well, as long as that's clear to you, Mr Fowler. Emily is *not* mad, *not* mad, *not* mad. I can't tell you how often I have to reassure her on the subject.'

* * *

Julia knew nothing of this fresh arrangement, otherwise she would have insisted on organizing it and providing some food. No, at the termination of Lorenzo's informal lecture, she had wiped her eyes again and hurried to Farringford for the second time that day, possibly wishing (as she ran along, panting and sweating, with her shawls a-flap) that some clever engineer would soon get around to inventing the safety bicycle. A dozen copies of the perfect-gift periodical lay in a basket across her arm. There was also a hammer and some nails, and some paste made from flour and water. Myopic pompous ingrate though Alfred was, he would certainly find his review before the day was out. He would rejoice in the *Westminster*'s good opinion, if the effort killed her.

Arriving at the house, she first established that Alfred had not returned, and that Emily was lying down upstairs. Then she made twelve quick decisions, distributing the copies in cunning places and completing the task in as many minutes. She paused for breath on the lawn, adjusted her lace cap (which was always getting askew), and departed for Dimbola Lodge again. Today she would photograph Mary Ann in the pose of

Friendship, which oddly she now knew to be a small organ of the brain positioned just back from the ear. Perhaps Mr Fowler could stimulate that organ in some of Julia's acquaintance, she thought. 'Then we might be getting somewhere.'

*   *   *

Dodgson meanwhile kept to his room at Dimbola, dreaming of the quiet life in Oxford. This morning he had seen Lorenzo Fowler enter the house, but no sign of the red-headed daughter, thank goodness. Dodgson was relieved. The last thing he needed was to be separated from his wits again by that demon in infant form.

Detached observers might assume that where Dodgson was concerned, the Fowlers owed an apology. After all, their antics had deranged a complete stranger—and while he was on his holidays, too. But the Fowlers saw it quite the other way about. Dodgson had many reasons to apologize to *them*. For one, he was a pervert. For another, he had ruined their show. Most important of all, however, he had interfered with their takings. Lorenzo was therefore not the ideal person to minister to Dodgson in his current fragile state.

'Sir!' shouted Lorenzo, catching the invalid logician weakly buffing his lens with a cloth. Dodgson dropped the lens on his bedroom carpet, and gaped. Such violence of manner in a gentleman's bedroom went well beyond decent practice. But worse was to come. With a flourish, Lorenzo shut the door behind him, and locked it.

'Mr F-F—! I must pr—protest.'

Dodgson looked round in panic. The room seemed a lot smaller with Lorenzo in it.

'Have you come to ap-p—pologize? I'm much b—better now.'

Lorenzo laughed.

'Apologize? No, I have come to tell you that I know exactly what you're up to.'

Dodgson thought quickly. What *was* he up to? Only failing to get Tennyson's blessing for his book, as far as he could see. At worst, he was pilfering a few bits of bric-à-brac. There was nothing deserving this kind of beastliness.

'I don't think it's any of y—your business,' he declared.

'It's the business of any decent man,' said Lorenzo. 'Every American has a God-given duty to defend the weak!'

Dodgson was completely baffled. He sat down and pushed a lock of hair behind his ear. Not for the first time, he wished he had a big bushy Moses beard like every other Victorian man of consequence. He was sure it was his smooth chops that did for him.

'And what's this?' said Lorenzo, lighting on the picture of Daisy.

'A present,' explained Dodgson, lamely.

Lorenzo read the inscription and his jaw dropped to his chest. It appeared to concern a proposed elopement between Dodgson and little Daisy Bradley.

'You are a fiend, sir!' said Lorenzo. 'I can tell you at once that you will go nowhere with this child!'

And Dodgson blinked in amazement as the phrenologist left the room and locked the door behind him.

*   *   *

While all this was going on, Ellen strolled in the garden with Alfred.

'Why won't you pose for Mrs Cameron?' she asked. 'It would make her so happy.'

'Happy? But, my dear, Mrs Cameron's happiness in this matter is neither here nor there.'

'It isn't?'

'Consider what she does when she has a person's photograph. She exhibits it, she gives copies to anybody who calls. She gives away albums.'

'She has a generous nature.'

'And I have a desire for seclusion. Why do you think I live on the Isle of Wight?'

Ellen thought this was a proper question, and answered it.

'Because the Queen likes it? And she once said she might visit you? And then you might get a knighthood?'

Alfred conceded the point. 'Yes, but aside from that. I simply will not accept that, just because I am a poet, people should know what I look like—'

'Well, everyone knows what *I* look like.'

'Take this point, my dear,' interrupted Alfred. 'On a walking holiday last year, my companion shouted "Tennyson!" in the hotel, and the price of our simple lodging was doubled at once. Already visitors come to our house, pushing their noses at the windows, frightening Emily, disturbing the boys. People send me their poetry to read. They want to intrude on my private life in a most unseemly manner. I fear for this development, my dear, especially if the railway comes to Freshwater. Even in death I will not be safe. For there is a fashion for writing lives of poets, publishing their diaries and letters.'

'Yes, but that's to show how important they are,' urged Ellen. 'Poets are dreadfully important.'

But Tennyson would not be cajoled. 'But such scoundrels might tell the world that a man was mad, or dirty, or worse! And he has no defence! You may have seen my poem on the subject, entitled "To—, After Reading a Life and Letters"?'

'To whom?' asked Ellen. 'I'm sorry, I didn't quite—'

'No, it's called "To—". A blank, you know. It's a poetic tradition, protecting people from exactly the presumptuous intrusion to which I respond.'

'I see.'

'I shall quote to you what I wrote. Stand back, my dear.'

She did so. She folded her hands.

Tennyson ahem-ed, closed his eyes, and rocked back and forth on the balls of his feet. He opened his eyes again. 'I'm starting in the middle,' he explained. She nodded. He closed his eyes, and from deep within him his poetry-reading voice erupted with such force that around Ellen where she stood, lilies shivered on their stalks. Tennyson had a mournful, barking recital manner reminiscent of an expiring moose.

'For now the Poet cannot die,
Nor leave his music as of old,
But round him ere he scarce be cold
Begins the scandal and the cry:

"Proclaim the faults he would not show:
Break lock and seal: betray the trust:
Keep nothing sacred: 'tis but just
The many-headed beast should know."'

Ellen put her hands together to clap, but Tennyson pressed on. Maids pegging washing in the kitchen garden beyond had popped their heads over the wall, to see the cause of the commotion. The laureate did seem very passionate about all this.

'Ah shameless! For he did but sing
A song that pleased us from its worth;
No public *life was his on earth,*
No blazon'd statesman he, nor king.'

Ellen clapped now, and Tennyson let out a long breath.

'You won't hear anything better than that on the subject,' he said.

'I am sure I won't. But don't you agree that fame has its price, Mr Tennyson?'

'It has *a* price,' he agreed, 'but I firmly believe that no one can make you pay it.'

* * *

Watts stood back from his canvas, after explaining its emblems and symbols to an impressed phrenologist. Watts hoped soon to broach the subject of Lorenzo modelling for him. For his own part, Lorenzo was definitely warming to the old goat, but he still couldn't quite see the attraction for Ellen. The man had a head so flat at the back it suggested he'd been struck with a frying pan.

'It is a very beautiful picture,' Lorenzo agreed. 'The brash camellia, the humble violets, a lovely conceit.'

'Thank you.'

'If you could just show me the humble violets again. I can't quite—'

'There.'

'Oh yes. No. Is that—?'

'There.'

Lorenzo clapped him on the back, slightly too hard so that Watts dropped his palette.

'Got it!' he said.

* * *

'It's no fun down here without Mr Dodgson,' pouted Daisy, her shrimp net limp in her hand.

Jessie looked at her pityingly. They were paddling in rock pools, as usual, under the eye of their respective maids.

'Daisy, tell me you're not serious,' she said. 'That man gives me *cholera*.'

Daisy huffed, and stamped her foot in the water, splashing them both.

'You don't understand about Mr Dodgson and me,' she said. 'It's very special. I think he really loves me. We're planning to run away. I've already packed a little bag.'

Jessie sat down on a rock.

'Jessie?'

The girl did not reply.

'Jessie? Speak to me.'

*   *   *

At two o'clock Emily Tennyson rose from her nap, and read the note sent by Alfred in the care of Julia's gardener's boy. Some Americans were coming to tea, apparently—an odd proposition from Alfred, since Americans were precisely the sort of people she was usually expected to shield him from.

In fact, if Americans turned up at the house, the Tennysons had a well-oiled routine for dealing with them. Emily would greet them hurriedly, leave them in the hall, and disappear to the dining room, immediately below Alfred's library. There she would take a long-handled broom and bang the ceiling with it three times. Re-emerging in the hall with telltale ceiling plaster on her hair and shoulders, she would point the way upstairs to Alfred's study, and then listen for Alfred's scuffle as he ran down his secret staircase, threw open the garden door and hared across the lawn to the cliffs.

People sometimes objected that they had travelled six thousand miles to see the Poet Laureate, to which Emily would always riposte (though only mentally) that oddly enough, Alfred would not have crossed Lombard Street to meet *them*.

So she made the arrangements for tea (with food, this time), and got surprisingly busy. She was one of those invalids who has to lie down a lot, and sometimes can't lift a bread knife, but can shift a mahogany wardrobe if the fancy is upon her to see it in a different place. To Alfred, she always tried to show her more feeble side, because it reminded him of his mother. To his friends, she emphasized the sacrifices she willingly made for her lord, so that they agreed in secret she was too good for him. To her children, she played the rewarding role of domestic saint.

This daily checking for madness, for example, she conducted in the following fashion:

'What day is it, Hallam?'

'Tuesday, Mother?' he lisped.

'Lionel?'

'Oh Tuesday, too, I'd say.'

'Does either of you happen to know the name of the Prime Minister?'

'No idea,' they chorused.

'Excellent,' she said, and packed them off to play.

Her boys were very beautiful, she thought, and she would keep their hair curly against all objections for as long as she could—possibly until the day they left her house to be married. Other boys were sent off to school, but Emily employed a succession of governesses to teach her boys at home. As she often argued to Alfred, this only *sounds* like an expensive option, but in fact it was completely free. Each governess would stay about a year before realizing she was never going to be paid. And then she would leave, and another would replace her.

As she reached the bottom of the stairs, Emily decided that she felt very well. She might even take a turn in the garden. So vigorous were her spirits, in fact, that when she first discovered a copy of the *Westminster Quarterly* perched on the umbrella stand next to the peg where Alfred's best hat was hanging, she simply removed it and tore it up. Only when she found another copy suspended from the door-knocker, and another attached to the collar of Alfred's favourite wolf hound, did she start to suspect that things were dangerously out of the ordinary. Three copies of the *Westminster*? How? Why? Was this another bad dream like the wallpaper? She sat down and fanned herself. It suddenly seemed very hot. How could she bear it if things ran this much out of control?

* * *

'So listen, Jessie, I want you to be on your very best behaviour.'

'You got it, Pa.'

Lorenzo looked down at his little girl, determinedly marching beside him in her little purple bonnet and lace-up boots, and he felt a surge of pride. He paused and kissed her hand.

'If I could bottle this moment,' he said, taking a deep breath, 'I could become a millionaire.'

'What shall we talk about at Farringford, Pa?'

'Between ourselves, Jessie, I have made an agreement with Mr Tennyson that I will check his sons for signs of madness.'

'What?'

Jessie stopped and adjusted a boot. She was a very independent little girl.

'Yes, the Tennysons are all mad, you see,' said Lorenzo. 'Tennyson's father used to spend an hour and a half each day choosing which peg to hang his hat on. So naturally, the present Mr Tennyson worries now that Hallam and Lionel are chips off the old block.'

Jessie had never heard you could inherit madness. She thought madness was something that just happened to people in Shakespeare when the wind got up.

'Lionel's not mad,' she said flatly. 'But I can't speak for Hallam. I don't think I've ever seen him.'

'Nor has anybody. They say he's very shy.'

'What about their mother? Does she have to be mad, too, for the boys to have caught it?'

'She doesn't have to be. Mr Tennyson says she has nothing to do with the black blood of the Tennysons. He was suspiciously emphatic on the point.'

'So you believed him?'

'Not for a second.'

'Good for you, Pa.'

Lorenzo rubbed his hands.

'My, I am really looking forward to this. If that old lady isn't a tile or two short of the full dome, I promise you, Jessie: I'll eat the hat shop on Ludgate Hill.'

* * *

To her increasing disbelief and concern, Emily found three more copies of the *Westminster* before the Fowlers arrived. One was peeking from under the hall carpet; another was on the seventh step of Alfred's special stairs; and the third was in the fireplace. It *was* the wallpaper dream, only worse. Where could these things be coming from? Who could be doing this to her? She wanted to scream. Help! Help!

Yet she must appear normal, at all costs. Waiting therefore in a relaxed family tableau before the fireplace—boys at her skirt—for Alfred to deliver his new friends into her presence, she gripped her sons' necks so tightly they started to see stars.

'Mother!' whimpered Hallam, as his legs gave way beneath him.

'Quiet!' she snapped.

Lionel broke free, and waved something.

'Look what I found inside one of Father's shoes,' he said, producing copy seven of the *Westminster*. She gasped, snatched it from him, and just as Alfred entered with his Americans, hurled it with considerable force across the room so that it landed behind a sofa. The Fowlers saw it fly. They looked at each other. Alfred, of course, saw nothing but a blur. 'But it had a review of father's new book,' Lionel started to say, but he managed only 'But it had—' before Emily, in desperation, stamped smartly on his foot.

'Good afternoon,' she said, moving forward with as much grace as she could, while Lionel yelled with pain and fell over backwards holding his leg.

'I think you've met Lionel,' she indicated the squawking child rolling on the hearth rug. 'Such a madcap!'

'Emily, is there a bird in the room?' said Alfred.

Emily laughed nervously. 'A bird?' she repeated. 'No, no.' She looked at Jessie Fowler, who stared back. 'Although very possibly a bat,' she added. 'You know how it is.'

Alfred merely grimaced and led the way to the garden, while Lionel regained his composure and hopped along behind. He stuck his tongue out at Jessie, who stuck her tongue out in return.

Lorenzo gripped Jessie's hand tightly, and gave it an excited squeeze. Already secrets and violence! Here was definitely something to tell the folks at home.

Things went relatively well for the rosy picture of mental health at Farringford until, seated in the garden, Lorenzo asked about the Wellingtonia.

'Garibaldi planted it,' said Tennyson, airily. 'He just turned up in April, and we didn't know why, so we put him to work with a shovel.'

Everyone laughed politely, as though it was a joke, although actually this version of events was pretty close to the truth.

'But I have been meaning to ask about Count Cavour, my dear,' Tennyson added. 'You saw him the other day from the window, but he never came in.'

Lorenzo butted in, assuming this was a joke as well. 'Did he come to mow the grass, Mrs Tennyson? Should we check that the man in the wide-awake tending the roses is not King Victor Emmanuel?'

The laughter continued, but Emily looked uncomfortable.

'I didn't say I saw Count Cavour.'

'You did.'

'I didn't.'

Alfred gripped her arm. He lowered his voice.

'You're not mad, Emily.'

'I never said I was.'

'But you pointed out of the window, and I got up to look.'

Emily smiled at her guests.

'It must have been a joke,' she explained.

Alfred spluttered. 'Well, if it was, it's the first one you ever made!'

'Perhaps you would like to see the tree itself, it is very fine,' said Emily. Alfred agreed that this was a good way to change the subject and led the way.

'Tell Mrs Tennyson about your fascinating experiences in phrenology, Mr Fowler,' Alfred urged, but strangely Lorenzo could not be drawn. For once in his life, a Phrenological Fowler preferred not to have an audience. On this occasion it was far more interesting to have a spectacle. Never before had he seen a woman more tightly wound up than Emily Tennyson. Not only was she hallucinating about North Italian politicians, but she was craning her head in all directions, as though anticipating an ambush in her own garden.

'Hello, what's this?' said Alfred. They had reached the Wellingtonia, and Alfred now leaned forward to pluck a small pamphlet from the trunk (where it was nailed).

Emily yelped in alarm. The *Westminster*! They all looked at her. What could she do?

'Alfred. You're right!' she blurted, desperately. 'I did see Count Cavour! I remember now! He came by gig!' The others said nothing. Alfred turned back to the pamphlet and reached out his hand.

'He was dressed in a patriotic flag!' she added, conclusively.

At which Alfred turned away from the tree, to say 'I knew you saw him really!'—thereby leaving *Westminster* copy eight safe for the meantime from discovery.

Copy number nine was an easier one. While the men went for a little game of croquet and the women drank tea, Emily asked little Jessie about herself, and noticed that the child was flicking through yet another manifestation of the *Westminster*. 'It was attached to the seat of my chair,' Jessie explained, as Emily took it gently from her.

'Do you like games?' Emily asked this strangely serious little girl.

'Not much,' admitted Jessie.

'Well, here's one anyway. See if you can bury this periodical in that flower bed using only a teaspoon.'

Unsurprisingly, the child was not excited by the suggestion.

'Why?' she said.

'Very well, I'll do it myself !' snapped Emily. And to Jessie's astonishment, that's precisely what she did.

It was only four o'clock and already Emily felt she could drop from exhaustion. Her head swam. Her whole body was so tensed for action that she tasted acid in her mouth. Besides which, the atmospheric pressure seemed to be rising, as if there would soon be a storm. Copy number ten was stuck to the tray on which the maid brought the tea; Emily upset the milk with a karate chop to the jug, and sent back for more. 'Bring a different tray, I never liked that one!' she added, twitching. It was clear by now that Alfred need have taken no pains to hide his phrenological intentions from her. Lorenzo could have put the boys in straitjackets this afternoon, shaved their girly hair, and ordered a black maria for their removal to Carisbrooke, and she would have noticed nothing.

As it was, however, Lorenzo was just examining Hallam's head and proclaiming a massive healthy intellect when Alfred, suddenly aware of a discomfort in his hat, took it off and looked inside it. It was copy number eleven.

'Look, Emily,' he said. 'What's this?' And Emily,

pulling out all the stops of her ingenuity, snatched the hat, turned her back on the company, and promptly vomited inside it. She gave it back to him.

'Emily!' he said. He was very fond of that hat.

It was the final straw.

'I do apologize to your guests, Alfred,' she said, almost in tears. 'Please do help yourself to some food, but I think I must lie down indoors. This heat, you know.'

'You have all our sympathy,' said Lorenzo, standing up to bow. She made a last desperate scan of the tea-table—no sign of another copy! she even checked in the teapot!—and took a few feeble steps towards the house. But she had gone only a few yards when the words 'What's this?' assailed her ears for the very last time that day.

'What's this?' said Lorenzo. For he was just cutting a piece of apple pie for Jessie (Alfred's favourite) when his knife made contact with a papery thing. Copy number twelve of the *Westminster Quarterly* had been *baked inside an apple pie*. Lorenzo broke open the crust, and pulled out the magazine, which emerged in a shower of crumbs.

'It's the new *Westminster Quarterly*, my dear,' called Alfred, delightedly, cleaning it against his waistcoat. 'Emily, however did it get *here*? Do you think there may be a notice of *Enoch Arden*?'

But as he turned to see what his dear wife had to say on the matter, her skinny body fell to the grass, twitched once and lay still.

Alfred shrugged, and opened his review.

'She's not mad, you know,' he remarked.

Lorenzo put a hand on his shoulder.

'Nobody said she was.'

Eleven

That evening the weather broke. It was still Tuesday—a day of great events; and it was far from over yet. For the first time in several weeks, rain fell softly on the West Wight, and Mrs Cameron danced in her rose garden, under a small ornamental umbrella, intoxicated by the elements. The earth exhaled rich, dank odours in the rain, and as her skirt grew sodden at its hem she sniffed the peculiar stewed-apple scent exuded by her beloved briar rose. Stewed apple? Was this a pathetic fallacy of some sort? No, it was just the authentic smell of damp briar rose. As Alfred might have said, *ask any botanist*.

Anyway, what with Alfred's surprise apple pie, what could be more apt? Yes, she decided, stewed apple was Alfred's particular wonderful smell—if you didn't count the tobacco smoke, the dog hair, and all the other unmentionable ones brought about by not washing. 'Ah,' she sighed. 'The proof of the pudding is in the eating! The eating of the proof is in the pudding!' And she did a little twirl of victory beside the Tennyson gate.

Her husband watched her from his bedroom window, Watts at his side. Two great sage beards together—Watts's wiry and deceptively virile; Cameron's soft and white, like flax on a distaff.

'She is a strange woman,' observed Cameron. 'But I would not exchange her for all the cracked pots in Staffordshire.'

Watts looked impressed. It was a sentiment that did the old man credit.

Watts coughed. 'Julia is in great spirits,' he explained, 'because we have news from Farringford that Mr Tennyson has received a good review. He found it in an apple pie, and it is accounted a miracle. Mrs Tennyson is said to have fainted.'

'A good review for *Enoch Arden*?' said Cameron. 'I am surprised the very church bells don't clamour!' And then he made an oddly un-sage-like ejaculation, which sounded suspiciously like 'tee-hee'.

Watts enjoyed the company of Julia's ancient husband Charles. Man to man, they could talk abstractions tirelessly, for hours by the clock. 'Trust is the mother of deceit' they might sagely concur, and apply the precept to Jane Austen and the Greek dramatists. The last time they had enjoyed such a seminar, however, their theme had been 'Marriage is the tomb of love'—but they had been obliged to cease this manly discussion when Watts, unaccountably, burst into tears.

As a man sensitive to metaphor, Watts was well aware that if marriage was generally the tomb of love, his own marriage was the Great Mausoleum at Halicarnassus. But what could he do? He had the will to change it, but not the imagination. What made married people happy? He didn't know. That helpful expression 'full intimacy' had not been quite helpful enough. On his wedding night he had gathered all his courage, and then confided in Ellen his guilty childhood story of the little cockney sparrow whose head he shut in a door.

How he wept as he remembered the tragedy of the little bird. 'I killed the thing I loved!' he sobbed. 'I never told anyone this before!' and she felt very sorry for him. Once this was off his chest, however, things continued to run weirdly when he went on to explain how badly he felt about old Haydon, who had slashed at his throat with a razor after first failing to put a bullet in his brain. 'Remember Westminster!' had made its first, fateful appearance. And then, having whipped up rather unusual wedding-night emotions in his beautiful young bride, he rolled over and went to sleep. That was it. Full intimacy, G. F. Watts-style.

Cameron, on the other hand, did not regard marriage as the tomb of love; very much the reverse. Julia's great spirit inspired him perpetually. It was like watching waves roll in, or an avalanche tumble—thrilling, just so long as you stood to one side and hung on to your hat.

On top of this, their children had been a great success—some of them were still quite young and hanging around the house, he believed. He had seen some recent photographs. Oh yes, there was much about life at Dimbola Lodge to amuse Mr Cameron. He even volunteered for occasional photographic modelling duty, although it was true that he ruined most sessions by cracking up laughing. 'Well, you must admit this is *funny*,' he would say, indicating his monkish garb and all the maids clustered round him in smocks with their hair down. But nobody else could see the comical side. So he just wiped his eyes and recomposed himself. He was the man who gave the lie to the old adage about laugh and the world laughs with you.

'Did Julia tell you about the exciting phrenologist?' asked Watts.

'Ah yes. I was very pleased for her. It seems that

Julia need no longer bark at her sitters to keep still and hold their expression.'

'Really? Why not?' Watts could remember no talk of this.

'Mr Fowler can mesmerize people, can he not? He practises animal magnetism. From what I have read about phrenology—which is all nonsense, of course—he can isolate an abstract emotion on the sitter's head. Thus Hope, Benevolence, Love, Friendship, Caution—each will be written on the sitter's face if the organ is excited. All Julia needs do is take the picture! All you need do, my dear fellow, is paint it! There's a moral there, somewhere, Watts, if only we search hard enough!'

Watts, however, looked pole-axed. Cameron couldn't see why.

'I thought you would be pleased, Mr Watts. In your own work, surely, Mr Fowler's intervention will be a help? You could stop using anchors and broken lyres, and other such emblematic fol-de-rol. He comes to dinner this evening. I am sure he will confirm what I say.'

Watts felt giddy. He saw his whole life unravel before his eyes. 'No,' he said. 'Oh no, no.' He felt for a chair, and sat down. 'My work is art, Mr Cameron, not trickery, not—' he struggled for the right word—'psychometry!'

Cameron was happy enough to drop the subject. 'Then think no more about it,' he said, and clapped Watts on the back.

Cameron climbed into bed, picked up a small volume of Pindar, arranged his white hair across the pillow and fell instantly asleep. Watts observed him in genuine admiration. If he had seen Bellini making with the hog's bristle, or Michelangelo with his big mallet, he could not have been more impressed. Conscious of his own amateur (but aspiring) status as Great Victorian Snoozer, he lay on a convenient chaise-longue and watched the rain pelt on Mr Cameron's bedroom window. Outside it was growing dark early. The panes rattled in the wind. He tried to count the gusts, and in a minute or less, he was happily impersonating 'Homer sometimes nods'.

* * *

Dressing for dinner, Ellen was—as usual—in a more animated state than her husband. Lorenzo Fowler had been asked to dine at Dimbola Lodge, and was expected shortly. She tried everything in her wardrobe twice, then a third time, and finally sat down on a heap of clothes with her wedding dress uppermost.

'What's fiddle-de-dee in Gaelic?' she asked Mary Ryan, who had been sent to help.

'Fiddle-de-dee isn't English, madam.'

'No, you're right,' said Ellen. 'It isn't.'

She didn't know what was wrong, but her feelings were all jangled together. She wanted to see Lorenzo; she wanted to share him with her friends. She had asked for his help in an important project, and nothing must interfere with its success. But on the other hand, she had spent so many hours dreaming of that exceptional moment when, in the dark, he reached out to touch the rim of her hat! Blushing again, she fanned herself with a glove, tried it on, and discarded it. She thought of Mr Dodgson's funny book. More than ever, she felt like little Alice.

Once you have glimpsed the glorious garden through the little pokey hole, nothing will prevent you from striving to see it again.

'May I ask you something, Mrs Watts?' asked Mary Ryan, to Ellen's surprise. She was pinning Ellen's golden hair.

'Of course, Mary. What is it?'

'I wondered if you could tell me what Mr Fowler said about me, at the lecture, about my marriage, and all.'

Ellen's eyes swivelled shiftily.

'At the lecture? At the *public* lecture?'

'Yes, madam.'

Ellen turned around to face her.

'Did you see me there, Mary?'

'Oh madam, sure but I didn't know it was yourself. Nobody did. But then didn't I see you again the other night in the trousers and Mr Fowler kissing his hand farewell from the window? And also, don't I iron your clothes and find boys' ones in the wardrobe? And isn't Mary Ann in love with you?'

Ellen listened with a mixture of horror and excitement. This maid knew her secret! Her innocent secret! Her guilty secret! She tried both ways of putting it. Both sounded all right.

She went straight to the real issue.

'*Did* he kiss his hand?'

'Oh he did that.'

Ellen tried to pull herself together.

'Things are not as they seem, Mary. Mr Fowler has agreed to help me in a device. Subterfuge was a necessity.'

'Honest to God, madam, I'd never have mentioned it. But aren't I *busting* to know what Mr

Fowler said about me grand weddin' chances! And you were there! Couldn't you tell me?'

'Do you really not remember, Mary?'

'Not a blind, blessed thing. One minute he's looking in me eyes, the next I'm waking up again laughing. *Anything* could have happened!' Mary laughed. Ellen studied her in the glass. She was very pretty when she cheered up a bit. She was only sixteen, after all.

'Then I'll tell you, Mary. He made you very confident in yourself, and you declared your own intention to marry well. He wasn't fortune-telling. He asked you about yourself, and you gave him your genuine opinion.'

Mary seemed disappointed. 'So it was *my* idea, the marrying? Then I'll not be married at all?'

'That's up to you, Mary. That's the point.'

Mary finished the pinning.

'You look very beautiful, madam,' she said. 'I think it's a shame to hide this hair under a silly boy's hat.'

Ellen studied her own face in the glass. She turned to a profile, and tipped back her head.

'My Caution is very small,' said Ellen, almost to herself. 'But I have Hope, Mary. I have phenomenal Hope.'

* * *

Dodgson waited all day for Mrs Cameron's household to realize that a madman had locked him in his room. But what with all the uproar from Farringford, and now the excitement of the rain, it somehow never did. A couple of people tried the door, but when they found it locked, they assumed he had turned the key himself, in the cause of peace and quiet.

He resigned himself to his captivity with surprisingly good grace. Being trapped unnecessarily in a nice room with writing materials was very similar to his own voluntary everyday existence, actually. If there was ever a man who lived in his head it was Charles Lutwidge Dodgson. In the time it might take a more active person to row up the Isis and back, Dodgson would construct a cracking full-length parody of a Tennyson poem—*Maud*, say—complete with funny illustrations and knock-em-dead puns.

He spent his day productively, therefore, first warming up with a few letters to 'child friends' (meaning girls), a practice he maintained throughout his exceptionally boring life. These missives were condescending, yet also ingenious, and some he wrote cunningly back-to-front, while others were painstakingly composed of pictograms. Finding at luncheon that still nobody came (he heard a tray left outside the door), he devised a new system for logging and answering correspondence, and then addressed himself to a word puzzle with which to delight young minds. Lorenzo Fowler was wrong about Dodgson. He was not a pervert. He did not want to do unspeakable things to little girls. But he was—oh yes, he was—a very sad case.

His latest invention was a game in which the player must convert one word into another, changing a single letter each time. Thus, HEAD becomes TAIL if it progresses thus:

HEAD
HEAL
TEAL
TELL
TALL
TAIL

—which looks quite simple until you try to do it yourself. He was now busy converting COMB into HAIR, ELLEN into ALICE, and WINTER into SUMMER. Currently the last required thirteen variants (or 'links') in between. How dull he was today!

It is no surprise that Dodgson should be captivated by the arbitrary nature of words, when you consider how often people wrongly anticipated what he was trying to say. Last night he had attempted to ask the maid for some water, and by the time they'd run the gamut from walnuts to whelks via wisteria, he had settled, fairly happily, for a walking stick.

* * *

'Will we *ever* have such an amusing afternoon again, Pa?' asked Jessie, drawing lines on the condensation of the rain-lashed window, as the waves boomed into the bay beneath their sitting room at the Albion.

'I honestly doubt it,' agreed Lorenzo, crossing his legs. He sat dressed for dinner in a resplendent waistcoat, which he now tugged a little. He was rather fond of fine clothes.

'You should have seen the old lady digging with the teaspoon, Pa! And when she was sick in that

hat, I thought I'd die!'

Lorenzo picked up his daughter and sat her on the arm of his chair. She gave him a brief hug.

'This thing we are doing tonight, Pa; is it anything to do with the Organ of Gratitude?'

'Oh yes, in a roundabout way. We are helping Mrs Watts in a delicate matter concerning her relationship with her husband. It's a grown-up thing. How's the costume? Have you practised?'

'So what's that got to do with the Organ of Gratitude?'

'We are a gift; a love-gift from a wife to a husband. We will see how much he loves her for it. Mr Watts is our only hope, Jessie. Everyone says he is gratitude personified, while nobody else here shows any signs of gratitude at all. We may have to give up the quest. It is possible that gratitude is an illusion.'

Jessie pulled a face and kicked a chair. She didn't know Mr Watts. But she had seen Mrs Watts on the beach, with Lionel, and she certainly didn't like her. Why should they help her with her marriage? One day Jessie would be grown up, and the world wouldn't know what had hit it.

'Why don't you just give Mrs Watts the leaflet Uncle Orson sent? The one you keep in the lid of the portmanteau. That's all about what to do when you are married, isn't it?'

Lorenzo's nostrils flared dangerously, but he resisted an unprecedented impulse to box the ears of his favourite child.

'Jessie,' he said firmly, 'I absolutely forbid you to look at that pamphlet.'

Jessie slid off the chair.

'I already read it, Pa. It's silly. What does

"lashing up" mean? I noticed you'd underscored it. Does it involve ropes?'

Lorenzo sighed. So much for parental authority. He stood up, and reached for his jacket.

'Have you got the head?' he asked, resignedly. Confining Jessie to the childish realm was as pointless as expecting curtsies from a buffalo.

'Head ready!' she saluted, and jerked her own head towards a hat-box.

'Flag?' he asked.

'Got it.'

'Bread knife?'

'Yes.'

'Let's go.'

'What about Mr Dodgson, Pa? Will he be there?'

'Dodgson?' Lorenzo stopped in his tracks and then burst out laughing. 'I'd forgotten all about him!'

* * *

Searching the house for her husband, Ellen discovered the canvas of 'Choosing' erected on an easel in his bedroom. She was touched. George hadn't told her he was bringing it. 'I'd swear those violets are getting bigger,' she said aloud, peering closely, and then passed on in her search, making calls at all the favourite sofas and window seats where her lord usually chose to make himself comfortable. She finally found him in Cameron's room, which, to judge from the rhythmical rise and fall of facial hair, seemed to have been converted temporarily into a sort of Dorm of Prophecy.

Ellen tiptoed to her husband's side. She had to

admit it: Watts always looked lovely when he was asleep. She knelt beside him and studied his face—his strong nose and excellent temples, his large eyes and fine lids. It melted her heart. Ever since she first met Watts at Little Holland House, she had longed to hold that noble face in her young hands, stroke its features, make it smile for joy.

'I love you, George,' she whispered in his ear.

He made no move.

'And after tonight, who knows? You may feel free to love me too. I would do *anything*.'

She reached out her hand, and laid it tenderly on his beard. Her fingers caressed it, and lightly she laid her cheek on his chest. Her husband did not wake.

* * *

Tennyson normally loathed the business of going out to dinner, but tonight was different. For one thing, he had an excellent review to celebrate. For another, Emily was in bed and not much company. And for another, there would be no apple pie at home, for obvious reasons! So Julia's invitation could not have come at a more suitable moment. As he gave his hair its first brush for a fortnight (and large particles of greasy loam fell on his shoulders), he rehearsed the review in his mind. He was particularly pleased with the sections refuting his previous critics.

'George Gilfillan should not have said Alfred Tennyson was not a great poet,' was a sentence which, to his mind, displayed an admirable combination of elegance and sagacity. Likewise, 'Mr Ruskin displayed considerable botanical ignorance when he questioned the rosiness of daisies in Tennyson's masterpiece *Maud*.'

He wondered whether to take the review with him, or merely quote it from memory. Better to take it, so that everyone could see.

He popped in to see Emily before he left. She lifted her head for an instant, but it sank back again under its own weight. Her Christian forbearance had rarely withstood more demanding tests than today.

'What do you think of my fine review, my dear?'

He performed a short Irish jig, by way of expressing his own opinion of it.

'It makes my birthday complete, Alfred,' she said, wanly.

'Birthday? Was it your birthday? Oh.'

He couldn't think what to say. 'Happy' and 'Birthday' would have been quite adequate, but they weren't the sort of words he knew.

'Did you get any presents?' he managed at last.

'Well, the silks from Julia at breakfast. But that seems a very long time ago now; at least a year or two, I'd say.'

Alfred came close and gazed into her haggard face.

'You certainly *look* like you've aged a year or two,' he said. 'It's a good thing you're not coming out. People would feel tired just to look at you!'

Emily smiled. 'I pray for strength.'

Alfred showed her his hands, turning them from backs to palms to backs again.

'What do you think?' he asked.

'Go on,' she said wearily.

* * *

'Your wife has planned some entertainment for us tonight, I believe,' said Julia, meeting Watts on the stairs. 'I have made a little podium in the drawing room, and a curtain. There is nothing like tableaux vivants to aid digestion.'

Watts was pleased to discover his host in such a good mood, but he didn't like the sound of this entertainment.

'I hope it will be nothing improper,' he whispered. 'Ellen once entertained us at Little Holland House, and I can't tell you—'

'George, please don't worry. We will also ask Mr Fowler to give a demonstration of phreno-magnetism. We will do that while we eat. I always think it absurd to leave all the conversation to the pudding. Astonishingly, my husband has agreed to sit for Mr Fowler. He wants to know whether the Organ of Mirthfulness can be stimulated and held. In which case, he says, I can take pictures of people looking cheerful instead of sad and morbid! Have you ever heard of such a thing?'

Watts tried to make an objection, but Julia loved talking about her husband, and could not be stopped.

'Charles is always full of mirth, of course, he hardly needs the good man's fingers making it worse. Do you know his favourite jest, George? It concerns a horse entering a hostelry—a horse!—and the tapster inquiring, "Tell me, why do you have such a long face tonight?" He laughs for hours. But I don't think that's so *very* funny, do you, George? Why the long face? Because a horse *has* a long face, I say, it can't help having a long face. But Charles just won't listen once he's away with his laughing.'

She paused for breath.

'I hate to cast a dour note, Julia,' interjected Watts, 'But I think we should take care of Mr Fowler. He is hardly the artistic equal of the company tonight. He is a mere showman, after all. He hardly shares our elevated aims. In fact I am surprised you have already included Mr Tennyson in his company twice.'

They stood in the hall now, and Ellen, unseen at the top of the stairs, stopped to listen, when she heard Lorenzo's name.

'But Mr Fowler is a fine man, George,' exclaimed Julia below. 'This morning you were talking of asking him to pose as Physical Energy. Your little wife is such an enthusiast too!'

'But I have learned more of him now,' hissed Watts. 'And I fear the man may be a positive scoundrel. He is most certainly a purveyor of low ideas which could contaminate our art. As for Ellen's enthusiasm, as you call it, I shall forbid it at once. As you well know, my little wife's ideas are quite low enough already.' And they passed on through to the drawing room, out of Ellen's hearing.

Dismayed, Ellen sat on the top step. She had been told off before, but she had never heard such a hurtful opinion from her husband's lips. Low ideas? Little wife? A tear tumbled down her face. She wanted to drag herself along the ground to hide in a chink in the wall. How could Watts be so cruel? Now she knew how that little cockney sparrow must have felt, when its head got squashed.

Was this her husband's true evaluation of her?

Her face dissolved in anguish, as she realized how foolish she had been. She had been living under a massive delusion, no doubt engendered by that damn enormous Hope of hers. For she always thought (stupid!) that she had done Watts a favour by marrying him—that this enormous act of unlikely charity (lovely young woman with dull old man) made him somehow beholden to her. But what nonsense this now appeared. Apparently Watts thought the favour had gone quite the other way. In his eyes, she was not a princess condescending to love him, but a tiresome child to be fathered.

Wretched and weeping, she stood up, gathered her gown and ran to her room, her eyes blind with tears. But almost at once, she heard a crash, and found that her elbow had knocked a vase from a stand, breaking it to fragments. Mary Ryan ran to meet her.

'Oh madam,' she said kindly, surprised to find Ellen sunk to the floor, sobbing over the pieces. 'Don't take on. Isn't it only a silly pot that's broken?'

'If only you knew, Mary. It is more than a pot that's been broken tonight.'

The Irish girl patted her shoulder, and gathered the pieces into her apron. Mrs Watts suddenly seemed like quite a little girl.

'And what's this? A little key, is it?'

Ellen picked up the key, and sniffed. She looked at it closely, and felt some comfort. She remembered how Watts had posed her once for a drawing of Hope trapped inside Pandora's box, when the lid was slammed and all the bad stuff got out. This key! She had been meant to find this key!

She must not despair! She realized they were outside Mr Dodgson's room.

Mary Ryan nudged her. 'Mr Dodgson has not opened his door all day,' she said.

'You don't think—?'

'Mr Dodgson?' Ellen whispered at the door. She put the key in the lock. It fitted!

* * *

Downstairs, Julia thought about all that Watts had said. Of course phrenology was not to be bracketed with high art and high poetry, it was probably irreligious, too. But as Watts ought to accept by now (he had mentioned Haydon's ignominy frequently enough), sometimes it was the midget you paid to see at the Egyptian Hall, not the heroic paintings.

'George, you are unbearably stuffy tonight, and I won't listen to another word.'

'Stuffy?'

Upstairs they heard a crash, but Julia shrugged. She didn't care.

'Mr Fowler is my guest this evening. His little girl will eat with my boys and be introduced to us later. Alfred is in the best of spirits, and if we can persuade Mr Dodgson to unlock his door, we will have an evening of exceptional lions! Personally, I can't wait. I just can't wait. And if you'll only be honest about it, George, neither can you.'

* * *

Ellen opened Dodgson's door to find, not Hope exactly, but something like it: Mr Dodgson absorbed in some origami. In fact, he was concentrating so hard upon its puzzles and folds that he hardly noticed rescue was finally at hand. On his chair were already grouped the letters shaped meticulously from paper—HELPIAMLOCKE—and he was just finishing the DIN, and considering how to hang them in the window with cotton and safety pins. A captive rarely looked less agitated. In fact, he saw at once that Miss Terry was in far greater distress than himself.

'Mrs Watts!'

'Mr Dodgson!'

To his great alarm, she ran to him, embraced him, and sobbed big tears against his chest, which was curiously stiff and ungiving to the cheek, actually; rather like a linen press. Sensing that something was required, Dodgson did not of course embrace the tearful woman, but tapped her on the shoulder a couple of times, as though telling a wrestler to break his hold.

'Mr Dodgson, Mr Dodgson,' sobbed Ellen. 'My true friend.'

She finally let him go, and sank on his chair instead.

Dodgson pointed at the chair—'Don't!' he warned—but it was too late. She had crushed the origami.

Ellen caught his hand in hers and kissed it, in a Shakespearean gesture which excited him despite himself. Good grief, normally he'd have to pay 1/6d for this. But he was not prepared for the sentiment that followed.

'I am so honoured that *Alice* was written for me, Mr Dodgson!' said Ellen. 'It is the greatest—

indeed the only kindness anyone has ever shown!'

How could he deny it now? Dodgson said nothing. He stared out of the window at the distant sea, sighed deeply, and wondered whether Mrs Watts's mistake could at least be turned to his advantage. She seemed to be a great friend of Mr Tennyson's, after all. And Mr Tennyson was coming to dinner.

And so they remained for some time—Ellen's wet swollen face upturned to Dodgson's; his own face turned away in calculation. If G. F. Watts had witnessed this tableau, he would have recognized it at once. It was, of course, 'Trust is the Mother of Deceit'.

Twelve

Julia's dinners were always a success, mainly because she took infinite pains to accommodate, and anticipate, the most difficult of tastes. Watts she provided with simple fare and a carafe of water (he never drank alcohol); Mr Fowler received a special vegetarian dish, requiring a lot of argument with a puzzled cook; and for Alfred she ordered a plain apple pie (a replacement, as it were, for the one she spoiled), plus two bottles of port and a good lamp nearby so that he could launch into a hooting moose-call recital of *Enoch Arden* whenever the whim overtook him. It would almost certainly be an *Enoch Arden* night tonight, she fancied. She loved it when Alfred read aloud. His presence filled the room, and even though he paused after each line to comment on its beauties and effects, the greatness of the sentiments invariably reduced her still to tears.

Of course he recited for adulation, but then Julia prided herself on giving the best adulation in England. This ensured that even at the risk of returning to Emily laden with unwanted decorating materials, Alfred would always remain her loyal friend. Julia had a particular way of telling people they were the greatest poet in the language which could really set up a chap, especially when he had tendencies of a mopish sort. And her paeans were not forced, either. Flattery was Mrs Cameron's second nature. It had been an essential part of her infant curriculum in Calcutta, along with French, Hindustani and the Appreciation of the Sublime.

So this evening Julia joyfully buttered Lorenzo, while not neglecting her duty to Alfred and Charles and Dodgson and Watts, all of whom relied on her to make them feel big, tall and important. The procedure was a bit like spinning plates. With an initial effort, she would get all her guests spinning individually, and then—when they started to wobble or flag—they required just a practised touch at the right moment. Alfred needed the word 'Review!' thrown in his direction, for example; 'Genius' sufficed for a weakening Watts, 'Clever' for Dodgson; 'Wise' for Charles. The trickiest moment for this exemplary hostess had been introducing Alfred to Dodgson, because Alfred squinted at him and boomed confidently, 'Hello, we've never met, Mr Carroll! I hope you have recovered your senses. Can't stand madmen, make me nervous.'

But the awkward moment had passed, and now, save for the presence of the mad and dangerous Lorenzo, Dodgson was in paradise. Whenever Julia caught his eye, or called him clever, he raised a glass. Never before had he socialized with Tennyson, and tonight he was doubly privileged, because the laureate was in a mood that was certainly overbearing, but might otherwise be described as good. With Tennyson, overbearing was not optional. All Dodgson's hopes for his little dedication were revived, like the flowers in the garden outside, emboldened by the sudden rain. 'Tonight's the night!' thought Dodgson happily, and almost drank some wine by mistake.

Beside him sat a subdued but brave Mrs Watts,

whom Mrs Cameron noticeably omitted from her flatterings. Poor Mrs Watts was a very highly wrought young woman, he decided. His waistcoat was still unpleasantly damp from the lady's tears. Such emotion perplexed him, and he wished to be no part of it. Yet she was a lovely girl, and so talented, and she looked so very disconsolate. So he regaled her with stories of his visits to Drury Lane, and complimented her on many performances given, in fact, by her sister. Luckily for him, she was much too confused to notice.

'What's this?' he asked, kindly. Ellen was feeling deeply hurt, yet somehow that damned enormous Hope of hers was egging her on. She had worn her wedding dress to dinner, and the pretty pearls; and she blushed continually, aware of Lorenzo Fowler's eyes upon her; aware of Watts paying her no attention whatsoever.

Yet 'I *will* make him love me,' she muttered to herself. In salt on the table, she had written the words LOW IDEAS, and was sadly pushing the grains with a fork. Dodgson saw what she had done, and made a quick calculation in his head. 'Wild Easo,' he whispered, pointing to the letters. 'No, no, We Sold AI'. She smiled wanly. Good grief, the man was doing anagrams. He pushed his fingers together, thought a bit, and then thumped the table with his fork. 'Solid Awe,' he said, triumphant.

'What's that?' said Julia, turning with a smile from her conversation with Watts. Solid awe was something she knew all about.

'Mr Dodgson was just seeing how many words you could make from "low ideas". Apparently another way of putting it is "Solid Awe",' said

Ellen, fixing a look of entreaty at her husband.

Mrs Cameron noticed Dodgson was looking thoughtful, and immediately agreed aloud with her husband that *Alice's Adventures in Wonderland* was quite the cleverest book they had ever read. Dodgson perked up immediately, shot an anxious look at Tennyson to see whether he heard (he didn't; he was busy lighting his pipe), and replied with some spirit that Mrs Cameron's photographs were the marvel of the age. And so it went on, quite merrily, all plates spinning, and Mrs Cameron asked Lorenzo Fowler whether he could enlighten the company on the subject of Phreno-Magnetism.

'Nothing to it!' blurted the always tactful Alfred. 'I mesmerized dear Emily of the headache.'

Lorenzo bowed his head.

'With the greatest respect,' he smiled, 'I once mesmerized a patient during the removal of a tumour. I have cured people of delusions and addictions. The vile weed tobacco, for example.'

Julia and her husband exchanged glances, but Alfred merely continued to puff energetically on his pipe, until he had encased himself in a sepia shroud.

'What I was wondering,' said Cameron, 'is this. Can you magnetize people to hold a certain expression for five minutes while they have their photograph taken? A person who might otherwise laugh?'

Cameron shot a mischievous glance at Watts, who made an impatient flapping commotion with his napkin. 'Low ideas,' he mumbled, but only to himself.

'I believe it may be possible,' replied Lorenzo.

‘Mrs Cameron, I think we should make the experiment. Perhaps your lovely assistant—?’ He indicated Mary Ann Hillier, who didn’t notice, being engrossed at that moment at the sideboard, disentangling her hair from a calves-foot jelly. Since she fell in love with young Herbert, her streak of stupidity had noticeably broadened.

More laughter, more clinking of crystal, more lamps. Mrs Cameron surveyed her table with pleasure. The odd tweak of selfishness assailed her when she considered how Alfred must never acknowledge her as the source of his happiness, but it was bearable, certainly bearable. The calves-foot jelly was found most acceptable, though not of course by Lorenzo, but he resisted the natural urge to tell the company their brains were clouded by animal fat. Instead, he drank a pint of water, talked to Mrs Cameron about photography, and cast a rather bold look at Mrs Watts, who surprisingly cast a bold look right back again.

‘And Viola, Mrs Watts! What a mag-g—nificent Viola,’ exclaimed Dodgson.

‘Thank you,’ said Ellen, turning back to her neighbour. ‘I seem to have a special affinity with Viola, I don’t know why.’

‘She is very lovely!’

‘I have been reading a book of flowers, and it appears that violets are for modesty, you know, while big red camellias are unpretending excellence.’

Dodgson wondered where the camellias had suddenly sprung from, but he knew about the language of flowers. Daisies, for example, were for innocence, which was funny enough in itself.

Ellen raised her voice a little so that Watts could

hear. The modulation of vocal projection was, of course, rather her forte. 'Oh, I mention camellias because my husband has been attempting an allegorical painting in which I choose between the two—between violet and camellia, modesty and excellence, you see—which rather suggests, don't it, that *you can't have both*.'

She surveyed this table of notable Victorian big-heads, and pursed her lips. 'Do you think excellence precludes modesty, Mr Dodgson? Perhaps it does, you know. But you must see my husband's picture, it is diverting. If you can spot the violets, I will give you half a crown.'

'Shall I read from our *Alice*, later?'

'I do hope so, Mr Dodgson. Give us the courtroom scene, in which little Alice realizes that the people she has been frightened of—who have terrorized her, and made her feel an inch tall—are nothing but a *pack of cards*.'

As she said the last phrase, she thumped the table with her knife, drawing an impatient 'Shh' from Watts, who was currently informing old Mr Cameron of the interesting verity that friends tie their purse with a cobweb thread.

'Talking of *Alice*,' said Dodgson, with his voice lowered and his eye on Tennyson, 'A thought has j-j—just come to me!'

He pretended to laugh light-heartedly.

'What is it, Mr Dodgson?'

'Do you think Mr T-T-T—'

'Tennyson?'

Dodgson nodded. 'Would allow us to d-dedi-c—cate the book to his s-s—'

'Sister?'

He shook his head, and indicated with a flat

hand the height of a young Tennyson.

'Schooldays?'

He took a slurp of water. Ellen had another inspiration.

'Serpent's tooth?'

He took a big breath.

'Sons,' he said.

Ellen frowned.

'Do you want me to ask him?'

'You seem to have influ-infl—'

'Influenza? La grippe?'

'Influence.'

Ellen didn't know what he was talking about. But on the other hand, she had no need to throw caution to the wind. Her Caution was so naturally small it had been lost in a light gust at birth.

* * *

Outside, the elements battled, and the rain still fell, and little Daisy Bradley curled up beside the briar hedge. She couldn't help noticing she was getting rather muddy, but on the other hand things in an adventure were supposed to be out of the ordinary; they were supposed to vex you a little bit. Had she picked the right evening to elope? Should she go home and think about eloping tomorrow? But then she remembered she had slammed the door behind her, and she didn't have a key.

The wind was sharp with rain. In order to stop feeling frightened, she sang quietly to herself the song she had learned from Mr Dodgson, 'Will you walk a little faster, said the whiting to the snail', but then faltered and stopped. His words were strangely uncheering for a little girl, actually. The odd thing about Mr Dodgson's story, she realized, was that the people in it were all so horrible to each other, on account of being mad and selfish; and in particular they kept threatening Alice, and calling her stupid, and trapping her with rules of etiquette that she couldn't possibly know.

For the first time since she met him, she asked herself whether Mr Dodgson was really the sunny personality she had at first imagined. Did she honestly want to spend the rest of her life with him, setting up home in a bathing machine, and living on what she could catch in a shrimp net? She pulled a face, stood up, brushed her frock. She was only eight, she told herself. As Jessie Fowler had pointed out this afternoon, a girl of eight needn't say yes to the first man who says he loves his love with a D. 'Panic about spinsterhood when you are ten and a half,' said the worldly Jessie. 'But really, not before.'

* * *

Meanwhile Jessie sat bored in the kitchen of Dimbola while the Cameron boys talked about lessons and Latin and ball games, and dull, dull things without any interest to a girl of avid brain power or searching imagination. Much more interesting to the little girl were the hissed discussions between the maids as they scurried about collecting platters of obscene roasted flesh. The one with the impenetrable Isle of Wight accent kept neglecting her duties, and mooning about by the window, and the Irish one was getting cross.

'Is it your blessed hair again?' demanded Mary Ryan, producing some nail scissors (she had started to carry them around on purpose).

Mary Ann sniffed, and looked sad.

'Will you take the roast tongue, Mary Ann! We've not all night.'

But Mary Ann broke down.

'It's not Herbert you're thinking on, is it?' asked the Irish one. 'Haven't I told you he'll be back in London by now?'

Herbert? Jessie's grip of her chair arm tightened, but otherwise she hardly moved a muscle. Herbert was the young man from the lecture that Lorenzo liked so much. Had the servant girl fallen in love with him? Here was some interest at last. Here was something to tell Pa.

Mary Ann snivelled. 'I be in a terbul pucker about it,' she managed at last.

'Look.' And reaching into her apron pocket, she produced Herbert's hat.

'That's Mr Herbert's hat,' said Mary Ryan.

Mary Ann sniffed some more.

'Did you take it from him?' asked Mary Ryan, confused. 'Where did you find it?'

Mary Ann broke down. 'In Mz Watts's room!'

She sobbed unpleasantly on to the plate of roast tongue.

'Dooan't jaw me, Mary Ryan! I be all uptipped! But I shan't goo without I knows!'

And Mary Ann boo-hooed and sniffed in a highly unbeautiful manner.

Mary Ryan felt somewhat uptipped too. Poor fool, she thought, to be in love with Herbert, who beneath his jerkin clearly had big breasts and womanly hips. More foolish still to be jealous in this confusing, ludicrous way.

'Now Mary,' she hissed, gripping the girl by the

arm. Jessie strained to listen through the clash of pans. This was excellent.

'I want you to pull yourself together, and not to think such thoughts about Mrs Watts. Aren't I telling you there is nothing between Mrs Watts and Herbert?'

Mary Ann wailed, and Mary Ryan made a decision.

'Never mention this to a living soul, but—'

'What?'

Mary Ryan lowered her voice further still. 'Mrs Watts is involved already with Mr Fowler,' she whispered. 'And is possibly beloved of Mr Tennyson as well.'

Mary Ann fell back in shock and nearly dropped the plate.

Mary Ryan shooshed her.

'And don't say Swap me bob.'

On that bombshell, they cantered back to the dining room, and the Cameron boys turned round to include Jessie in a joke about donkeys, only to find her staring like the dog in 'The Tinder Box'—the one with the eyes as big as windmills.

'Jessie?' said Henry Cameron.

'Jessie, what's wrong?'

But Jessie was lost in shock. She felt weightless and betrayed. Her head reverberated as if she had been boxed on both ears at once. 'Mrs Watts already involved with Mr Fowler'? Pa? *Pa*? For a couple of minutes, she scarcely remembered to breathe.

But how? They had been in Freshwater less than a week!

What did 'involved' mean? Did it have anything to do with those mutual ropings in Uncle Orson's pamphlet? Had Pa known this woman before this holiday? Had he brought his little innocent darling eight-year-old daughter to this dreary back end of nowhere filled with nincompoops just so that he could do lashings with Mrs Bloody Watts?

'There's something wrong with Jessie, Mother,' the boys told Mrs Cameron, who had popped behind the scenes to check on the hold-up with the food.

'Oh my dear, my dear! What can I give you? I am at my wits' end! Your father quite refuses tongue!'

Jessie's face was unreadable. Luckily Americans are often deaf to innuendo.

'My dear girl, I would give anything.'

'Are we still doing the tableaux later on?' Jessie asked at last, with her mouth set.

'Yes, I believe so.'

'Well then there is one thing I'd like, Mrs Cameron. I've brought a bread knife, but it's not right for what we are planning to do. Could I have a sharper one please? A really sharp one?'

Mrs Cameron hugged her, and Jessie wriggled.

'What a curious little girl you are!' she said.

* * *

Julia had been absent from the room three minutes. When she returned, however, she knew her lovely dinner had collapsed before she even opened the door. The hub-bub had dissipated to an awkward silence, and the maids were hurriedly removing themselves, Mary Ann with an ornate silver gravy boat attached and dangling against her chest. Julia stood at the door aghast. Turn your back on spinning plates for the merest instant, and they wobble, clatter and crash. Food lay uneaten, a glass was overturned, and Watts was staring at the ceiling with a martyred expression, indicative of one of his heads. Some fracas seemed to have broken out, but what on earth could it be?

'Do you see this impudence, Julia?' Tennyson barked, waving his arms.

Julia rushed to his side. 'What impudence, my dear Alfred? Show me and I will dispel it. This is a great day for you, Alfred, and I will not have it spoiled.'

'The young man here—' he pointed at Dodgson, whom he could only vaguely make out—'Gets your friend's little wife to ask me—' He spluttered. He couldn't go on.

'I merely asked him on behalf of Mr Dodgson,' spoke up Ellen, 'whether *Alice* might be dedicated to Hallam and Lionel, who are Mr Dodgson's special friends.'

Julia now understood why her dinner party was in ruins. How could anyone be so *stupid*?

'Did you say your name was Dodgson?' boomed the laureate, peering. 'You're not the damn photographer fellow too?'

Dodgson gripped the back of his chair. 'I have n—never given cause for s—such treatment,' he objected, hotly.

'And I have never given cause for this hounding and baiting and confounded cockney cheek!' shouted the bard, bashing the table as he stood up. 'I am surprised you would allow such disgraceful fellows into your intimate circle, Julia. I am surprised, and I am disappointed.'

Julia started to cry. The lovely review! What

about the lovely review?

'Now I am going home,' he continued. 'I had hoped this would be a pleasant evening among friends at which I could make an announcement. When I came here tonight I wanted you all to share my well-earned happiness, since none of you will ever earn happiness half as good for yourselves. In fact I was willing to read *for four hours* if necessary. But I find that circumstances have changed all that. So let me just say this. The review I received today confirmed what I and my real friends already knew, that *Enoch Arden* is the work which will make my fortune. I have therefore decided to thank you all for your kindness—especially Julia—and tell you that I intend to leave Farringford when my lease expires in two months. There is nothing to keep me here. I shall never set foot on this island again. Good night.'

He swept from the room, and all eyes turned to Dodgson, who stood up.

'I must say,' he began, but was interrupted by the sound of Julia weeping on her husband's chest.

'Mr Dodgson, don't you have some eloping to do, or something?' asked Lorenzo, pointedly. Dodgson, affronted now beyond endurance, left the room.

Julia glared at Ellen.

'I don't see what *I've* done,' said Ellen. 'Shall I follow Mr Tennyson? He seems quite fond of me usually.'

'No!' shouted Julia, so vehemently that her guests jumped. 'No, I will,' she added in a more normal voice. 'May I, Charles?'

'If it makes you happy,' said her lord, as always.

'You do your tableaux without me,' she said,

gathering her skirts. And she ran off to plead with the man she loved best in the world.

*　　　*　　　*

Ellen and Lorenzo looked at one another, and were just unfortunately swapping loaded glances when Jessie entered, to find out whether the show was ready.

'What the blazes happened here?' she asked, flatly. Even when mourning for her tragic young life, she couldn't help noticing that half her audience had split before curtain-up. The ones who remained were an unlikely crowd, too.

'You don't want to know,' said Lorenzo. 'But come and meet everybody.' Jessie curtsied to them all in turn, and gave each a steady look, especially the shaky Mrs Watts. 'You look as bad as I feel,' she said generally, which was impudent but accurate.

'Shouldn't we do this another night?' said Watts. The strain of the evening ought to be over now, surely. He had the distinctive look of a man who, though he has never had a stiff drink, yet suddenly feels the need of a stiff drink and tragically doesn't know that a stiff drink is the thing he needs.

But Ellen was not to be denied her chance. Perhaps she did have low ideas, but surely he would forgive her—if not absolutely adore her—for using them in the cause of love. So she took all the lamps and candles and arranged them at the foot of the curtain, and then made a short speech.

'In this first tableau, I represent Inspiration. I think my husband will guess who the other figure is.'

Cameron nudged Watts; Watts shrugged back.

He wished his wife would be sensible. He wished they could just go to bed. But then Lorenzo drew back the curtain, and what was behind it? It was—oh horrible!—the head of Haydon.

'No, no!' whispered Watts.

'Isn't this good, George?' said Ellen.

Haydon's head was set on a clothed dummy, made of rags, with its right arm cunningly raised to hold a paintbrush. The clothes were the ones usually worn by Herbert. Ellen had dressed the plaster head in a wig, and coloured its features with theatrical make-up. It was Haydon to the life! An apparition! Watts nearly choked. In the distance he heard a knocking and clamouring at the front door, but he was transfixed by the horror of this vision.

'Haydon!' he gasped.

Cameron (the only other person left at the table) watched Watts's face. Little Ellen had certainly captured her husband's attention, he thought. What a clever girl. And then he drifted off into a pleasant doze.

Ellen stood just behind the curtain, holding a handkerchief as though waving farewell. The curtain closed, and she stepped forward.

'That was, of course, Inspiration Deserts Benjamin Robert Haydon,' she explained. 'You see, George, it was nothing to do with you at all. He just dried up.'

'Why are you doing this?' Watts croaked.

Ellen, whose jangling emotions were now heightened by the thrill of the stage, made a solemn answer.

'Because I love you,' she said. 'And now—'

Watts called out to her from the darkness, 'Ellen, I forbid you—'

But then the curtain opened again on Haydon, and this time his companion was not Inspiration, but the precocious American child wrapped in a union flag, holding a flashing blade to Haydon's throat, and snarling.

The curtain closed again. 'That was General Tom Thumb, Famous American Midget, Kills Benjamin Robert Haydon.'

'Ellen, please! This is most unseemly! The man is dead!'

But the curtain swung open for the last time, and Jessie, smiling grimly, held the detached head in her hands, from which bright red blood appeared to be trickling.

Ellen applauded, but she was the only one. Watts had his hand before his eyes.

'Westminster!' he whimpered.

'That's the end,' Ellen explained to Watts. She turned to the child. 'Jessie, you clever girl, how ever did you manage the blood? It's so lifelike.'

But Jessie was wobbling a bit. Which was not surprising when she had just cut herself rather deeply on purpose.

She pushed Ellen away.

'Pa,' yelled Jessie. 'Get this woman away from me or I'll cut her too.'

Ellen fell back in alarm. 'Mr Fowler, come quickly. She's done something with this knife!'

'Jessie!' he yelled.

'I hate you, Pa. I love you. How could you do it?' Jessie's voice sounded a bit funny. She dropped the knife and it clattered at her feet.

* * *

Outside, in the garden, Julia caught up with Alfred Tennyson, as the wind lashed the trees above their heads, and the rain fell on their faces like—well, you know, God's angry tears or something. For a man who hotly resisted accusations of the pathetic fallacy, these stormy conditions were just too bad.

'Alfred!' yelled Julia above the wind.

'It's no good, Julia. My mind is made up.'

'Alfred!'

They could have gone on like this, but fortunately Julia thought of sheltering in the glass house, where at least they could hear each other speak. And so they entered Julia's hallowed place, where Alfred had never stepped before, and the conflicting emotions Julia had demanded from Mr Watts as Ulysses were as nothing to the feelings now fighting in her own breast like cross winds tearing at a sail.

'I can't believe you would leave me, Alfred,' she wailed. 'Just because I have never spoken to you of my feelings, you must surely know what they are.'

'Julia, I think we should discuss this tomorrow. Or perhaps, even better, we should never discuss it at all. It pains me to see you like this.'

'It pains you!'

'It's a figure of speech, Julia. It means I don't want to talk about it. And that such passion in a plain dumpy woman is ugly and absurd.'

Julia gaped. Alfred on the defensive was clearly a very dangerous man. He was still very angry.

'Correct me, Julia, but you seem to believe that I owe you something. I don't, and nor does Emily. We did not ask you to move here. We did not ask you for the wallpaper or the ponchos. We don't even know what a poncho is. We do not need your permission to settle our own affairs and enjoy the success that my talent has earned me, away from constant outrageous requests for photographs and dedications!'

Julia looked around. There was something about the setting. She never thought she would see Alfred in her glass house. She had wanted it so much that it had nearly broken her heart.

'Sit for me, Alfred,' she said quietly.

'You do not listen, madam!'

'But I do, Alfred. I do. And each word you speak pains me a great deal more than it pains you. But tell me, will your friends see the review in the *Westminster*? Will they be pleased and impressed?'

Alfred tugged his cloak. 'Yes, they will.'

'And will your enemies choke on their breakfast?'

'I sincerely hope so.'

'I really didn't want you to know this, Alfred, and I would never have told you for my own sake, but you simply need to know. I wrote that review. Sara used her influence with the editor to print it.'

Tennyson stood up impatiently. Why was he listening to such silly invention?

'And why would you do that?' he snapped.

'Because I love you,' she said. 'And because I wanted you to have a present from me that did not demand thanks. That way your usual brutal disregard for my feelings could not hurt me.'

'I don't believe you.'

'Oh Alfred. Your blindness is such a curse. Why do you think the review disputes with George Gilfillan and John Ruskin? Who else but your closest friends would know your tiresome preoccupation with their trifling passing comments?'

'They were a lot more than passing comments. They were wounds, Julia, *wounds*.'

'All right then. Look at it another way. How do you think the review got into the apple pie?'

He heard what she was saying. He sat thinking for a while, and the more he thought, the angrier he got.

'So do you expect thanks now? Is that why you do these stupid extravagant things, for the thanks? Well, you won't get any. Do you know what you have done, you silly woman?'

'Yes thank you,' said Julia. 'I thought I was doing you a favour, when in fact I have done one for myself.'

'I don't understand,' he said.

She drew a deep breath. 'I could tell the world the review was mine, Alfred. Your reputation would never recover.'

'You wouldn't.'

She raised her eyebrows.

'Julia. Julia, you are a nice person. In all the turmoil this evening, you seem to have forgotten.'

'Sit for me, Alfred. I love you.'

They sat in the dark, and the rain lashed the windows.

'I love you,' she repeated. 'Remember the *Westminster*. Sit for me.'

* * *

Dodgson rushed in to the dining room.

'It's Daisy Bradley!' he shouted. 'They say she's gone m—m-missing!'

Jessie dropped Haydon's head, and it smashed

on the edge of the podium. Blood trickled from her fingers' ends.

'I love you, Pa,' she said, and Lorenzo screamed as he ran to catch her in his arms.

It was quite a scene. In fact Mr Cameron woke up at that moment, took a look round the darkened room and—not surprisingly—applauded vigorously. It was quite the best tableau he'd ever seen—Watts with his hand across his eyes, Ellen aghast, Lorenzo with the bleeding child, and Dodgson frozen in the doorway.

'Very fine!' he called. 'Mark my words. Put that on in Drury Lane and people would pay good money to see it, I assure you!'

Part Three

Hats In The Air

Thirteen

Lionel Tennyson sat up in bed and laughed with delight. His beautiful little face was framed by hair curled in papers (at his mother's insistence), but he didn't mind. He hardly even noticed the discomfort in his foot, caused by his mother stamping on it so unexpectedly that afternoon. While Hallam slumbered inoffensively in an adjacent bed, Lionel held up a candle and continued to read a parody of his father's famous poem 'The Two Voices'. The parody, published anonymously, had been sent to Lionel by Mr Dodgson a couple of years ago. But Lionel, rightly believing Dodgson to be rather *infra dig* at the time, had never got around to reading it.

'The Two Voices' is not much read nowadays, but Lionel knew it very well indeed. Even though it was a grave and grown-up poem about the arguments for and against suicide, Lionel had known his father's poem since his earliest youth. The last-but-one governess had read it compulsively and had made both boys learn sections of it by heart. The children used to wonder, actually, whether she was quite all right in the head. At local children's parties, therefore, when games took place, other infants might lisp 'Humpty Dumpty sat on a wall', while the Tennyson boys were apt to fold their hands and begin,

A still small voice spake unto me,
'Thou art so full of misery,
Were it not better not to be?'

They would conclude their recitals thirty minutes later, among a party of blubbing and demoralized kiddies, and parents in despair.

So there had been general relief when that gloomy governess had gone, and another had replaced her. Like Tennyson himself, she would have been outraged by Mr Dodgson's version, 'The Three Voices', which concerned a chap determined, not to kill himself, but rather to be extremely cheerful at the seaside. But then a sea breeze carries his hat athwart the glooming flat (good Tennysonian words, 'glooming' and 'athwart'), where it is speared by the umbrella of a female philosopher whose aim is to make him see misery in everything. For someone who himself lived beside the sea, Lionel appreciated, if nothing else, the way Mr Dodgson set so many of his poems on the beach.

A while like one in dreams he stood,
Then faltered forth his gratitude
In words just short of being rude:

For it [his hat] had lost its shape and shine,
And it had cost him four-and-nine,
And he was going out to dine.

Lionel hugged himself. It wasn't that the parody was so very funny. It was that his father would be so very mad when he read it that he wouldn't know which leg to hop on.

'To dine!' she shrieked in dragon-wrath,
'To swallow wines all foam and froth!
To simper at a table cloth!

'Say, can thy noble spirit stoop
To join the gormandizing troop
Who find a solace in the soup?

'Canst thou desire of pie or puff?
Thy well-bred manners were enough,
Without such gross material stuff.'

'Yet well-bred men,' he faintly said,
'Are not unwilling to be fed:
Nor are they well without the bread.'

There was no doubt about it. 'The Three Voices' was dynamite. Dodgson had written doggerel stuff about dinner and hats! In fact Lionel was so engrossed in this wonderful fare that when a handful of pebbles rattled at his window, he ignored them. After all, it was a stormy night with sudden gusts. With any luck the Garibaldi tree would fall over, and do them all a favour. (Lionel had already loosened it secretly around the roots, to get it started.)

Another pebble hit the casement, however, and Lionel went to look. Outside, below, was Daisy Bradley, waving a small bag.

Lionel opened the window.

'Daisy! It's ten o'clock!'

'Lionel! What happened to your head?'

Lionel squirmed as he remembered the curling papers.

'I'll come down,' he said. 'Stay there.'

*   *   *

Down on the shore, Dodgson's boater had blown off, but no lady philosopher speared it. It bowled inland, spinning and scooping, and was never seen by a living soul again.

'Daisy!' he yelled.

Behind him, battling with the breeze from the sea, were Mrs Cameron and Tennyson, and Watts and Ellen, all doing their best, though not really knowing where to start. Before Jessie passed out at Dimbola, she whispered to Lorenzo that Daisy might have headed for the bathing machines (Jessie was privy to Daisy's somewhat flawed domestic intentions), which was why the household's luminaries had now crowded to the bay in low tide and pitch dark, calling and peering, while Daisy's other family and friends searched inland.

Alfred was not much use on a search party. Each time he called, 'Here she is! I have found the child!' he was discovered to be pointing at a big rock or a piece of old donkey blanket caught on a bush. But he felt that he needed to be there. He needed to come out and do something rugged and masculine after his frightful encounter with Julia in the chicken-house. Above all, he needed to feel good about himself again. Somehow or other, Julia's frank words (particularly 'I love you') had knocked him quite off balance.

'Daisy!' 'Daisy!' they called.

Dodgson felt wretched, and not just about the loss of his hat. Everyone knew Daisy's disappearance was his fault. Jessie had told everybody about the safety pins before she fainted away; and they had all shaken their heads and said 'Shame'. What could he do to redeem himself? Not take a picture, or write a parody, or sing a comic song. All his usual repertoire for ingratiation was useless in this company. So he must find Daisy. At all costs, he must find her before anyone else.

Ellen jumped from rock to rock like—oh Puck or Ariel, or something; while Watts poked at the ground with his stick, as though Daisy might be a shell fish burrowed there. Perhaps he was looking for dropped florins. He held up a large handkerchief and wiped a tear. This had been an emotional evening for him; it felt curiously final, as though nothing would ever be the same. Ellen had paraded his Haydon obsession for all to see! If a child was lost tonight—especially a child called Daisy—the metaphorical implications were simply too enormous to ignore.

'We'll find her,' Julia reassured him, loudly, directly in his ear. 'She is a very level-headed little girl normally.'

'But people do mad things when they love, Julia. Look at me. I married Ellen. That was mad, was it not? Tonight Ellen broke my heart with her little entertainment, apparently thinking to *win my affection*. That too was quite insane.'

But Julia couldn't hear him for the waves crashing and the wind pushing the tide up the shingly beach. Besides, this was hardly the time or place for introspection. Much as she loved him, sometimes Watts was enough to try the patience of an oyster. So she left him to his bemoanings and banged on the side of a bathing machine with a big stick.

Alfred was suddenly struck by a thought. 'The scream of a maddened beach dragged down by the wave,' he said, mainly to himself. 'I wrote that, you know. It's very fine, very fine. I doubt anyone else could have done it.' He tried substituting different words—

The scream of a maddened beach dragged
down by the tide;
The shriek of a maddened beach pulled
down to the deep;
The sound of some pebbly rocks sucked back
by a tow

—and decided he had probably got it right the first time, and that he was, despite all his other failings as a human being, a genius of a poet.

'Julia!' he called.

She ran to his side. 'Yes Alfred.'

She thought he had found the child. But of course he was thinking about himself again.

'I just wanted to remind you, Julia, that I have a very great gift.'

Julia's eyes filled with tears. Perhaps it was the wind.

'Oh you do have a gift, Alfred,' she shouted directly in his ear. She had to stand so close, she could feel his beard touch her face. 'A great gift. If only you could learn to appreciate it.'

Alfred was nonplussed. A man cannot bear so many home truths in one night.

'I will return to Emily,' he boomed. And before Julia could say anything, he had gathered his cloak and gone.

It was Dodgson who first noticed the light on the boat, thirty yards out in the black water. 'A light,' he shouted, pointing. 'C—Can anyone swim?'

Of course they couldn't. Nor could he. But he was actually ready to strip off and dive in when Mrs Cameron held his arm.

'It's not Daisy,' she shouted.

It was true. The boat, with its lantern swinging, which tossed against the choppy water, was not stationary and helpless, but moved quite quickly towards the beach. And if their eyes did not deceive them, it was rowed by a woman.

Who could this be? They watched in a line (and amazement) as this woman rower deftly caught the wave to ram her boat ashore, then jumped out quickly and dragged it up the beach. Rather too late, Mrs Cameron ran to help.

'Why, hello!' shouted the woman, in a friendly fashion. They looked at her. She held her lantern closer to her face. She was a complete stranger.

'Hello again,' she yelled, with an American accent. 'My, this wind.'

It was as though she had dropped out of the sky. In fact it would hardly have been more remarkable if she had. Who was this extraordinary woman? She wore a large tweed cape, sodden with rain and sea-water, which she flung back carelessly as though it were the lightest shawl. If she had worn thigh-boots, and slapped them, it would hardly have looked much out of place.

'I really didn't expect to see anybody, arriving so late,' she shouted, shaking hands with each of them, and ignoring their rude gaping. 'Out for a walk in the storm? A fine idea. Feel the electricity in these elements. Those nincompoops at

Lymington refused to sail, so I hired this boat and travelled under some steam of my own.'

'You didn't row around the Needles?' asked Julia, aghast.

'The tall chalk stacks? I did, yes. That was the very best part.'

She removed some thick waterproof boots and tucked them under her arm.

'But now, what's this? Great luck. It is the Albion Hotel and my journey's goal.'

'Excuse my rudeness,' said Julia, 'but what are you doing here?'

'I have come to meet my husband and daughter. What a surprise I will give them both. They think I am in Boston. How do you do? My name is Lydia Fowler.'

The others stared.

'But tell you what,' she added, 'seeing as we're friends already, you can call me Professor.'

* * *

'So what happened, Daisy?'

Lionel sat with Daisy in a large armchair. Sophia had brought some drinks, and Daisy had changed from her wet clothes. In her little bag was found a very nice floor-length cotton nightie, so she now wore that, and flicked her hair back over her shoulders.

'I was mad,' she said.

'To fancy Mr Dodo? I'll say.'

'It was just that he said he loved me.'

'Hmm. But Daisy, he says that to all the girls.'

Daisy shrugged.

'I expect so.'

'Come on, Daisy, I know so. Someone told Hallam that Alice Liddell's mother stopped letting him write to her.'

'Who's Alice Liddell?'

'Don't you know anything? She's the girl he wrote *Alice's Adventures* for.'

Daisy whimpered. She couldn't help it. Nobody told her there was a real Alice. Mr Dodgson had kept that very quiet.

'Oh,' she said.

'What's wrong?'

'Nothing.'

She pretended she didn't care, but it was a bit of a shock. Alice Liddell, eh? Alice Liddell. She blinked a lot, but did not cry.

'The Liddells sometimes holiday in Freshwater,' Lionel explained.

'You mean he even sees her here?'

'And at Oxford, of course.'

She shook her head. Mr Dodgson's character got worse and worse.

'Does he love her?'

'Daisy, forget it. He's thirty-two and she's twelve.'

Daisy twiddled with a bit of her hair. It was all a bit much to take in.

'Let's change the subject,' urged Lionel.

She nodded, and tried to think about something else.

'What does she look like?'

'Daisy!'

'I know, I know. I'm sorry.'

'Won't anyone be looking for you, Daisy?'

'I shouldn't think so. I left very quietly.'

'Oh good.'

*   *   *

Back at Dimbola, Jessie languished in her father's arms, while the maids looked grim and mopped the blood off the dining room floor.

'What have I done?' Lorenzo moaned. His darling child! His prodigy! He caressed her ghastly ringlets with his big hands, and hugged her closely to him, careful not to touch her bandaged arm. For yes, Jessie had really cut herself with the sharp knife from the kitchen, and it was a madder act than anything a black-blooded Tennyson had ever done, despite the imperatives of heredity.

'What have I done?' he repeated. 'Jessie, just tell me, what did I do?'

She opened an eye. 'You lashed up your senses with Mrs Watts, didn't you Pa?' It was the thought in her head, but she did not speak it aloud. She was enjoying the attention far too much to jeopardize the mood. So she snuggled nearer and let out a faraway moan.

'I will send for Ada,' he declared. But as he said it, his heart broke and he began to sob over the actually not-at-all lifeless body of his little girl.

'Jessie, you are everything to me. Don't take yourself away.'

'Oh really, Lorry,' said Lydia, standing at the door. 'Can't you see the child is acting?'

Lorenzo looked around. 'What?'

His wife? Lydia? Leaning on oars in Mrs Cameron's drawing room?

Jessie sprang into life.

'Mama!' she yelled, and sat up straight.

'What?' said Lorenzo again, releasing his hold.

Was Jessie all right? Or was Lydia a phantasm?

'Oops,' said Jessie, looking up at him. 'Sorry, Pa.'

'Jessie,' called Lydia. 'My own brat prodigy.'

'Mama! Or should I say Professor!'

*   *   *

Finding Lydia was certainly a bonus, but as far as Dodgson was concerned, it didn't quite compensate for losing Daisy. Alone, therefore, he set off into the darkness. For someone with a logical mind, it was tragic the way he had lost all power of consecutive thought this evening. He sat down for a moment on a little post, and tried to pull himself together. Perhaps he could deduce Daisy's whereabouts by means of his intellectual training. So he had a go at it, out there in the dark, setting his mighty syllogistic brain to work in a practical cause, using all the available data. Through force of habit, however, the propositions came out something like this:

1. No one takes *The Times* unless he is well educated.
2. Daisy Bradley is missing.
3. No birds, except ostriches, are nine feet high.
4. Guinea pigs are hopelessly ignorant of music.
5. Rainbows are not worth writing odes to.
6. A fish that cannot dance a minuet is contemptible.

Even a cursory perusal told him there was not much to be deduced here, so he tried to focus more narrowly on the matter in hand.

1. Daisy Bradley loves me.
2. Daisy Bradley is eight years old.
3. Eight-year-old girls sometimes cut themselves deeply with sharp knives.
4. If you drink from a bottle marked poison, it is bound to disagree with you, sooner or later.

Dodgson put back his head and screamed. Then he chose the logical course again, and argued thus.

1. Daisy has friends at Dimbola and Farringford.
2. She is not at Dimbola.

The word 'ergo' had certainly been invented for such moments.

* * *

Jessie, jumping into her mother's arms, found that she could administer a little kick in Mrs Watts's pretty little face, which cheered her up immensely, and also brought a smile to Mrs Cameron. No bothersome questions of how, why, or what interfered with her infant joy. Mama was home!

Lorenzo, however, was overwhelmed—a sensation he recognized, and adored. Lydia had overwhelmed Lorenzo from their earliest days as phrenologists together, and had thereafter never left off. Readers of this story may have assumed Lorenzo was a widower; certainly his new friends in Freshwater had jumped to that mistake. But Lydia was not dead, she was merely in the United States, which is not the same. She had travelled home with a few tidying-up missions: to reorganize the national practice of obstetrics, for example.

Lorenzo, who up to now looked pretty energetic in the context of Freshwater Bay, dwindled beside Lydia like a candle set before a furnace. It was Lydia the child took after, not Lorenzo. The song about Lydia, oh Lydia, that encyclo-piddia was not actually written about Lydia Fowler, for she had no tattoos. But in her family, she was nevertheless known as Piddia, for her obvious know-all tendencies.

'Greet me, Lorry,' she said.

He jumped to his feet, quickly adjusted his beard, and ran to her side. It pained him to do this in front of sweet little Mrs Watts, but it couldn't be helped.

'Goddess,' he breathed. And taking her by the back of the neck, he kissed her, for a not inconsiderable period, full on the lips, while Jessie looked on proudly.

The others, still damp from the elements, coughed and shuffled disapprovingly, a bit like Wonderland creatures waiting for a Caucus race.

'Mrs Fowler rowed across the Solent in a rainstorm,' said Julia conversationally, as though the kiss had finished (it hadn't).

'She has won medals for rowing,' said Jessie, proudly. 'She is Marblehead champion.'

'Oh, what's Marblehead?' asked Julia, hoping to fill time while the kiss continued.

'It's a place,' said Jessie. 'Near where Uncle Orson lives. We thought he ought to live in Marblehead, really. Because of the name being so apt.'

The kiss shifted a little; it stopped for air. But it did not conclude.

'We didn't actually know there was a Mrs Fowler,' said Ellen, with an attempted gay laugh.

'Oh no?'

But the kiss did not stop.

Jessie piped up. 'Did you find Daisy?'

The grown-ups hung their heads. In the excitement of Lydia, they had forgotten.

'Oh, she'll be all right,' Jessie assured them. 'But if she isn't, she has only herself to blame. I mean, fancy falling for Mr Dodo. Give me typhoid any day.'

The Fowler clinch had now broken, much to the relief of the host nation, but the couple were still not ready for general chat.

Lorenzo went down on one knee. 'Diana! Juno! Explain!'

'I found you had left London, and here I am. I have brought five hundred copies of Orson's latest pamphlet. We start lecturing tomorrow.'

'Oh Ma,' squealed Jessie, 'we've missed you so much.'

A few minutes later, a message arrived from Farringford, to say that Alfred had returned home to find Daisy safe in her nightie. The worried Bradley family had been calmed. The hunt was off. The only person who did not know this, of course, was Mr Dodgson, who could now not be found himself.

'Let's ask Ada to find him,' said Jessie. 'She would love to be out on a night like this. It's exactly her kind of thing. She's awful gloomy, Ma.'

'Ada?' queried Lydia. She seemed surprised.

'We engaged Ada Wilson four months ago, just before you left for America, my dear. You surely remember?'

‘But Lorry, I left instructions for the girl to be dismissed.’

‘Why?’

‘I found her writing anonymous letters. I considered her dangerous.’

Lorenzo and Jessie looked at each other, nonplussed.

‘But Ada’s a real silly, Ma. She’s a misery, but also what you call a nincompoop. Pa says her brain has been fogged by pig and cow.’

‘Let us send for the girl at once,’ said Lydia. ‘But let us also consider the evidence. I left you a letter about the wickedness of the girl, secreting it carefully in your dressing table. *You did not receive it*. So the girl *must* be wicked. Did you not read her head, Lorry? She has Destructiveness so big that her ears stick out at an angle, unable to support the arms of spectacles. Her Organ of Gratitude is the size of a wizened pea.’

Lorenzo and Jessie looked at one another. ‘Ada?’ ‘Organ of Gratitude?’ was the astounded look on both their faces.

‘What sort of anonymous letters?’ asked Julia, intrigued.

‘Very threatening, to judge by the one I read. The girl was mad, I think. Mad with a grudge. She actually mentioned pushing some mean old lady in an invalid carriage off a cliff!’

Julia stopped breathing.

‘To whom did she send these anonymous letters?’ she asked.

‘To Alfred Tennyson, the Poet Laureate,’ said Lydia, almost laughing. ‘So preposterous.’

*   *   *

Dodgson trudged up the lane toward Farringford, unaware that deep within that lifeless house, Alfred was reading 'The Three Voices', and hopping on both legs at once. Which was ironic really, because Dodgson was currently reciting to himself the Tennyson original, and recognizing for the first time the full force of the argument for self-slaughter.

Alfred, on the other hand, could hardly believe his eyes. All the deep philosophy of the poem was mocked here, transformed into nonsensical bantering. He had never been so insulted—not by George Gilfillan, not by anybody. The hero in the Dodgson poem doesn't even know what the Voice is talking about!

Fixing her eyes upon the beach,
As though unconscious of his speech,
She said 'Each gives to more than each.'

He could not answer yea or nay:
He faltered 'Gifts may pass away.'
Yet knew not what he meant to say.

Gifts may pass away? Well, this gift certainly would. Alfred thundered so loud when he read this sacrilege that Emily was forced to come downstairs to investigate. She found two giggling children (one of them not her own), and her lord in apoplexy, holding a brown magazine which looked, at first glance, similar to the *Westminster*.

'Is the review less good than you first imagined, Alfred? I knew you would find cause to hate it before long.'

Alfred folded the magazine and pushed it inside his coat pocket. He would not allow anyone else to see this monstrous thing; Lionel should certainly not keep it; the child would delight too much in learning the poem by rote.

'Dodgson is in Freshwater, my love,' he blurted. 'Damn the man.'

'The Oxford photographist?'

'The very same.'

'Oh.' Emily had never told Alfred of the letter from Dodgson. She had thereby saved a week of relative peace.

'He's been here for several days,' said Lionel, helpfully. 'In fact, he's been here long enough for Daisy to fall in love with him, plan an elopement, and then think better of it.'

'Lionel!' said everybody together—including Daisy, who kicked him.

'He ruined the dinner at Julia's this evening,' said Alfred. 'I didn't get my apple pie—twice!'

'Poor Alfred.'

'Scoundrel,' spat Alfred.

'Scoundrel,' agreed his dear, weary wife.

'Photographist.'

'Scoundrel.'

'If he comes near me, I shan't be responsible for my actions, Emily. Do you know, he even wrote a parody of "The Two Voices"?'

'No!'

*   *   *

Back at Dimbola, they sent to the Albion for Ada Wilson, but received the reply that she had packed and gone, immediately after Lydia's luggage had been delivered to the rooms. Vanished, they said.

Jessie and Lorenzo did not wish to believe it, but the evidence was mounting. The child now recollected how Ada had always hidden behind the bathing machines when Lionel Tennyson was on the beach; she had also pumped Jessie for every detail of their afternoon at Farringford. Mrs Cameron thought about her own sweet-tempered maids, and thanked the almighty for her good fortune. Mary Ryan might be disaffected, but she was not (as yet, anyway) murderously insane.

'But what can she have against the Tennysons?' was what they all pondered. Yes, sometimes Tennyson's poetry was a bit depressing, but you didn't *have* to read it.

Jessie shrugged. She was just glad the girl had left them. 'Mama, did you mention Ada's Organ of Gratitude just now?'

'Wizened,' said her mother. 'Pitiful.'

Jessie knew she must pluck up the courage to ask. 'Where is it?'

'It's in the lobes of the ear, Jessie.'

All around the room, people fingered their ear-lobes thoughtfully.

'Who found it?' said Lorenzo, trying to sound casual.

'I did. Are you pleased? Brother Orson said it was the discovery of the age, especially since almost nobody has got one.'

Around the room, people stopped bothering.

'But what are we doing about Ada? Do you think she is positively dangerous?'

*   *   *

Dodgson was just about to find out, when he noticed on the road ahead of him a woman in a dark cloak hurrying in the same direction.

'Madam,' he cried, and scampered to catch up.

The woman stopped and turned, and he soon arrived at her side. He recognized her from the beach, but he didn't know her name.

'I am going as far as F-F—Farringford,' he volunteered. 'May I—?'

She looked at him as if he were mad. 'I can find my own way to Farringford, thank you.'

There was something very odd about her, he thought. She sounded much too well educated to be a maid, but he was sure that's what she was.

'Do you have business at Farringford, so late at night?' he asked.

'I do.'

'So they are expecting you?'

The woman shrieked with laughter. 'No!'

'Are you familiar with the temper of Mr Tennyson?'

'I know his wife much better.'

'To tell you the truth,' said Dodgson, 'I am a little fr-fr—'

'Friendless?'

Dodgson shrugged thoughtfully; 'friendless' wasn't far off the mark, but it wasn't what he was trying to say. He waved his hands.

'Frisky?'

He shook his head, but not vehemently. He put his fingers in his mouth.

'Frost-bitten?'

'Frightened.'

Which really he was right to be, because once they were announced at the door—Mr Dodgson and Miss Wilson—they discovered a less than welcoming group of Tennysons sitting in the semi-dark.

'Miss Wilson?' repeated a puzzled Emily, as the couple approached.

'She's the governess who made Hallam and me learn "The Two Voices", mother,' hissed Lionel. 'She left when you didn't pay her.' And then, spotting Dodgson, his eyes lit up.

'Stay there,' he told Daisy.

'What?'

'I've got an idea,' he said, and scampered to the hall.

'Miss Wilson, what an unexpected pleasure.'

But Emily had only just stepped forward to greet her ex-employee when she was almost knocked down by Dodgson. To his enormous relief, he had spied the little girl in her night dress. He ran towards her and fell at her feet.

'Daisy!' he exclaimed.

'Eek,' said Daisy. 'Get off !'

'You *scoundrel*,' said Tennyson, rising.

'Shall I do it, father?'

Dodgson looked around. What was happening? Lionel had leapt on to a convenient chair and had raised a croquet mallet. Dodgson looked up at Tennyson.

'Yes, do it,' said Tennyson.

So Lionel Tennyson struck Dodgson on the head with a croquet mallet, as he had so long hoped to do. As Dodgson keeled over on the hearth rug, Tennyson and Emily broke into spontaneous applause.

'I never require you to check the boys for signs of madness again, my dear,' said Alfred, with his broadest smile, patting his breathless son on the shoulder. 'If that was not the act of a sane mind, I really don't know what is.'

Fourteen

That night, Watts informed Ellen they were going home. He sent her a little note, by means of Mary Ryan, advising her to pack her bags at once. Now, with the Irish maid offering her bits of things to decide on—and surreptitiously returning the purloined Herbert hat to its rightful place—Ellen sat amid the debris of her ransacked wardrobe, and felt pretty glum. Perhaps it was time to accept that the marriage was over. The Haydon extravaganza had gone down quite badly. Her satin wedding dress had been ruined in the rain.

Damn this small Caution; damn this big Hope. She felt terribly confused. She wanted Watts to love her; but if she was honest, she wanted Lorenzo Fowler to love her too. If only Watts had set up house with her, the marriage might have been different. If they had taken up an independent life, they would have stood a chance. But Watts was a poor man. Haydon had lived an independent life, and look what happened to him. All that remained of him now was a moral tale, a set of gloomy diaries, and a plaster head in fragments.

'The Absence of Hope'? It was all Watts really desired, of course; to depict moments of desolation and spiritual defeat. How stupid she had been to think she could turn him into Mister Cheeryble just by effort and example. It was as pointless as re-writing 'The Two Voices' as 'The Three Voices', or trying to pose for a Julia Margaret Cameron photograph ('Wait! I come to thee! I die!') with a grin from ear to ear. It was just no good. It did not accord. Despite all his wife's best efforts, Old Greybeard's doomy life force had prevailed. 'And the moral of that is?' Watts seemed to whisper in her ear. All too easily, she thought of the apt motto. Let the cobbler stick to his last.

Of course, the considerable shock of Lydia Fowler's arrival was still negotiating its way through Ellen's nervous system, and many, many hours would pass before it settled. The great magnetic Fowler kiss was unlike anything previously seen in polite society, and as a spectacle of raw marital desire, it uptipped this little virgin quite. Lorenzo and Lydia had seemed clamped together, locked in place, their bodies humming the same tremendous note in a major key. 'Goddess,' Lorenzo said, and Ellen nearly swooned with longing.

She fingered her Herbert costume, and considered putting it on again, but her Herbertian adventure seemed so paltry now. Compared with rowing around the Needles in a night storm to join the man who worshipped you, dressing up as a boy for a bit of strained flirtation with someone else's husband was very small potatoes. It hadn't helped, either, that Lydia had handed everyone a copy of Uncle Orson's explicit pamphlet before bidding goodnight and gathering child and husband back to her omnicompetent skirts. Ellen had read it at once, and a lot of matters of an unmentionable physical nature had finally fallen into place. 'Full intimacy', for example, covered all sorts of things between a man and wife, but it had nothing to do with dead pets.

Somewhat feverish at the recollection, Ellen now

found herself alone at bed-time letting down her hair, and unbuttoning the top bit of her nightie. Up to now, Ellen's sexual frustration had been to her a puzzling sensation, something like a faraway itch, or a door opening to the garden but nobody coming in. But after Lorenzo said 'Goddess', the world changed; she saw it differently, and she felt the full, bitter force of missing out on the action. At the Albion Hotel, at this very minute, Mr and Mrs Fowler would doubtless be engaging in vigorous marital relations precisely as prescribed by O. S. Fowler. Ellen had the mental picture of a battering ram, flames, cheers, and boiling oil—which was odd, really, because there was nothing alluding to medieval siegecraft in the book. Watts, by contrast, would be lolling in the next bedroom by himself, feebly wiping his dribbling brushes on a linseed rag.

Ellen made up her mind. Five months was long enough to wait for marital love, whatever the quality. What would she lose now by forcing the issue? Nothing. She undid another button and stepped into the corridor. It was time to take the bull by the horns. It was time to forget Westminster.

'George?'

She rapped lightly on his door.

'George?'

'Mm?'

There was a scrabbling noise in the room, but before her husband could say, 'Wait!' Ellen entered on exaggerated tiptoe, getting ready to pull her nightie over her head. But it was a mistake. Oh dear, this was a mistake. As the door swung open, Watts leapt to his feet in embarrassment—

'George! But—'

'No!'

'How could you?'

'Leave this room at once!'

—and Ellen had returned to the corridor pole-axed with astonishment within thirty seconds.

It was the last body-blow of her visit to Freshwater, and it was conclusive. Her marriage was now definitely over. George Frederic Watts had deceived and betrayed his wife in the worst possible way. For no, she had not surprised him molesting a chambermaid, or a child, or her best friend, or even the St Bernard, as other disappointed wives have done throughout history. When she entered her husband's room on that black night in Freshwater Bay, she had surprised him counting an enormous pile of money.

*   *   *

Cameron sat up in bed and persuaded his wife that a further mercy dash to Farringford was out of the question. The hour was too late.

'But they must be told of Ada Wilson,' she exclaimed. 'Alfred has often mentioned an anonymous letter, but think how brave he has been, if the wicked missives have continued. Perhaps he did not wish to alarm Emily. Think of that, Charles. There is some good in the man, you must not deny it. I would give *anything* for this not to have happened to my dear, dear friends.'

'I know you would. You would give anything to anybody. It is to the infinite glory of God that each time I wake up I find my bed still under my body. But you can inform them of this silly Ada business in the morning, Julia. Tell me, how many times have you visited Farringford today already?'

Julia nodded that he was right, as always. She had been there twice, and both times without benefit of wheeled propulsion. She was nearly fifty, and her legs were feeling the strain. She recollected this morning's first visit, when she tripped over the Elgin Marbles wallpaper in Tennyson's staircase. How much could happen in a single day.

'I found the wallpaper, incidentally,' she told Cameron, absent-mindedly rubbing her shin at the memory of its discovery. 'I brought a roll back with me, in fact.'

'Did you?' He was amused. 'Was that quite proper, do you think?'

'Well, they don't want it. They have made that clear enough. Besides, I'm afraid I was hurt and angry, Charles; I believe I vowed to burn the stuff in the fireplace. But now that I look at it, it is so *very* fine I think I might give it to Mrs Fowler as a present. I would so like to have that lady's good opinion.'

'My dear, as you know, I admire you in all things save your impulsively charitable first impressions.'

Julia said nothing.

'But Julia, you surprise me. How can you take back a gift you have given? It is no longer yours. Aside from the propriety of the thing, if you don't return it, they will suspect the servants or the children.'

Julia bit her lip.

'I was in a passion, Charles.'

'I know.'

'This has been a terrible day.'

'No, no. There I must disagree. From the entertainment point of view, it was more than satisfactory.'

'But you are right, Charles. I will return the wallpaper tomorrow. You are always right. That's why I love you.'

Cameron smiled and settled his head. He did not regard this as something requiring an answer, let alone a reciprocation.

Julia differed from him in this opinion, however. 'I said I love you, Charles,' she repeated, with meaningful emphasis.

'Good for you,' he said, comfortably.

* * *

Staggering hatless from Farringford in the direction of the sea, Dodgson decided it was time to make his excuses to Freshwater society and leave before lunch tomorrow. However much people begged him to reconsider, he would just have to disappoint them. His week's sojourn at this delightful holiday place had been at best a grim race against brain damage, and he considered it wise to quit while he—and his head—were still ahead.

There were just a few details to tidy up in the morning. For example, he would require Daisy Bradley to return his safety pins; and he intended to lend some photographs to Mrs Cameron (to demonstrate how photography should be done). As for Mr Tennyson, his own offences against the great man were still well beyond his power to comprehend, but the evidence of his own ringing ear told him that Tennyson was definitely offended. In retrospect he thanked goodness that at least Lionel had reached for the croquet mallet and not the mock-baronial axe above the mantel.

His other major task before leaving Freshwater was to detach *Alice* from little Miss Terry, who still unaccountably believed the work to be somehow their joint creation. Having finally accepted that Tennyson's answer was a No, he would instead dedicate the book with a poem to Alice Liddell, which was only fair—despite that ungrateful little girl's insistence on growing up and spoiling everything. Hopefully, other little girls would heed the warnings in *Alice* about getting so big suddenly that you fill the room, and your arm goes out of the window and your foot goes up the chimney. But in Dodgson's experience, there was no reasoning with the little angels once their grosser hormones kicked in and they stopped wearing the wings. Meanwhile, as the rain finally stopped, he was thinking of a clever poem for Ellen which he might slip into the book somewhere as a way of pretending to say thank you.

So he was just pacing along with his head down, practising rhymes, when he bumped into the rather arresting figure of Mary Ann Hillier, swathed in black, lighting up the dark with her moonglow profile and expression of infinite sadness. Such beauty was truly astonishing, he had to admit it. The Pre-Raphaelites would stripe themselves pink with envy.

'Mary Ann?'

'Meester Dadgson?' she said. Dodgson winced as the vision fled.

'If you wants to go hooam I shall be gwine outlong in a minute or two,' she said. Which was nice of her, if not particularly nicely done. Nobody around here, he noticed, seemed to have much grace when they offered you a kindness.

They walked along in silence for a short while, but Mary Ann clearly had something she wanted to discuss.

'Be you a-minding o that lecture t'other day?' she asked, as they walked along in the dark.

'How could I forget it?' said Dodgson.

'Waall, I caast eyes on a buoy, swap me bob, that tore my heart all to libbets!'

'You d—did?' Dodgson wanted to ask what a libbet was, but he dared not disrupt the flow. Mary Ann seemed to be telling him she was in love, but he didn't see what he could do about it, and he was hardly in the mood for maids' confessions. Even at the best of times, in fact, such intimacies made him want to scratch vigorously at the rough skin on his elbows.

'And the boy?' he asked. 'Do you mean young Herbert?'

Her eyes lit up.

'I do.'

'Well, if you look down the road there, you'll see he's j—just emerging from D-D—'

'Dimbooala Lodge!' exclaimed the girl. 'I knowed it! That Mary Ryan'll git sich a whistersniff in the chops one day!' And she scurried off after Herbert, while Dodgson—glad to take his mind off his current problems—couldn't help speculating how long he would have to stammer 'W-w-w—' before anyone guessed he was trying to say whistersniff.

* * *

'Ada has taken some of the pamphlets, Lorry,' declared Lydia, surveying a sorry mess in the

Fowler quarters, which had got quite a lot worse during a rather wild hello-it's-me-back-from-Boston conjugal intimacy.

'Mm,' said Lorenzo, still lazing in his stewy sheets. 'But we can easily hire another maid, Lydia. Please don't exercise yourself about it, my Aphrodite. You have, after all, just rowed a very dangerous shipping channel before performing as a fully participant female in a quite exhausting marital act. You must surely deserve a breath or two, or even'—he looked at her steadily—'a drink.'

'Lorenzo Niles Fowler!' she exclaimed.

Any other teetotal couple might have laughed at this suggestion. The Fowlers were not light-hearted, however; it was the secret of their marriage. Now each gripped the other's hand fiercely, as though rescuing somebody from the sea. They looked searchingly into each other's eyes, and held the pose for two minutes. And when this odd, non-dancing tango was released, they got back to normal again.

'Besides, the girl seems to have done no other harm,' said Lorenzo.

'But when I think what she might have done to Jessie!'

'All she did to Jessie was offer her ham at breakfast. Oh, but there is something to tell you about our Infant Phrenologist. I meant to mention it earlier.'

'Apart from the cut to her arm?'

'Yes, apart from that.' Lorenzo had still not fully convinced Lydia that the cut was part of a party game that went wrong.

'No. The fact is, Jessie read Orson's pamphlet one day when I wasn't looking.'

Lydia thought about it. He studied her face. Was she shocked? She wasn't.

'Jessie is remarkable, isn't she, Lorry?'

'She is.'

'How old is she again?'

'Eight.'

'Good heavens.'

Lydia tidied part of a demountable brain into a box. It was the Fowlers' special delight to employ, in their passions, not only their own Organs of Amativeness, but someone else's too.

'Shall we leave tomorrow?'

Lorenzo remembered he had an appointment with Mrs Cameron, to test the applications of phrenology on photographic models. The lady was counting on him, dammit, and he owed her a good turn. Briefly, he wrestled with his conscience.

'I'm with you, divine one,' he decided. 'Let's go!'

Lydia rose from her bed to draw back a curtain. She had firm views about fresh air at night; she had once written a hundred-page monograph about its benefits that had sold particularly well in the western frontier states, and had led to many readers being attacked in their beds by coyotes.

'That's odd,' she said, as she climbed back into bed. 'There is a youth outside sitting on the sea wall with a cap on. And beside him is a girl with very long hair. It's late for romantic trysts, don't you think? I hope they won't steal my boat.'

Lorenzo sat up.

'Shall I go and see?'

She kissed him.

'God,' she breathed.

She was not swearing. A Fowler never swore. She was simply doing the 'goddess' thing in reverse.

She drank a pint of water in a manner that set her husband's loins aflame. Which was why another half hour elapsed before Lorenzo could investigate the callow couple outside.

*　　*　　*

Dodgson had been right, you see, that the figure was Herbert. The lad made his last outing that night before being burned, with a horrible smell, in a kitchen stove at Dimbola Lodge the following day.

'What is that? Is it wool?' asked Cook, as Mary Ryan wiggled the tweed with a poker.

'Ah, isn't it such stuff as dreams are made on?' said Mary Ryan, significantly. As we mentioned earlier, Mary Ryan had been no slouch in the literature department.

Ellen adopted Herbert once more because she needed time to think, and no longer could she bear to stay indoors. The rain had subsided, and though a wind still blew, it was warm. She walked to the bay, where she watched the waves, and tried to sort out her life, starting with the most important thing, to wit, the astounding news that Watts had money. She kept saying it to herself. Watts has money. Watts has money. Watts—who has made his proud wife behave as little more than a mendicant—actually possesses heaps of the stuff that rents houses and buys food, and secures respectable independence away from interfering, condescending patrons.

Watts had accumulated the money, of course, by taking care of the pence and looking blank and helpless whenever the cost of a ticket to the seaside was mentioned. He was paid for his portraits. He won £300 in the Westminster competition. She could never forgive him. In particular, she could never forgive him for instructing her to live on ninepence a week, and giving her nothing by way of presents except a cut-price proverb book at Waterloo Station. It is normally the case that when poverty comes in at the door, love flies out of the window. But Ellen stopped loving Watts only when she finally found out about his dosh.

It was as she sat there, staring at the sea, that Mary Ann Hillier first watched her from the shadows, tragically retaining her firm hold of the wrong end of the stick. It would be a shame to transcribe the exact words of this lovely girl on this occasion, especially if whistersniff or rantipike were among them. Besides, when Ellen ever after looked back on this tragical-comical scene, she remembered it rather differently:

O, what a deal of scorn looks beautiful
In the contempt and anger of his lip!

said Mary Ann (aside), her face all blind admiration. ('Poor lady!' thought Ellen; 'She were better love a dream.')

A murd'rous guilt shows not itself more soon (said Mary Ann)
Than love that would seem hid: love's night is noon.
O Herbert, by the roses of the spring,
By maidihood, honour, truth and every thing,
I love thee so that, maugre all thy pride,
Nor wit nor reason can my passion hide.

Mary Ann gasped at the realization of what she was saying.

Do not extort thy reasons from this clause,
For that I woo, thou therefore hast no cause;
But rather reason thus with reason fetter:
Love sought is good, but giv'n unsought is better.

Mary Ann Hillier did not say any of this, obviously. Her heart was tore in libbets. Was it true, in any case, that love sought was good but given unsought was better? That's how it felt to the martyred giver, certainly; but to the receiver, love unsought was a pain in the neck. It did not flatter; it was beaten off with a bad grace, or shunned altogether. It was like unwanted wallpaper. Here was the lesson that Julia Margaret Cameron failed to learn every day of her life: simply, that one-way passion scares people off; it doesn't work. Ellen saw Mary Ann's hopeless attachment, and felt sorry for it. She suddenly realized how impossible it was to love in return just because someone loves you very much first.

The delicacy of the situation required Shakespeare to help her out. Forever after, when Ellen played Viola to crowds of adoring play-goers, her heart broke for her own dear Olivia, the sweet and beautiful (but very dim) Mary Ann, whom gently she rejected that momentous night in Freshwater.

By innocence I swear, and by my youth,
I have one heart, one bosom, and one truth,

And that no woman has; nor never none
Shall mistress be of it, save I alone.

* * *

If Julia thought the day had been a long one, for Emily Tennyson it was the worst birthday since Alfred had asked her in the first year of marriage what was in her pocket. Thinking it was a game, she gaily produced a thimble, and was astounded when he solemnly gave it back to her as a present. 'I beg you to receive this elegant thimble,' he said. Since then she had largely hidden the fact of her birthday, and enjoyed it more. Alfred had performed one kindness today, however, by removing a roll of that awful wallpaper and disposing of it. No one could find it anywhere. She meant to thank him as soon as she could. It was a thoughtful deed worthy of a great man, and all the better for being utterly uncharacteristic.

In all other respects, however, Emily's birthday had laid her low completely. The battle with the dozen *Westminster*s had been so enervating that after the arrival of the late-night guests she could not even struggle up to bed unaided, and required Lionel and Alfred to carry her. In the pocket of her night gown she found this morning's 'Yours in aversion' letter which she was about to slip into her bureau with the others when she realized—with a certain *frisson*—that it had been delivered by hand.

Was 'Yours in aversion' a local, then? If only her husband were like other men, if only he could stand a bit of mild criticism, none of this tiring subterfuge would be necessary. It was true to say that the more you take on, the more you will be taken advantage of. All lay load on the willing horse.

Strangely, it had been quite comforting to see Wilson, the old governess. Emily had no idea Wilson might bear a grudge about not being paid. Was Emily herself paid for her duties in this household? Of course not. What price could be placed on feminine duties? No, she and Wilson had shared almost two happy years, and yes, there had been occasional quarrels over money, but Emily had always forgiven the outbursts. Wilson's unjust sense of furious grievance would expend itself (she did have quite a temper), and then the two women would get along famously again.

'Wilson! It is a pleasure to see you, even at this unlikely time of night.'

Emily had thus taken the young woman aside while Alfred and Lionel picked up Dodgson from the carpet and carried him to the door. The whacking of Dodgson did not alarm the old governess. Being accustomed to the Tennysons, she wondered as little as anybody at the croquet mallet forming part of the house's hospitality.

'No chance of tea, I suppose?' Wilson said. Emily laughed and rocked.

'You and your strange wit, just like old times!'

In the bedroom now, Alfred entered and found her smiling. He decided to take advantage of the good mood.

'Emily, do you think I should pose for Julia?'

'No, I don't.'

'What if I must?'

'Must?'

'Must.'

She pursed her lips tight.

'Must?' she demanded again.

'We will discuss it tomorrow, Alfred. Wilson was saying I looked peaky, and I believe she is right. You must take us both with you on your walk tomorrow.'

'Must?' Alfred began.

'Yes, must,' she barked, and then sank to her pillow, all energies disbursed.

* * *

Ellen sat alone again. Mary Ann—or Shakespeare's Olivia, it was all melting together in her mind—had left her. It was no fun reducing a beautiful woman to tears, Ellen thought; why did Watts admire his own handiwork so much? She wiped her eyes and stood up.

'Mrs Watts?'

She looked around.

'Mrs Watts?'

It was Lorenzo. Oh heavens, how thrilling. Whenever she saw this man, she felt acutely self-aware, as though her body were swelled by electricity, and moreover outlined by sparks of blue fire.

'I thought I saw you from upstairs,' he explained. 'We are leaving tomorrow.'

Ellen felt a mortal pang, although she knew she was not entitled to it.

'As are we,' she admitted.

'Were the tableaux a success? Was Mr Watts cured of his problem?'

'Not entirely. He has forgotten Westminster, but unfortunately remembered something else.'

She smiled at him. She wanted very much to

touch his arm, but she held back. She was half afraid the contact might kill him. She lowered her eyes instead.

'I think my husband and I will soon conclude—oh, that all good things must come to an end.'

'Ah. I hope there were other reasons to enjoy your stay?'

Ellen's body sang so loudly she was amazed he couldn't hear it. Or perhaps he could.

'Mr Fowler, I would not have missed it. It's the sea, you know. The sea throws up all manner of things.' She raised her eyes. 'Mrs Fowler, for example.'

Lorenzo did not comment. There was no call for an apology. His wife was a fact. He sniffed his fingers in the dark.

'You seem unhappy,' he said at last, tenderly.

'Not unhappy at all, thank you. I just need courage.'

They looked at the black waves together.

'You have great courage, Mrs Watts.'

'Do I?'

Oh dear, they were getting personal again. Why did every conversation with Lorenzo Fowler have to scream with the sub-text, *Please, please, for pity's sake, touch my head*?

He looked at her. She looked at him.

'Will you take your hat off this time, Mrs Watts?'

'I think I will, Mr Fowler.'

And as the moon broke through cloud above the ink-black bay, Ellen shook the hair out of her hat, pouring it like gold into his hands.

Fifteen

Next morning, Alfred was just reading mad Uncle Orson's startling description of sexual frenzy when Emily was wheeled in by Wilson. In her black, pram-like invalid carriage, she looked like a squeezed doll, an image of weakness quite belying either her authority in the household or her influence over the big strapping man who stood myopically before her, his back to the fireplace in authentic baronial manner, while a grey shaggy deer-hound lay at his feet. It was quite true, she reflected, what they said about people and their dogs.

'Reading your excellent review again, my dear?'

Tennyson took a quick look at the brown cover of the Orson pamphlet. Actually, in appearance it was not unlike the *Westminster*, a coincidence which might later come in handy—if he wanted, say, to read it again in bed.

'I am indeed, Emily. Fine words, fine words, and correct in every particular.'

'May I see it now, Alfred?'

'Mm?'

'Will you hand it to me? I think I have strength enough.'

Tennyson hesitated. He doubted his wife would ever have strength enough for the contents of the matter he was reading—which was a shame, but there you go. Thinking quickly, he reached into his coat pocket and withdrew the true—*Westminster*.

'Another copy,' he announced ingeniously, and continued to read feverishly about the abomination of women who don't want to take part.

How had Orson Fowler's curious document found its way into his home? Alfred had no idea that Wilson had brought it. All he knew was that, ambling vaguely down the main stairs this morning, he had discovered it hanging by a thread, exactly placed so that it bumped into his forehead as he made his way to breakfast. What with the apple pie yesterday, and today the contraption with string, people were finally finding ways of drawing things to his attention.

'This appears to be a periodical called *The Train*,' pronounced Emily at last, 'And it contains Mr Dodgson's scandalous version of "The Two Voices".'

Tennyson snatched it back, searched his pocket again, and found the *Westminster*. These papers all looked too similar. He wondered how librarians managed things at all. Impatiently he took all three pamphlets into one bundle, and cast them on the piano.

'Do you think we should all go out at once, Emily?' He wanted to walk alone this morning. He had lots of things on his mind.

'Why ever should we not?'

Alfred thought for a reason. He grasped at straws.

'What if the Queen came, for example?'

'Alfred!'

'Well, must Wilson accompany us, then?' he demanded. 'She is not pleasant company, you must confess. I firmly believe she did not deserve the wages you did not pay her.'

There was an awkward silence, broken by Wilson humming 'Rock of Ages', just behind his ear.

Emily cleared her throat.

'She is standing in the room, Alfred.'

'Is she?' he whispered.

'Three yards to your left, before the window.'

'Oh good.' He thought quickly again. 'I thought you were a sideboard, my dear!'

He waved an arm of explanation. 'You admit yourself that you are thick set? Broad of beam? Hm? Shall we be off ?'

* * *

And so it was that half an hour later three small black figures could be seen on the down—approaching the high point of the seven-hundred foot cliffs—when Julia set out uphill from Dimbola Lodge with her wretched roll of wallpaper. Cameron had refused to let her spoil the Tennysons' breakfast with the news of Ada, but she broke out of the house as early as she could.

There was an air of finality about the day, for Mr Watts had announced his imminent departure, as had Mr Dodgson, who pored over a piece of paper at breakfast while mysteriously holding a yellow cushion to the side of his head. She had also received a note from Mr Fowler saying that his family must return to London, so bang went the science-meets-art Absence of Hope enterprise as well. Julia hated endings, yet also loved them. She doted on the high-minded melancholy they produced. 'He is gone, he is gone!' was the sort of picture she loved above all to produce—a long face in profile, bereft of love. Luckily, Mary Ann had been looking positively hangdog recently. A period of excellent droopy-servant Art was therefore on the cards.

*   *   *

Dodgson spent his morning trading in safety pins and pictures, and bits of ornament, and writing a tortured letter to Ellen. It was conceived in kindness, as a present, but luckily Mrs Watts had become accustomed to presents of a cheap, disappointing nature. For here was yet another.

> My dear Mrs Watts [he wrote]
> I hope you will indulge an author's wish, and allow me to include this little poem in my Alice, so that you may then justly claim to have inspired my book in some small, private way (if not in any big one). You will recognize at once its close allusions to the proceedings of this strange week at Freshwater, but at the same time appreciate my efforts to cloak them in terms that will make the poem a private matter between us. The system for decoding the below is a simple one, and I shall never disclose it to a living soul.

(Here followed a highly complicated system of 'him' for 'her' in lines of even number, and so on. It was obvious to anybody that this was not a system at all, but an excuse for an insulting and empty gift.)

The matter of the safety pins in stanza three

[he concluded] can be readily comprehended when I tell you that Mr Bradley will send them to you this morning. He has sent me a most polite note telling me I need not call for them myself.

Ellen had no idea what Mr Dodgson's instructions meant. She also had no idea why he would write her a poem about safety pins. He seemed to be telling her, in certain terms, that Alice was not written for her, but at least this poem was. So she tossed the instructions aside and read the attached.

They told me you had been to her
And mentioned me to him:
She gave me a good character,
But said I could not swim.

('Well, that last bit is true at least,' thought Ellen. 'Come, this is not too difficult.')

He sent them word I had not gone
(We know it to be true):
If she should push the matter on,
What would become of you?

('What indeed?' she commented.)

I gave her one, they gave him two,
You gave us three or more;
They all returned from him to you
Though they were mine before.

(Ellen's heart began to sink. She re-read the

stanza twice, and pushed on.)

If I or she should chance to be
Involved in this affair,
He trusts to you to set them free
Exactly as they were.

Ellen stopped reading. She had reached the bottom of the sheet. She turned over. There was more.

My notion was that you had been
(Before she had this fit)
An obstacle that came between
Him, and ourselves, and it.

Don't let him know she liked them best,
For this must ever be
A secret kept from all the rest
Between yourself and me.

Ellen put it down. She felt her age had doubled since last night, and with the new-found authority of sadness (which suited her), she tore Mr Dodgson's poem in pieces. '*A secret kept from all the rest between yourself and me*,' she recited. 'It will certainly be that, Mr Dodgson. It will certainly be that.'

Watts opened the door. 'Are you ready?' he asked, coolly.

'I am,' said his little wife, in a grown-up voice. As she looked at him now, she could never imagine being in awe of him again.

He walked away, but she recalled him.

'Come back!' she cried, using a professional

diaphragm technique which would soon come in handy again.

'Come back, I have something important to say.'

This sounded promising; Watts turned.

'What is it?'

She smiled and raised her eyebrows. It was lucky she knew Mr Dodgson's book by heart.

'Keep your temper,' she said.

* * *

It was a fine day; the effect of last night's storm had been to break the hot weather, and today small clouds scudded inland over the Needles and across the chalk. At the bay, seaweed in ugly heaps had appeared on the sand, stirred up by last night's waves, and was now stinking like sulphur, making little girls run squealing, holding their noses. Julia loved the seaweed smell, for it was similar to her photographic chemicals, which betokened freedom and happiness, and a chance to do something beautiful in an otherwise humdrum life. In the confusions of the last few days she had taken few photographs; when her guests had all departed she would again have the leisure but not the subjects. It was annoying how things always worked out that way.

But she must hurry to Alfred. There were so many things to say. He would be walking on the down this fine morning, and she must tell him she was sorry for the review, and that of course he must sit for her only if he wished it in his heart. Second, that Ada Wilson was a threat to Emily (though she still did not believe it). Also, she would take the opportunity of returning the wallpaper—and let him toss it from the cliff if he wanted. So with the wallpaper in her arms, she toiled up the steep path to Tennyson's favourite walk, and was only half-way when she spied the tiny black figures and counted them. They were three. The upright one with the hat—a bit like a chimney-stack—was certainly Alfred; her heart leapt at that. The little box-shaped one was Emily (her heart subsided again). But who—dear God—was the third?

*   *   *

Back at Farringford, Lionel roamed the garden. He examined the Garibaldi tree, which alas, had not budged overnight; and though he pushed it hard with his good foot, it stood firm. Still pinned to it was a copy of the *Westminster Quarterly*, but it was drenched and ruined. Not for the first time, Lionel wished he could be sent away to school like other boys. At Freshwater, it was not much fun being a child, when all the interesting imaginative games were played exclusively by the grown-ups.

'Lionel!' He turned to see Jessie and a strange woman approaching the house.

Lionel gave them a cool wave, and sauntered towards them.

He was well aware that Jessie thought him handsome. He expected to work his charm on the woman too.

'Remember, Jessie,' Lydia whispered. 'We must not alarm Lionel by asking too directly about Ada. He is only a child.'

Jessie nodded in a grown-up fashion. How awful it must be, she thought, to have people regard you as only a child.

'This is my Mama,' said Jessie proudly. 'Are your folks about?'

'I'm afraid my Father and Mother are on the cliff,' he explained, showing a good profile as he turned to point.

'Oh,' said Lydia. This was all a bit delicate. How do you ask a ten-year-old boy whether a maniac has called, without alarming him?

'Are your parents well?' she asked, at last.

Lionel thought about it.

'Not exactly,' he answered candidly. 'But then they never are.'

He giggled, and Jessie joined in.

'We wondered whether anyone strange has been here,' Lydia continued. But again Lionel was obtuse.

'Define strange,' he said, wistfully.

At this point Jessie interceded. She couldn't see the point of all this pussyfoot.

'We are looking for Ada Wilson; she's dangerous,' she snapped.

'Why didn't you say so?' said Lionel. 'She's gone with my parents on their walk.'

Lydia handed her umbrella and hat to Jessie, and hitched up her skirts.

'Which way did they go?'

'Through the green gate, I expect. Father always goes that way.'

'May Jessie stay here with you?'

Lionel pursed his lips, and shrugged his assent. 'Come on, then,' he said, without much enthusiasm, and led his little guest indoors. Tennyson's second son may or may not have inherited the black blood of the family, but he was certainly a splinter off the old door-post in other ways.

Lydia Fowler picked up her heels and sprinted towards the cliff.

'I'll show you a parody Mr Dodgson wrote of father's poetry,' said Lionel, as they walked indoors.

'A poem by Mr Dodgson?' remarked the little girl, sardonically. 'That will be fun. Perhaps we could give each other smallpox as well.'

* * *

And where was Lorenzo? Lydia's husband was at Dimbola, to take his apologetic leave of Mrs Cameron (who was not there) and offer Ada's old job to Mary Ryan (who was). The house was otherwise deserted: the Wattses had left, and Mr Dodgson was on board a coach to Shanklin (unbelievably) for another seaside holiday, and another batch of little girls.

But what a bombshell for Mary Ryan. She was astonished at Mr Fowler's offer, and blushed a vivid pink. She shut the drawing room door behind her, and begged him to lower his voice. It would be terrible if Mary Ann heard anything of this—so it was unfortunate that when she shut the door, Mary Ann was lurking outside, and got her hair caught in the jamb.

They stood in the drawing room looking at each other, Mary Ryan and Mr Fowler. Mary Ryan didn't know what to say. Lorenzo, on the other hand, could think of plenty.

'You have such well developed Individuality, Mary,' explained Lorenzo. 'How can you stay here, away from the world? You have such spirit, it should not be squandered. And you have a desire for a good marriage, too. But whom will you meet if you stay here? We, the Phrenological Fowlers, can offer you travel and glamour, even trips to the United States of America. Really, Mary, you must leave Mrs Cameron and come with us. We could take you this very day!'

Mary hesitated. It was true she loved the sound of travel and glamour. And it was true that she felt frustrated at Dimbola Lodge. There comes a point when ministering to gloomy high-brows gets a bit samey. Also, her photographic modelling career was rubbish.

'I don't know.' Her face crumpled with indecision.

But it was then that Lorenzo Fowler—for all his experience in flattery, and for all his enormous Human Nature—made a bad move.

'We could take you away with us today,' he repeated. 'Mrs Cameron is a delightful employer, no doubt, but how can I forget what you said at my lecture—that you stay here only for indebtedness, not gratitude.'

Mary looked at him.

'Did I say that?'

'You did.'

'I would never say such a thing.'

'In your trance you said it, Mary. And anything said when mesmerized comes from the heart of hearts.'

Mary coloured up. She felt ashamed. Was she really not grateful to Mrs Cameron? Was she really such a bad, unchristian girl?

Lorenzo felt her slipping away, but didn't know what to do.

'Please don't condemn yourself for your lack of gratitude, Mary. It is the most natural thing in the world. We phrenologists have discovered scientific evidence that gratitude scarcely exists. See these earlobes of mine, for example?' And he thrust his face towards her.

Mary struggled, she bit her lip, she looked quizzically at his earlobes. Finally, she spoke. Her mind was made up.

'Thank you for your offer, Mr Fowler. I will always remember it. And I am sure I will never have another to match it. But perhaps my Individuality is too strongly developed for my own good. For, if only to prove to you that gratitude is not an accident of the earlobe, but a proper Christian virtue, I will remain with Mrs Cameron, who has been so kind to me. Without her kindness, I would probably be dead. Matrimonially, I shall take my chances here. Travel and glamour I hereby renounce.'

She sank in a chair. Such a big articulate speech was rarely required of the maids at Dimbola Lodge, but she always had it in her, and it came out very well indeed.

Lorenzo, who should really have applauded, was disgruntled, and left the room. Opening the door, he released Mary Ann, who sprang back, and then rushed in. Her mouth was agape like a big 'O'.

'Mary Ryan! Harken to you! Lor a massey!' she laughed in amazement, with her hands on her hips.

'Don't,' said Mary Ryan. 'Please don't.'

'Just wait till Mrs Caameron hear this, buoy!' exclaimed the stupid girl. 'Mary Ryan, if you doan't need your head examined!'

*   *   *

Up on the windy cliff, with no idea of the interest they were causing, the Tennysons proceeded in their usual manner.

'Emily, listen,' said Alfred

He marked a place in his book.

'With blackest moss the flower-plots
Were thickly crusted, one and all:
The rusted nails fell from the knots
That held the pear to the gable wall.'

'What of it?' asked Emily, leaning over to pick an orchid. 'It's *Mariana* again. You changed peach to pear, I know that.'

'I am considering further emendations, my dear. "Garden wall" to "gable wall". It is a great improvement?'

Emily shrugged.

'What do you think, Wilson?'

They both turned to the strange woman in black, who had hardly spoken.

'I think I'd like to take you for a little walk by ourselves,' she said. 'Poetry and fresh air never did mix.'

'Good idea!' boomed Tennyson, and turned to survey the blue of sea and sky, while Wilson, with a mad laugh, kicked off the brake of Emily's carriage, and pushed it fast in the direction of the cliff edge.

The carriage had been built for this clifftop terrain, but it was murder nevertheless. Its big wheels bucked and slithered at the best of times, and now Wilson was pushing it much too fast.

'Hold on, Wilson,' commanded Emily. The

bumping was making her teeth dance, and her brain bounce in her head.

'No, you hold on,' sneered Wilson.

'I beg your pardon?'

'Oh, it's not respectable to beg. I'm sure you told me that, Mrs Tennyson. I'm sure you mentioned it many times.'

The invalid carriage came to a halt in a little hollow, and Emily caught her breath. Something was wrong here. Wilson was much weirder than she remembered.

'Alfred!' she called. But either the wind was too loud, or her voice was too soft, because he could not hear. And as for seeing her, there never was a man to whom 'Out of sight, out of mind' more aptly applied. Currently, he was whispering 'garden-gable-garden-gable' to himself, oblivious.

'Wilson?'

'Yes, Mrs Tennyson.'

'Is there something you wish to say to me?'

Wilson laughed again.

Emily turned to look at her. 'I wish you'd stop laughing in that sinister way, and start explaining yourself. Look, Mrs Cameron is coming towards us. We will discuss any grievance you have when we return to the house, but at present, I wish to speak with my friend, even though—oh no, how can I bear it?—she is bringing me another roll of that infernal wallpaper.'

'Are you telling me you did not receive my letters?' said Wilson, nastily.

'Letters?'

'I wrote them twice a week for a year, Mrs Tennyson. A hard thing not to notice.'

Letters? Instinctively, Emily felt in her pocket,

and produced the latest 'Yours in aversion'.

'Is this you?'

'Yes.'

Emily could scarcely believe it. She had always pictured 'Yours in aversion' as a failed, impoverished poet expiring from the strength of his own body odour somewhere near Hungerford Stairs, with dandruff and no coals.

Emily looked at the letter and shook her head in disbelief. 'I have read none of these letters since the first,' she told Wilson, in firm tones. 'Anonymous letters are vile and cowardly, Wilson. I have—I have thrown them all away.'

'What?' Though Wilson stood behind her, Emily could tell she had struck home.

'And now,' said Emily, 'I will dispose of this one also.' Wilson reached forward to grab it from her hand, but Emily cast it in the air.

Caught by the wind, it soared away uphill like a child's kite. Wilson yelped.

'You beast!' she screamed, and scampered after her handiwork.

Emily laughed and slapped her knees. How stupid Wilson was. Alfred was right: the girl had not deserved the wages she had not been paid.

At which point, with Mrs Cameron toiling towards her just fifty yards off, Emily's invalid carriage started trundling downhill, brakeless and without a rudder.

'Alfred!' called Emily, as she felt the wheels begin to turn. 'Alfred!'

But the carriage was travelling quite fast now, downward and seaward, straight towards Julia, across the grass and chalk ('Alfred!'), gathering speed and bumping from wheel to wheel.

Julia, who heard the cry downwind, looked up and saw a sight which filled her with a mixture of panic and euphoria, guilt and elation. She stopped and put her hand to her mouth. For this was exactly the picture she had conjured jealously for herself a hundred times, Emily freewheeling towards a certain doom—except that sprinting over the hill behind came Lydia Fowler, waving and yelling.

'I'm coming,' shouted Lydia, pushing past Tennyson, who still gazed out to sea, impervious. 'Stop that carriage! Let me through, I'm a professor!'

'And I'm coming too!' yelled Julia.

Emily's carriage was bouncing and veering now like india rubber as it gathered speed, and it was hard to guess exactly the path it would take, but as it closed on Julia it swerved to the right, directly towards the cliff edge. Julia froze. Her heart drummed in her chest. What could she do? Well, she could get rid of this wallpaper for a start. And so it was that with fantastic presence of mind, Julia heaved the wallpaper into the air. It flew, it arced, and time stopped. And then it landed in front of the lady's wheels, just ten feet from the edge. The runaway carriage stopped with a jerk, its black-clad passenger shot out with a scream, and the rest was a blank, because Julia—understandably in the circumstances—collapsed in a dead faint.

When Alfred was finally roused to the situation, it was mostly under control. Lydia, with typical efficiency, had restored Emily to her carriage, revived Julia's unconscious form with a practised slap, and restrained the would-be murderess by wrapping her in wallpaper, which was the only material to hand.

'Very good quality stuff,' she remarked, as she worked.

'Well, I'm glad somebody thinks so,' said Julia.

Alfred was nonplussed by the presence of so many people on his cliff at once, but considering that two of them had helped save the life of his dearest Emily, decided to be big about it. He produced some embroidery silks from his pocket which helped tie the wallpaper more securely around the prisoner. And then, having decided definitely in favour of 'gable', he suggested they all walk home.

'She wanted to kill me, Alfred.'

Tennyson didn't know what to say. He looked around at the clouds and sky.

'Well, Emily. She couldn't have chosen a finer day.'

* * *

As they walked back across the down from their adventure, they little knew how they were spotted from afar by a lady in a fine carriage, bowling away from Farringford. It is always a nuisance to call on the off-chance and find the whole family from home, but it is even more of a nuisance if you are Queen Victoria and have popped in for an edifying recital of *In Memoriam*, to remind you of your poor dear dead Albert. It is worth remembering here that the Tennysons had lived in hopes of such a visit for ten years. As has been mentioned before, they even kept a plum-cake on the off-chance (or they thought they did—Lionel and Hallam had eaten it).

‘The Queen came, father,’ said Lionel, as the solemn bedraggled party made their way indoors.

Lydia laughed.

‘No, it’s true, Ma,’ said Jessie. ‘She was here ten minutes ago, you just missed her. Why is Ada done up like the Elgin Marbles? Is it a game?’

‘The Queen?’ said Tennyson, blankly. ‘The Queen? No, no.’

He sank into a chair, and allowed a small sob to escape him.

‘I hope you were courteous, Lionel,’ said Emily.

‘I gave her a copy of *Enoch Arden*, father, and she seemed very pleased to have it. And I also suggested that you would be glad to read it to her.’

‘Well done, boy.’

Alfred was torn between a desire to hug the boy, and to hack his own head off with a ceremonial axe.

‘But there was a strange thing,’ Lionel added, in that handsome nonchalant way of his. ‘When I left the room to get the book for her, there were three copies of that brown review thing over there on the piano. And when I came back, there were only two.’

‘She has taken your excellent review, my dear!’

Alfred and Julia exchanged glances. On the walk back from the cliff, she had explained about not expecting thanks for the review. She had explained that she was sorry. But now that Queen Victoria would read Julia’s handiwork, and be terribly impressed, she felt prouder than ever of her perfect gift.

‘Oh, may I see it, too?’ said Lydia. She went to have a look.

‘Ah yes, a copy of the *Westminster Quarterly*,’ she

said, picking it up. 'And *The Train*. I don't know this, is it good? You are fortunate, Mr Tennyson, that the Queen did not pick up the wrong thing here! They are so alike!'

Alfred was still so mentally enfeebled by his terrible luck at missing the monarch that he didn't at first appreciate the full force of Mrs Fowler's news.

'You seem pale, Alfred,' said Emily. 'Yet I am safe and sound! I think this is a special occasion. Come, we shall have some tea.'

Jessie and Lionel cheered.

'And we shall cut the plumcake!'

Jessie, unaccountably, found herself cheering alone.

But meanwhile Tennyson remained silent. He knew there was horror lurking in Mrs Fowler's innocent words. He just had to pin it down. Slowly he made a calculation. After the Queen left the room, the *Westminster* was still there; and *The Train*. Which meant—which meant—

As he finally fell in, the sound that escaped him was a suitable combination of gasping and drowning. The Queen, at this minute, rattling towards East Cowes, held the sexual ravings of Orson S. Fowler in her commodious black silk lap. Had Alfred been asked that morning the worst potential mishap that could befall Orson's time bomb, he might have pictured Lionel reading it, or Emily. Now, however, Queen Victoria would hop into her four-poster tonight at Osborne House, and scream the place down. He was ruined. It was all up.

All he could do was pray. No one would notice. He closed his eyes.

'Almighty God,' he began. 'Save me from this and I will—'

He paused. What bargain could he strike with the almighty? After all, he was already such a Christian man. He opened his eyes for a clue, and spied his dear friend Julia being brave about the Elgin Marbles wallpaper, while adjusting her bothersome lace cap. He closed his eyes again. In his heart of hearts, he knew what he had to do.

*   *   *

Two days later, Julia Margaret Cameron sat at her window in her quiet time, while Mary Ryan read to her from *Maud*. She had heard about Mary Ryan's stout and loyal speech to Lorenzo Fowler, and was so heartened by it that she promised the girl more starring parts in the photographs from now on, and also less water-carrying, which was a relief. Mary Ann, who had thought herself rather clever to pass on the story to her mistress, now cleaned silver in the exile of the kitchen, and couldn't quite work out what had happened.

Mary Ryan always read beautifully. She had a poetic soul. Julia listened to her now while watching Tennyson's gate, with tears rolling from her eyes.

'Come into the garden, Maud,
For the black bat, night, has flown,
Come into the garden, Maud,
I am here at the gate alone;
And the woodbine spices are wafted abroad,
And the musk of the rose is blown.

For a breeze of morning moves,
And the planet of Love is on high,
Beginning to faint in the light that she loves
On a bed of daffodil sky,
To faint in the light of the sun she loves,
To faint in his light, and to die.'

The air had taken a chill this morning. Julia shivered. Ah, yes. *To faint in the light of the sun she loves; to faint in his light and to die*. She wiped her cheeks with her shawl.

'Oh Mary. Mr Tennyson is a very great man.'

Kindly, Mary took her hand and squeezed it.

'He is so.'

'He has a great gift.'

'Is that the same?'

'He makes the sun come out.'

'I know.'

Julia was so taken with this thought that she didn't straight away notice the Tennyson gate swing open, and her darling Alfred appear, waving his hat at her window. Just like the vision of Emily on the cliff, it would be like a dream coming true.

'Come into the garden, Julia!' he called.

She looked down.

'Come into the garden,' he called again. And then she properly saw him, stark and black amongst her white roses, and her heart filled with joy.

She flung open the sash. 'Alfred!'

'I have a note from the Queen, my dear. All is well! All is very well indeed!'

He produced the letter from his pocket, and held it close to his eyes.

'She says she was never more happily diverted than by the reading matter she obtained from my house—that it made her think *more than ever* of her poor dear Albert!'

'Alfred, I am so glad she loved *Enoch Arden*. It is a great poem, full of loss.'

Alfred frowned. *Enoch Arden*? Who mentioned *Enoch Arden*? He scanned the note again, puzzled.

'Oh yes, here it is! Yes, she says thank you for the book of poems too.'

Julia had never seen him so playful or so handsome. She scurried from her bedroom and ran downstairs, reaching the garden just as he plucked a white rose—at last, a white rose!—and held it to his face.

Her heart broke.

'I'm so glad you came to tell me,' she said. 'And I hope you have forgiven me, Alfred. It's just that, well, I would give *anything*, and when—'

'I have decided to sit for you, Julia.'

Julia caught her breath and adjusted a shawl. She looked around at her lovely roses. The day was so very beautiful. The soul of the rose went into her blood.

'Sit for me? Oh, but Alfred! Only if your heart desires it.'

'I will sit for you—' and here he made a special, enormous effort, so difficult that you could almost hear his soul creak—'with pleasure.'

'You will?'

'I will.'

He removed his hat and bowed his amazing, famous, enormous head before her.

She reached out, as if to touch it.

'It's all for you,' he said.

Appendix

NEITHER MRS CAMERON NOR G. F. WATTS produced an 'Absence of Hope'. But Watts's curiously pessimistic painting 'Hope'—in which a blindfold figure on a buoy listens to the last string on a broken lyre, and doesn't look especially cheered up by it—became his best-known work. At one time, it was as famous as Holman Hunt's 'Light of the World', and it brought solace in unlikely places. After their defeat in the 1967 war, Egyptian troops were distributed with reproductions of 'Hope'. What they made of this peculiar choice of consolation prize is not recorded.

Mrs Cameron, meanwhile, decided that the phrenological route to perfect abstract expressions was not the only one, and to generate the right demeanour for her picture 'Despair' she simply locked the sitter in a cupboard.

JESSIE FOWLER became a famous phrenologist in her own right. She continued to help her parents in their lifetimes, and then pressed on alone, back in New York, writing widely on such arcane matters as 'The Psychology of Arkansas'. She became an expert on child psychology. She never married.

Meanwhile, Lorenzo—that 'prince of mental scientists'—lived to his eighties. Despite a stroke three years earlier, he accepted a model skull at the Phrenological Centenary in Queen's Hall, during a programme which included music from the Aeolian Ladies Orchestra, and a blindfold examination by Jessie. Back in Boston, Orson Fowler continued to hoe a lonely row, and was publicly reviled for such publications as *Private Lectures on Perfect Men, Women and Children, in Happy Families*, which included chapters on 'Just How Love-Making Should be Conducted' and 'Male and Female Electricity'. His *Sexual Science* at the Boston Public Library today has the obscure shelf-mark 'Inferno', and cannot be traced. Presumably, it was burned.

THE MARRIAGE of Ellen Terry and G. F. Watts did not survive many months. Ellen returned to her family home, where she received many visits from C. L. Dodgson. In the divorce proceedings, some years later, a difference of temperament was mentioned. In her chirpy memoirs, however, Ellen suggests that 'a difference of occupation' would have been nearer the mark. Bumping into Watts one day in a street in Brighton, she records, 'He told me I had grown!' Outside a jeweller's shop in Bond Street, she once saw Tennyson in his carriage. 'How very nice you look in daytime!' he remarked. 'Not like an actress.'

ALFRED TENNYSON sat for umpteen portraits by Julia Margaret Cameron. She took over 1,200 images in all, and is rightly regarded as a great pioneer photographer. In terms of exposure and aesthetic composition, her solemn big-head pictures are unparalleled.

Dimbola Lodge still stands, with its view of the sea intact, and is currently under renovation as a museum. Of her portraits of Tennyson, the poet's favourite showed a profile, in which the full glory of his unwashed neck is visible for the world to gaze on in perpetuity. He named it 'The Dirty Monk', and once wrote beneath it a characteristic imprimatur, 'This I like best of all my portraits, except one by Mayall.'

FARRINGFORD also still stands, as a hotel, with a pitch-and-putt on the lawn and croquet mallets in the hall. On Saturday nights is held a dinner-dance, to be avoided at all costs. Through some meteorological mishap, the Garibaldi tree is a gaunt bare trunk, but it is still sturdy and very tall, and pierces the horizon like a needle. Until recently, Alfred's study was reached by way of an entertaining sign in Gothic script, 'Tennyson's Library and Colour Television'. The base of his spiral staircase was blocked by a fruit machine.

MARY RYAN, though not a natural actress, appeared in photographs after this time, and made an amazingly good marriage as a result. Henry Cotton spotted her in Mrs Cameron's 'Prospero and Miranda' at the Colnaghi Gallery, and fell in love. They were married in 1867. Henry Cotton was later knighted. Mrs Cameron celebrated their love by posing them, rather thoughtlessly, as King Cophetua and the Beggar Maid.

ENOCH ARDEN sold extremely well, as did *Alice's Adventures in Wonderland*. One of these works has survived rather better than the other in the national memory, but no simple moral is to be deduced from this. A late flurry of bad feeling between Dodgson and Tennyson took place in

1870, when Dodgson applied to the poet—with extreme niceness—for his permission to read a bootlegged copy of a poem called 'The Window'.

There is a certain unpublished poem of yours, called 'The Window', which it seems was printed for private circulation only. However it has been transcribed, and is in my hands in the form of MS. A friend, who has had a MS copy given to him, has in his turn presented me with one. I have not even read it yet & shall do so with much greater pleasure when I know that you do not object to my possessing it. What I plead for is, first, that you will make me comfortable in possessing this copy by giving your consent to my preserving it—secondly, the further permission to show it to my friends. I can hardly go so far as ask leave to give away copies of it to friends, tho' I should esteem such permission as a great favour.

This is an extract from the whole letter. A shorter reply came from Emily Tennyson.

DEAR SIR,
It is useless troubling Mr Tennyson with a request which will only revive the annoyance he has already had on the subject & will add to it.

No doubt 'The Window' is circulated by means of the same unscrupulous person whose breach of confidence placed 'The Lover's Tale' in your hands.

It would be well that whatever may be done

by such people, a gentleman should understand that when an author does not give his works to the public he has his own reasons for it.

Yours truly,
EMILY TENNYSON

Dodgson insisted on an apology, but did not receive one. The friendship was at an end.

DAISY (Margaret Louisa) grew up to be a prolific novelist. She became Mrs Woods, and was seen by Dodgson acting Jessica in *The Merchant of Venice*. Her father, the Dean of Westminster, officiated at Tennyson's funeral in Westminster Abbey in 1892.

WATTS was commissioned to sculpt a statue of Tennyson after his death, and it stands in the Close at Lincoln Cathedral. It shows a stooped figure with a big dog, looking down at his open hand with a puzzled expression. It is known to locals as 'The Disappointed Cabbie'.

After his separation from Ellen Terry, Watts continued to paint excellent portraits and bad walls, still perversely preferring the latter. In the 1870s he bought a house of his own at Freshwater, which presumably surprised everyone. His second marriage was to another energetic woman, who built him a stunning Arts and Crafts chapel at Compton in Surrey. Mrs Cameron took a photograph of the second Mrs Watts with her sisters, all in their shifts. As if to make up for the *Maud* reference hidden in 'Choosing', the subject for the photograph was 'The Rosebud Garden of Girls'.

Despite his general good luck, Watts's most famous statement remains 'Often I sit among the ruins of my aspirations, watching the tide of time', and photographs show a man who appears to have had his backbone removed. He is due a revival, however, especially since he missed out so badly by not joining the Pre-Raphaelites (who didn't want him). On hearing that Watts was about to tackle the walls of a country house, William Morris is supposed to have commented, 'A coat of whitewash would soon set that right.'

In 1875, THE CAMERONS departed from Freshwater Bay. Mr Cameron announced a desire to see his estates in Ceylon, possibly to check that Julia had not given them away. Mrs Cameron died in Ceylon in 1879, looking at a sunset from her deathbed. Her last word was 'beautiful'.

Mr Cameron, twenty years her senior, miraculously survived her. Surrounded by his sons as he lay dying, he declared himself happier than Priam. A minister, waiting outside, sent in a message, offering to read the Bible to him. Mr Cameron considered the proposal. His last words therefore were, 'If you think it would be any comfort to him, let him come in.'